CR Content

Two years of Creative Review's Showcase section

This is CR Content, a compilation of two years' worth of Creative Review's Showcase section. Each month, Showcase brings together the best work from a particular sector. Content has been compiled from the following issues:

Music: April 04, January 05, June 05
Sport: November 03, July 04
Food and Drink: December 03, August 04, April 05
Self-Promotion: January 04, February 05
Arts and Culture: February 04, March 05
Fashion: March 04, October 04, May 05
Finance: June 04
Transport: November 04
Type and Typography: July 05
Home: August 03, May 04
Degree Shows: September 03, September 04
Charities/Not-for-Profit Organisations: October 03, December 04

Published by Centaur Publishing
Copyright © Centaur Publishing 2005

Design by Nathan Gale

Subscribing to Creative Review gets you more than just a magazine. 12 issues of the world's best creative title, featuring the world's best creative work... 2 DVDs with an extra 4 hours of new content on each... entry into the CR Members' Club with monthly savings on consumer goods and creative services... access to the CR editorial archive online... discounts on all CR events... a minimum 10% saving on the retail cover price... and a rather fine free gift!

Music

1

2

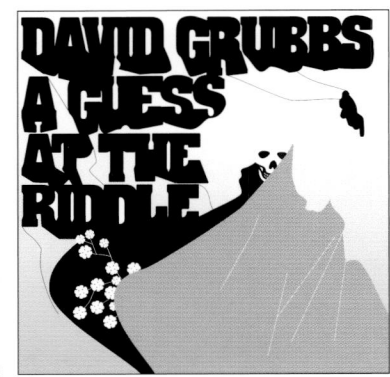

3

4

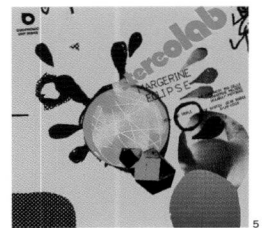

5

6

7

1. Illustrator Andrew Rae created this bear-headed boy as a logo for new electronic label Orson Records set up by artist Transparent Sound and Martin Bundock.

2. House bag for Bush Records, designed by Nathan Gale.

3. Cover for David Grubbs' A Guess At The Riddle for Drag City/FatCat Records, designed by Norway's Kim Hiorthøy.

Intro's Julian House designed these interchangeable covers for Stereolab's recent album, Margerine Eclipse, released on the Duophonic label (shown 4&5). "Sun Ra record covers, late 60s small press art and poetry magazines, Max Ernst and sci-fi comic books," were all key points of reference in the design, he tells us. House also created the covers for the Rock 'n' Roll Lies and Stumble & Fall singles from Mercury Records' new signing, Razorlight (shown 6&7).

8. Poster from Anthony Burrill, promoting "Balearica" night at London nightspot, The Social. "The curly lines and general waviness was me thinking about what it's like to be 'enjoying' yourself whilst listening to acid house music," says Burrill. This poster is the first in a series Burrill is designing for future "Balearica" nights at The Social.

9-11. Periodic table-inspired branding and shop graphics from de-construct for new London-based

music retailer, Carbon. The design aims to portray the brand's open and accessible attitude and runs throughout the store, incorporating identity work, wall graphics and section dividers

8

9

10

11

12 13 14 15 16 17

18

19

20

21

12-17. Punks from illustrator and toy designer par excellence, James Jarvis. Their names (from left to right) are Jean-Paul, Ferg, Bunty, "New-Wave" Dave, "Lieutenant" Les and Nige. "They are here to shake up a shabby Establishment and usher in a new age for the level headed," comments Jarvis. "The kids had better beware. Punk is not dead." The toys go on sale at the end of April, see www.amostoys.com

Berlin-based, self-taught graphic

designer Nathaniel Hamon has worked primarily in the music sector since 1997. Here are two of his most recent sleeves, one for Fridgelife's New And Improved 12" release on Proptronix label (18) and Kid606's latest album, Kill Sound Before Sound Kills You (19), released on Ipecac Recordings. To see more of his work go to www.slanginternational.org

When approached to design a logo for band Lucky Jim as a favour,

Brighton's Red Design loved the music so much they started their own record label, Red Records (now owned by Skint) in order to release it. The first single is shown (20).

21. Yacht Associates have designed the sleeve work for Martina Topley-Bird's latest single Soul Food. They worked with the singer on the sleeve for last year's album Quixotic and this is a continuation of the same theme. Photography: Jonathan Glynn-Smith for Morgan Lockyer.

Label: Independiente.

22. This screenprinted poster for band, The Fades, on Gene Pool Records was one of two designed and hand-coloured with felt-tips by London-based illustrator Luke Best.

23. Letterpressed CD covers from designer Adam Whitaker for his new music sourcing outlet lyrie! To find out more contact him direct at adamjwhitaker@mac.com

22

23

A wily fox sets his sights on making a meal out of a rather easily led young crow in this promo for Gomez' latest single Catch Me Up by Toronto-based Plates Animation. Label: Virgin

underbeat 1 noisy light
tubevoice
synth 00

emph beat

Monosum is a graphic representation of sampling in electronic music. This compelling black and white film features a typographical break-down of the different sampled components of a track, alongside fluid, organic graphics. Design and direction by Chris Turner and Sam Tootal at Spin. Music by Pho/Twin Valley Falls

Website for Brighton-based label Loca Records. Much of the output from this label is open source (free to download, distribute and modify). Designers Agitprop wanted to reflect this non-conformist attitude, while simultaneously portraying the label as a credible, financially viable organisation. The site is populated with mass media style blipverts and animations, incorporating everything from hand-drawn illustration to blocky bitmap graphics, that flash up as you navigate the site

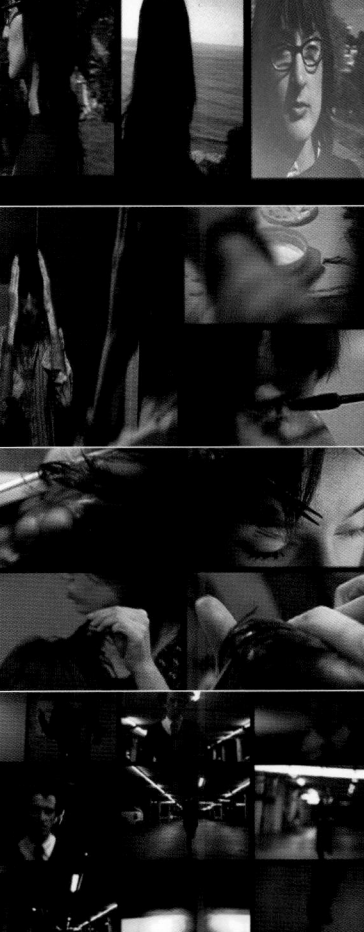

This video for band Clearlake's single Almost The Same follows a boy and a girl, independently going about a day's chores and shopping around the same city while slowly becoming more and more like each other as the track progresses. Directed by Cobra Kai. Label: Domino Records. Commissioned by Vez

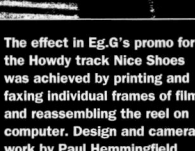

The effect in Eg.G's promo for the Howdy track Nice Shoes was achieved by printing and faxing individual frames of film and reassembling the reel on computer. Design and camera work by Paul Hemmingfield

Video by Matthias Hillner for ML track Automotive Hydraulic. The film features an extract from Helmut Heissenbüttel's poem Mittwochsgespräch which Hillner translated from German into English. The typeface he used is called Gravita (see www.virtualtypography.com). Label: Loca Records

North's logotype for Japanese sound/production studio Syn Entertainment metaphorically depicts sound as a viral organism: hence the morphing letterforms, which resemble dividing cell structures

1

2

3

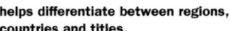

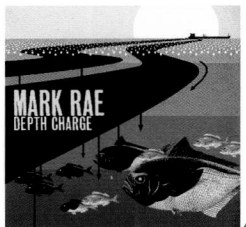

4

1. Swifty designed this sleeve for Brazilian guitar legend, Milton Nascimento's album of previously unreleased recordings from the 70s, Maria Maria Ultimo Trem. Label: Far Out Records. Swifty designed the bespoke typeface Bull (2) specially for the project – it will soon be available from www.swifty.co.uk

3&4. Two sleeves created for forthcoming album, Into The Depths, and single, Depth Charge, by Grand Central Records artist and founder

Mark Rae. Designed by London-based Stunning, the artwork for both sleeves was influenced by Rae's love of fishing and also by an illustrated 60s book called The Sea.

5. Nonesuch Explorer, a re-issue of over 90 archival world music CDs, designed by Stephen Doyle, Chuck Robertson and John Clifford at Doyle Partners, New York. The covers feature images by among others Marc Riboud and Henri Cartier-Bresson. A colour-coded system

helps differentiate between regions, countries and titles.

6. Non-Format employed the talents of Brazilian illustrator Tonho/Quinta-Feira to help create this CD digipak for Motohiro Nakashima's debut album And I Went To Sleep on Lo Recordings.

7. This cotton carrier bag featuring a lino-cut print has been produced to support the release of Icelandic band Múm's new album, Summer Make

Good. Label: FatCat Records.

8. Twelve inch sleeve for Angels Remix by Wax Poetic, featuring Norah Jones. Designed by Airside.

9. Malfunction by Will Saul on Simple records, designed by Build after Wim Crouwel. The grid device is a metaphor for the precision drum programming nature of the music, while the ghosting of the type refers to marks made by a photocopier that needs its cartridge replacing

5

6

7

8

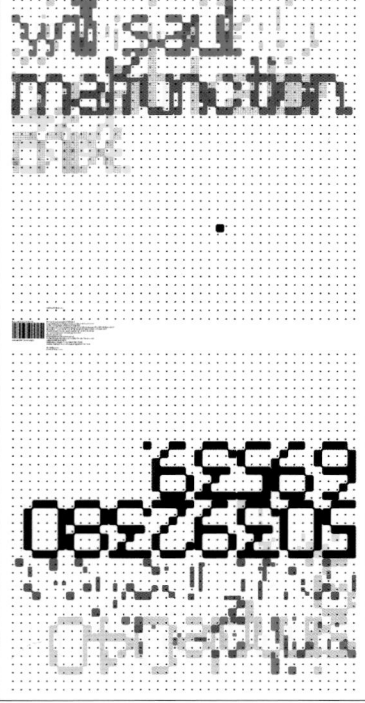

9

10

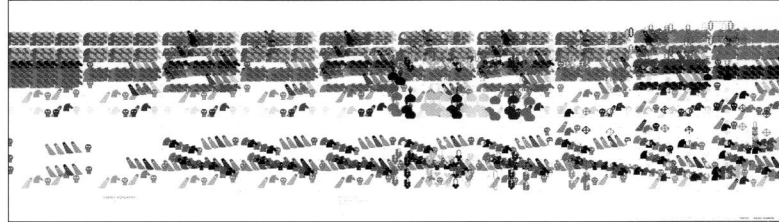

11

12

10. Plan-B Studio designed this sleeve for Dialect, the debut album by East Anglian Hip Hoppers, Vinyl Dialect. Label: Wall Of Sound.

11. Recent MA graduate from Central St Martin's, Maria Gandra, explores the visualisation of western classical music through colourful symbolic forms in her book SeeMusic. Shown here is a poster she devised for her MA show revealing her translation of Wagner's Ride Of The Valkyries.

Photographer Dennis Morris wasn't even 20 years old when he shot this image of Sex Pistols' Sid Vicious (13). To commemorate the twenty-fifth anniversary of Vicious' death, 25 images by Morris of Sid and those around him were exhibited at London's Blink Gallery through February. A pair of Converse All Stars created by Dennis Morris (shown, 12) was also displayed.

14. Design studio Traffic invited people on the EMI/Virgin database to take part in a casting for this year's sampler series CD covers. Twelve music fans were selected: one for each CD. The artwork also features text written by each cover star on the music they like and what it means to them. Shown is the first in the series. Photography Morten Laursen @ Webber.

Finland's Syrup Helsinki designed these covers for compilation series We Are Escalator Records (15&16). The two albums feature tracks from the label's ten-year history.

17. Gothenburg-based Io Design created this beautiful sleeve for band Isolation Years' EP Frosted Minds. Label: MNW Records.

18. Rick Myers' sleeve for Lowgold track The Same Way features a shot of the projections made by sunlight as it shone through a plastic rainbow money box in his kitchen. The sleeve also features Myers' distinctive hand-lettering. Label: Sanctuary

13

14

15

16

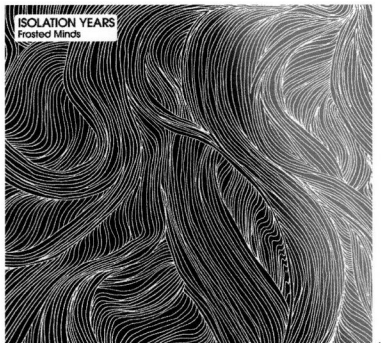

17

18

3

5

Frankfurt-based design studio Eikes Grafischer Hort, comprising the talents of founder and art director Eike König and art director Martin Lorenz, celebrates its tenth birthday this year. To mark the occasion the studio has just launched a new website, hort.org.uk to show, says König "that we do more than design record sleeves". EGH still exists for music industry work while The Hort website showcases their corporate design, illustrations and spreads for magazines etc. Here are their most

recently completed music projects.

1&2. Geschmeidig Zwei is the second edition of a compilation full of downbeat electronica. The word "Geschmeidig" means "smooth" but probably best equates to the english word "silky". For the artwork, EGH had the idea to depict athletes using their athletic, silky skills to liven-up mundane, everyday tasks such as going to the loo, or putting on a record. Label: Island Zeitgeist/ Universal Music.

The artwork for Mandy & Randy

album, Love For Eternity (cover shown, 3) on Sony/Home Records label, depicts Mandy and Randy as a lovestruck CG couple. The CD booklet takes the form of a lover's keepsake/scrapbook. It brings the characters to life by including images of framed photos of Mandy and Randy in different locations (6), photos of billboards advertising their music (5), plus written proclamations of love and drawings, as if penned and collected by the characters themselves. The booklet

is entirely free of credit info as this is all displayed around the point where the cd is attached to the case (4). 3D modelling by Soulpix.

The CD packaging of Finnish act Putsch's new album, Putsch 79, (7-9) is a more abstract affair based, according to König, on the meaning of the word Putsch. "It means to destroy something existing to create something new", he says. "We started with various images but broke them down, cut them up – to create something new." Label: Clone

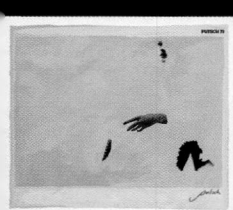

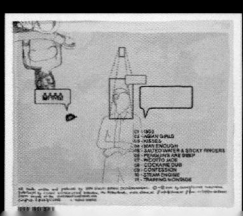

1

2

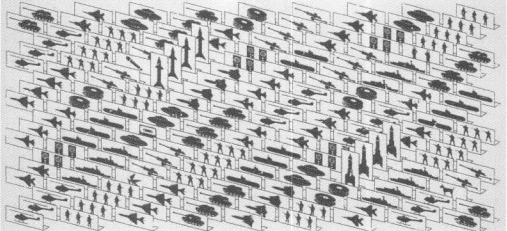

3

HOT CHIP DOWN WITH PRINCE

4

1. Lopetz from Swiss design group Büro Destruct designed this poster for club night Vienna Scientists for client Reitschule Bern.

2. Fold out the CD pack in American band, The Belles' new album, Omertá, to find this calming photograph of blue sky, completely free of text. Photography: Matthias Clamer. Label: Eat Sleep Records. Design: Amp Associates.

This sleeve for King Geedorah's

album, Take Me To Your Leader (inside of gatefold shown, 3) was devised by 25 Survivors. Influenced by the theme of the album itself and by generic war plan diagrams, the sleeve features cut out sets of military vehicles and weapons – although to lighten the tone there is also the odd speaker, dove, demo tape and flying saucer.

4. Darren Wall featured in our student round up two years ago (CR August 2002). Here is his sleeve

design for Hot Chip's debut release on the Moshi Moshi label.

5. Agency J Walter Thompson Italia's Milan office developed this poster for Heineken, to promote to lager's three day Jamming Festival... and what a line-up it appears to be. Creatives: Alessandro Sposetti, Francesco Muzzopappa, Pietro Maestri and Bruno Bertelli. Photographer: Davide Bodini.

6&7. Barry Smith's design for the

Motive Sounds compilation. "Both the relative youth of the project and the home production of a lot of the bands were the influences on the design and project direction," says Smith. "Elements like photocopier and typewriter keys were the starting point for an experiment in pattern and type. Metallic black ink was used to lift the halftone and photocopied collage." The cover was produced on a small budget so the CD can be sold at £7 to promote the webzine www.motivesounds.co.uk

8. Nottingham's Output Design created this sleeve for Drumsound & Bassline Smith's 12" release Tech023 on Technique Recordings.

9. Die-cut 12" sleeve designed by TDR for Access Rhythm by Jimmy Edgar. Label: Warp.

10. Cover for Keane's Somewhere Only We Know single designed by Madefire in collaboration with photographer Alex Lake

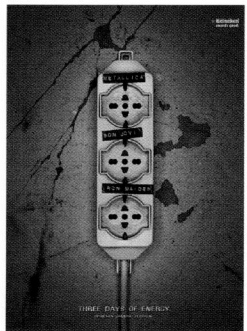

5

6

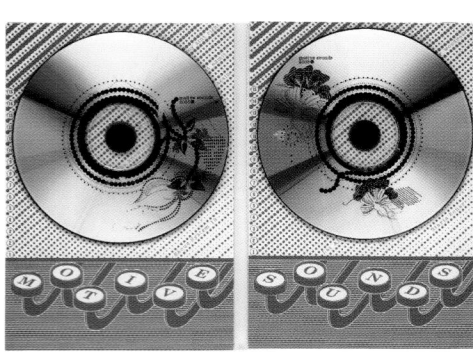

7

DRUMSOUND & BASSLINE SMITH
(A) TINMAN (AA) PALAMINO

8

JIMMY EDGAR

9

KEANE

10

11

12

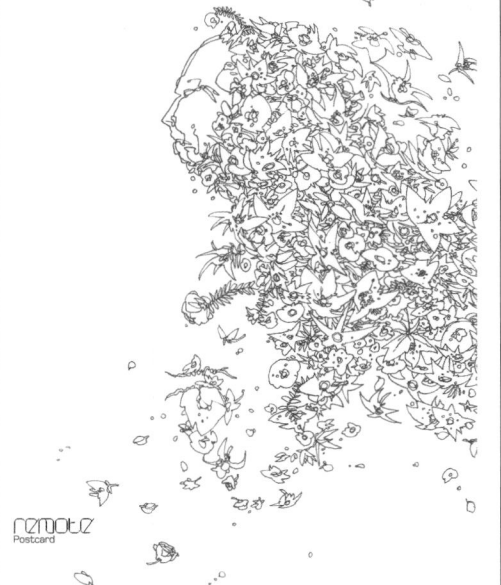

remote
Postcard

13

Mass Distraction, the debut album from SPAN, features cover and inner panel work (shown 11) from Big Active. The band (and design team) feature in the crowd scene covering the booklet. Design: Richard Andrews. Illustration: David Foldvari. 12. Design duo I Want Design, who work out of Stoke Newington, London, created this CD pack for new label Buzzin' Fly's first release, Volume One.

13. Detailed illustration work by

Lance Sells for Remote's latest release, Postcard. Design: Zip Design. Art direction: David Bowden.

14&15. Pages from forthcoming book by Andrew Rae compiling four years of flyers for Perverted Science

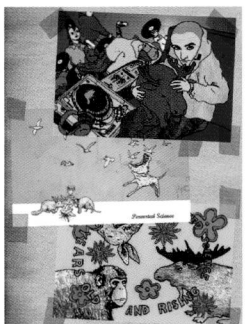

14

15

1

2

3

4

5

6

7

8

1-4. Pentagram New York partner Paula Scher, was commissioned to design the identity and environmental graphics for Jazz at Lincoln Center's new home in the Time Warner Center on Columbus Circle, New York. Scher has considerable experience working with jazz as she was East Coast art director for CBS Records in the 1970s and has designed hundreds of jazz album covers. She later worked for Blue Note in the early 80s. At an initial meeting, the client told Scher that jazz was about syncopation – where one beat is slightly out of time with the others. He also compared jazz to a square peg in a round hole. Both these ideas were made visible in the treatment of the letter "a" in the logo. The "a" also subtly changes colour very slowly: Scher and the client could not decide on a colour so she thought they could have a flashing sign which changed from one to the other. However, Scher was told by city authorities that the building could not sport such a sign: undeterred she devised one that changes colour almost imperceptibly. Interior murals are bright and colourful and use the graphic forms of the printing process to connect jazz to its popular roots. Designer: Rion Byrd. Photograph: Peter Mauss/Esto.

5. EMI's autumn catalogue of new releases was designed by Brighton design group Red Design.

6. The cover for DJ Magazine's Top 100 DJs poll features this "brain-bending" optical illusion by Nottingham-based studio Output. The sharp-eyed among you will see that the image is a portrait of poll winner Tiesto.

7&8. US designer Corey Holms created this logo for Miami record label, Fighting Records. The logo (8) represents both halves of the company's name: Fighting, by an abstract fist, Records, by an abstracted soundwave. Holms also designed this ambigram (7). An ambigram is a mark that can be read from different orientations – this one works both right-side-up and upside-down. It will be printed on the disc of a CD sampler

9

10

Oakland-based designer Jason Munn designs gig posters under the moniker The Small Stakes. Here are his recent poster designs for Rilo Kiley (9) and The Pixies (10).

11&12. For a feature in the January 2005 issue, Dazed & Confused asked various artists for their favourite song lyrics. They then provided Japanese design and illustration collective Delaware with photography of the artists and the lyrics chosen by them in order for Delaware to create these illustrations. The lyrical choices of Sam Herlihy of Hope of the States and The Duke Spirit's Liela Moss are illustrated on one spread (11), while Benjamin Zephania's and The Yeah Yeah Yeahs Karen O's choices get the Delaware treatment on another (12). Other artists featured include MF Doom and Talib Kweli.

13. Xmas acid house party poster by Anthony Burrill and Malcolm Goldie. PAM are Burrill, Goldie and collaborator Paul Plowman.

14. Each month, The Sunday Times produces a CD-Rom of additional content, designed by Mook. Subjects covered in The Month vary from music to film, games and TV. Say Mook: "The self-contained CD environment provides an enormous amount of creative freedom, and is ideal for extended editorial pieces... Unlike the web, there are few file size restrictions, and we could control the exact appearance of each page, which allowed us to play with typography, layout and elegant transitions." Musicians covered in The Month have included David Bowie, The Red Hot Chili Peppers, Oasis, The Beastie Boys and, in this instance, Fat Boy Slim.

15&16. Designer Mat Lazenby of The Morrice Partnership and musician/graffiti artist Part 2 (Keith Hopewell) developed these limited edition iPod cases. Described by Lazenby as "shamelessly lo-tec" they and other designs are available from www.part2ism.com

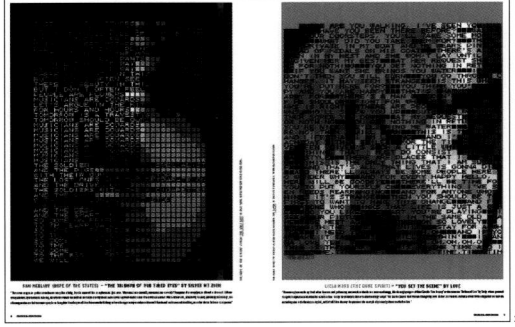

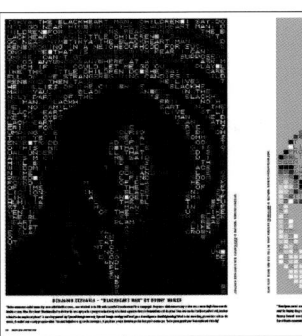

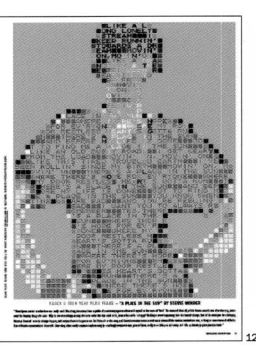

11

12

13

14

15

16

depeche remixes 81···04

depeche mode

1

2

4

depeche enjoy the silence·04

6

depeche mode
de
enjoy the silence·04

7

depeche enjoy the silence···04

8

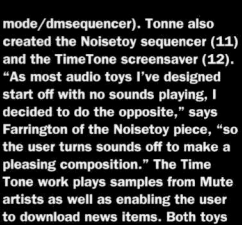

depeche enjoy the silence·04

Mute Records commissioned Mat Cook at Intro to create the graphics for the Depeche Mode Remixes 81-04 project. The work included a box set (cover shown, 1) with four 12" inner sleeves (2-5), and covers for different CD versions of the single, Enjoy the Silence (6 – with disc, 7 – and 9), and for the 12" version (8). Reminiscent of textile design, the visuals were generated by filming digital images on a computer monitor, resulting in a moiré effect.

The original hardness of the digital image was softened through this process (putting digital work through an analogue treatment), creating a hand-made effect; essentially "remixing" the imagery. For Mute's website, Studio Tonne (aka designer Paul Farrington) and Neil Rackett created the Depeche Mode Remix Toy sequencer (10). Users can remix loops and samples from the Mode's hefty back catalogue (www.mute.biz/depeche

mode/dmsequencer). Tonne also created the Noisetoy sequencer (11) and the TimeTone screensaver (12). "As most audio toys I've designed start off with no sounds playing, I decided to do the opposite," says Farrington of the Noisetoy piece, "so the user turns sounds off to make a pleasing composition." The Time Tone work plays samples from Mute artists as well as enabling the user to download news items. Both toys are at www.mute.com/distract

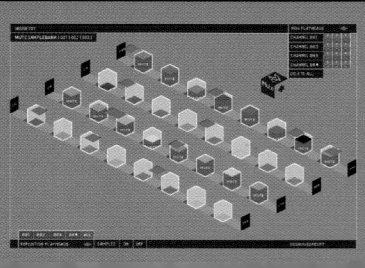

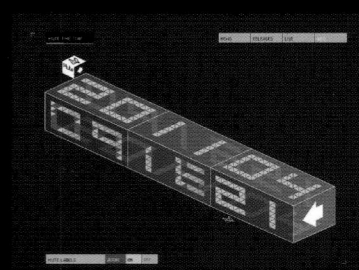

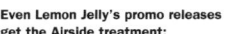

13

14

15

Most readers will be familiar with Lemon Jelly and their rather splendid looking record releases – all of which are created by band member Fred Deakin's design outfit, Airside. For their new album, titled '64-'95, due for release on 31 January, Lemon Jelly have taken this relationship a step further: Airside have produced a film to accompany each track of the album which will be released as a DVD/CD album.

These stills from the accompanying films for tracks Come Down On Me

(16); Make Things Right (17); Only Time (18); The Shouty Track (19) and The Slow Train (20) illustrate the variety of visual styles Airside have created for the different tracks on the album.

13. The recent single Stay With You is beautifully packaged with no text printed on the sleeve or on the disc's labels whatsoever – a removable sticker contains all the tracklisting info and credits, both on the 10" vinyl version and on the DVD/CD single version.

Even Lemon Jelly's promo releases get the Airside treatment:

14. A promo copy of the DVD album. The design screenprinted onto the disc marries up perfectly with the outline of the text printed on the clear plastic Ejector CD case.

15. The reverse of a very limited edition, one-sided 12" promo of Stay With You which was sent to DJs. The swirling design is actually etched onto the surface of the disc

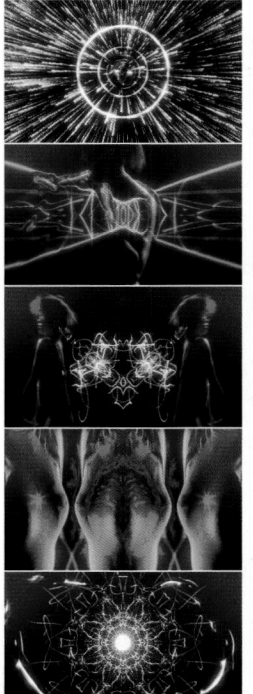
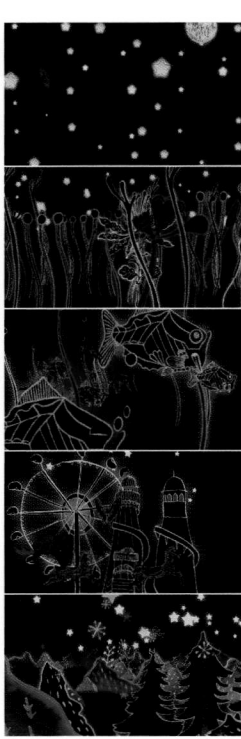
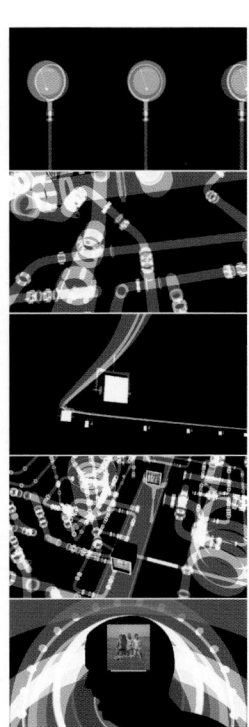

16

17

18

19

20

1

2

3

4

5

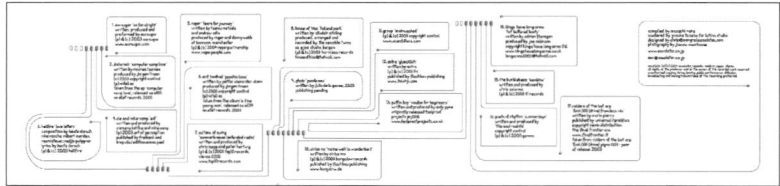

6

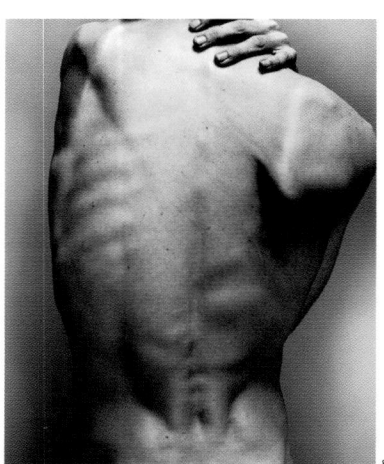

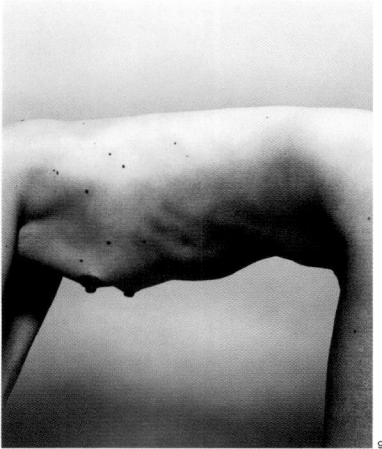

7

8

9

1. Frankfurt-based The Hort designed this sleeve for dance act Booka Shade's first album Memento on label Get Physical Music.

2. New Feeder album, Pushing The Senses, features original paintings by artist Ryan Wallace. "Grant from Feeder wanted a richer, more magical and dreamlike feeling," says Blue Source's Seb Marling. Art director/designer: Peter Richardson @ Blue Source.

3&4. These two sleeves were created by Helsinki-based studio Andsign for two sample 12" records on Japanese label Escalator. Andsign also devised the artwork for the same label's compilation Radio Escalator which comes packaged in a fold-out CD pack (exterior shown, 5; interior shown, 6).

7-9. Nadav Kander shot multiple black and white images of the members of Placebo for compilation CD Once More With Feeling, Singles 1996-2004. Design: Alex Cowper @ Virgin Art. Label: Virgin Records

10. Vinyl EP from The Fallout Trust on At Large records. Design by Jey Malaiperuman. Cover art by Stuart Pearson Wright.

10

16

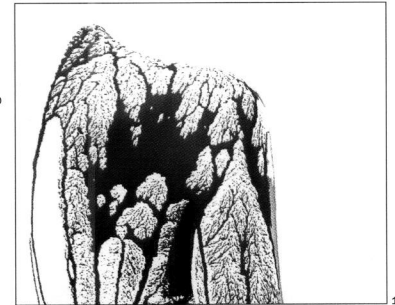

13

17

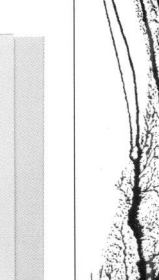

11

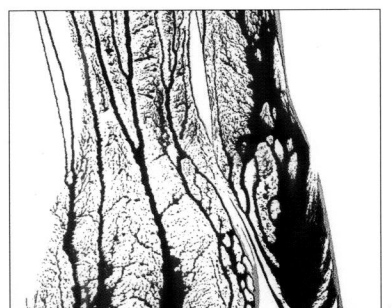

14

12

15

18

The packaging for Nick Cave and the Bad Seeds' new album, Abattoir Blues, and supporting singles was created by Tom Hingston Studio. The clothbound album slipcase (11) houses three CDs, the effect being that of a poetry anthology. The inner sleeves are in delicate pastel shades, as are the singles (Nature Boy shown, 12).

13-15. Farrow Design developed the packaging for the Manic Street Preachers' new album Life Blood. These three covers are for the single release Empty Souls. Like the artwork on Life Blood, they feature shots of a model with "blood" poured over her (the skin tones were removed digitally afterwards). Fans can buy three versions of the single, each with a different section of the blood image on the cover. Photographer: John Ross.

16. BMG Zomba are a music library. To add a bit more cred to their selection, they approached Lo Recordings to create this sampler three CD box set of sounds from the label. Packaging in clean black and white by design duo Non-Format.

17. For King Of Woolworths album Rediffusion, Non-Format utilised the photography of Natalie Stevens, whose images all appear at first to be of classic English meals at a rather posh table setting. On closer inspection, the food is mouldy and rotten. Non-Format also designed Milky Globe's Ode To A Beatbox 12" on Lo Recordings (18)

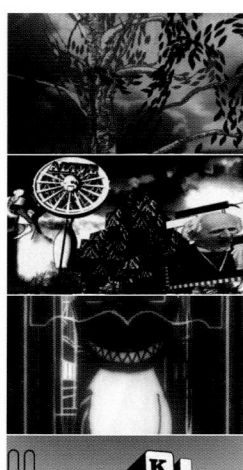

Directorial trio SSSR created the video for track F.K.O. by Subtle. The result: a beautiful animation that follows a strange character on a surreal, Monty Python-inspired adventure. Label: Lex Records

Sweet little imp Kylie Minogue dons sparkly eyebrows and dances in a cage of multi-coloured light in this new promo for track I Believe In You, directed by talented RSA newcomer Vernie Yeung

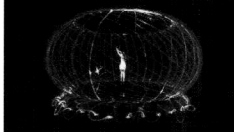

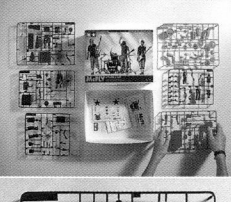

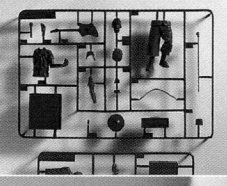

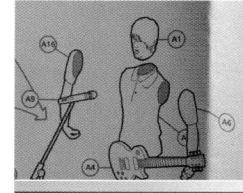

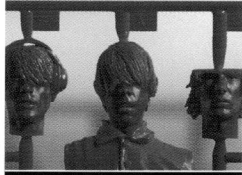

McFly's surprisingly good video to (Room On The 3rd Floor) was directed by Si&Ad at Academy: their model kit idea was carried through to the single packaging and a promo box of goodies (below)

Motion graphics team MK12 made this promo for Sleeping Beauty, a track from German electronica duo Funkstörung's DVD project, Isolated. In it, animated typography weaves in and out of the scenery

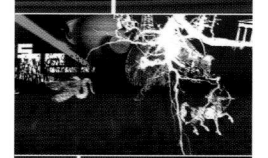

Merciless Boyzone send-up from Welsh sensations GoldieLookinChain for track You Knows I Love Ya. Fingers crossed it'll keep Band Aid off the number one spot. Director: Adam Smith at Colonel Blimp.

Muffin The Mule versus life on an inner city council estate: that's Dougal Wilson's promo for Dizzee Rascal track Dream. Best bit: two puppets nicking a widescreen telly. Production company: Colonel Blimp

Fallon's latest output for BBC Radio 1 includes this rather nice TV spot featuring solitary music fans across the land, all united in their love of music (in this instance, specifically, track Stumble and Fall by Razorlight). Also from Fallon are heraldic posters (one below) featuring the artwork of Joel Lardner, for Radio 1 DJ Zane Lowe. Creatives: Richard Flintham, Andy McLeod, Gary Anderson and Lawrence Seftel. Director (Razorlight): Ne-o. Production company: Stink

RADIO 1 FROM 7PM
ZANE LOWE
IN NEW MUSIC WE TRUST
BBC

The promo for REM's new single, Aftermath, features visual effects from LA-based A52, evoking a "live feed" transmission breaking up. Production Co: Bob Industries. Director: Peter Care

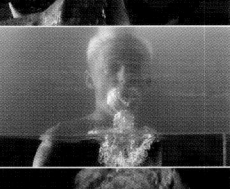
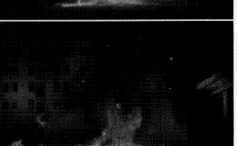
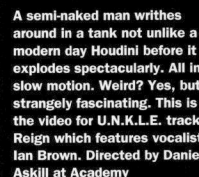

A semi-naked man writhes around in a tank not unlike a modern day Houdini before it explodes spectacularly. All in slow motion. Weird? Yes, but strangely fascinating. This is the video for U.N.K.L.E. track Reign which features vocalist Ian Brown. Directed by Daniel Askill at Academy

1

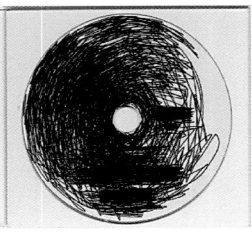

2

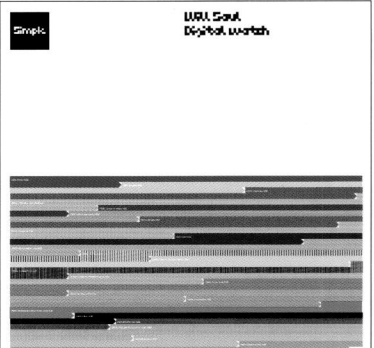

3

1. This CD of music put together by fashion designer Barbara Bui is intended to have a home-made feel. By Base Design.

2. Will Saul Digital Watch 12", designed by Blam at Neue. The stripes of colour relate to previous releases on the Simple label and the length of each track. "Because Will Saul is responsible for all A&R for the label," explains Blam, "this sleeve graphically represents the body of music he's signed to the label – a digital survey of the last 18 months of Simple Records."

3. House sleeve for New York label Record Camp devised by Build. Michael Place explains: "It's printed in spot UV with a die-cut (the curvy slash) to reveal the inner sleeve. The owner is encouraged to fill in the information themselves in the spaces provided as this is the house bag and each release will have its own unique inner sleeve."

4. From a series of atmospheric video graphics for Amsterdam's restaurant/bar/club, 11. Entitled Organically Synthetic Eleventh Heaven, the video is aired during dinner time to compliment the garden theme of the venue. Visuals: Matte. Animation: Pope.

5&6. Designer Matt Pyke of Universal Everything describes this fold-out front cover for Emo-Droidz by V.L.A.D as "Living, walking complexity"

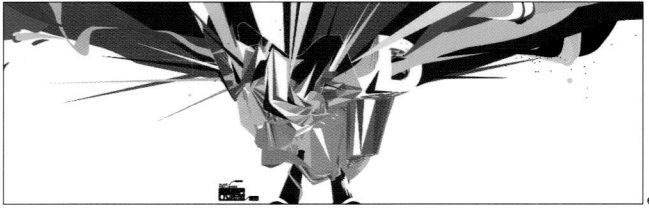

4

5

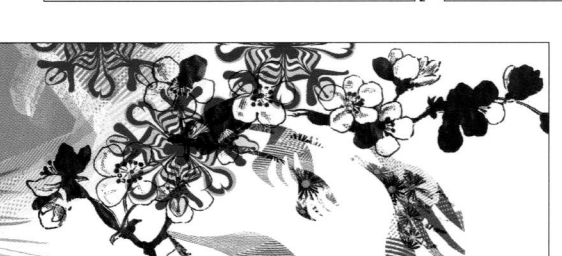

6

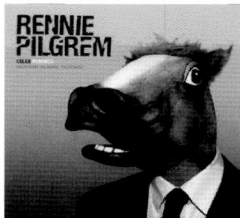

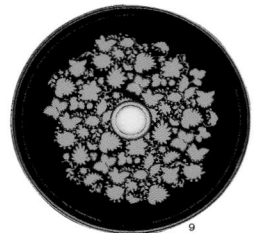

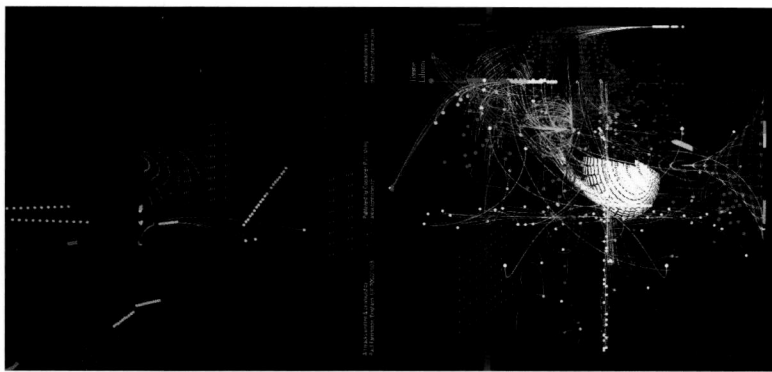

7. Taking its cues from the surname of the artist, man and beast are combined in this cover for Rennie Pilgrem's Celeb Remixes, taken from the album Pilgremage. Designed by Holborn.

8. Robot Dancing Vol 1 compilation album cover by Steve Rowland.

9. Redneck Manifesto's I Am Brazil CD is adorned with a leafy illustration courtesy of band member Matthew Bolger, also a designer at Dublin studio My Brain Design.

10. CD for German band, Warren Suicide. Graphics by Cherie.

Paul Farrington, the man behind Studio Tonne, is also a musician. He created the artwork for Lilium (11), his latest album, and also Epitome (12), a four-track EP by Lowfour, Lod, and Tomas Jirku – both released through Barcelona's Klitekture Records (www.klitekture.com).

13. Art director Patrick Duffy designed the sleeve for Whitey's debut album, The Light At The End Of The Tunnel Is A Train, on 1234 Records. The title was turned into a rebus (a puzzle where pictures and symbols represent words) using paintings by Chris Graham.

14&15. TDR/Matt Pyke designed this CD pack for Warp act Jimmy Edgar's release Bounce, Make, Model – making the most of a red UV plastic jewel case

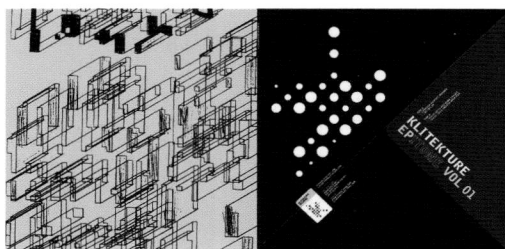

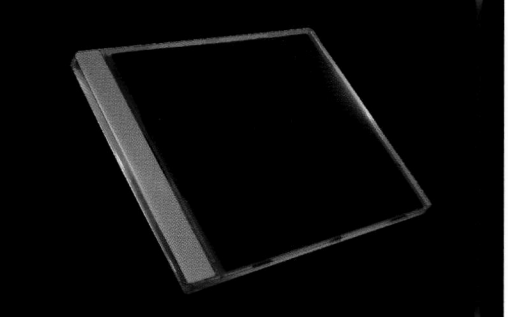

1. Traffic has just completed the artwork for new signings to Parlophone, Morning Runner. This is their first EP, Drawing Shapes. "The artwork takes the release title and uses hand drawn type to create a spiralling vortex", explains Traffic's Stuart Hardie.

2. Fold out the CD artwork of Optimo's latest release Psyche Out, and this mini poster is revealed. Explains designer Chris Bolton: "The typography was inspired by optical illusion artists of the 60s, such as Bridget Riley." Label: Eskimo Recordings. 3-6. Julian House of Intro's

70s inspired artwork for Stereolab boxed triple CD and DVD release Oscillons From The Anti-Sun, out now on Duophonic. 7-10. Math is a magazine based in Brighton run by student collective posikids! For its second issue, 20 designers, illustrators and artists were

each asked to respond to a different track donated by one of 20 bands. The results (including images by Faile, 9, and Earthstetic, 10), along with a compilation CD of all the donated tracks, form the main feature of math 2. Cover (7) and contents

spread (8) by Hugh Frost at posikids! Concept: Francesca Wade and Hugh Frost. For more about math, see www.posikids.org

11. Studio Output have developed the promotional material for Saturday nights at Nottingham club, Stealth. A cross-section of the

Stealth logo inspired the artwork which features ruled lines, colour gradient combinations and offset gridded type to hint, the designers explain, "at cell structures, space photography and LED displays"

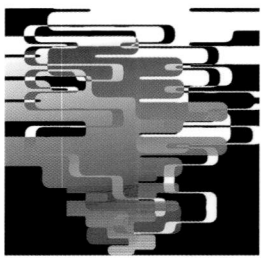

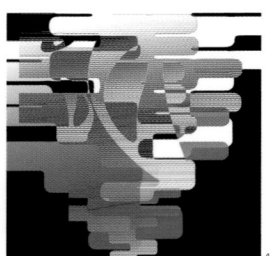

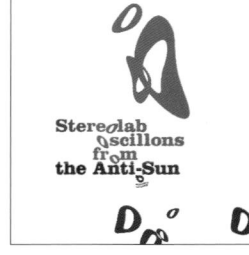

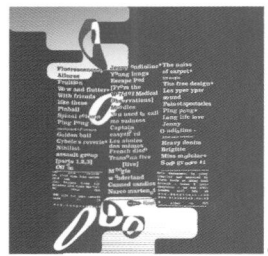

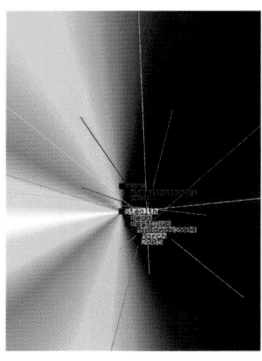

12. New single from Cristian Vogel, 1968. Holes. Art direction, illustration and design by Red Design. Label: Novamute.
13. Another beautiful sleeve from Lex Records, this time for act Fog's new album, 10th Avenue Freakout. Andrew Broder, the man behind Fog's music, came up with the front cover cave painting concept while all artwork and design has been done by ehquestionmark.
14-18. For Fischerspooner's second album, Odyssey, Alias created an abstract logo device which appears in different colour combinations through the album packaging and mutates into different patterns and shapes for the singles. "A logotype and typeface were drawn as a semi-classic counterbalance to this graphic aesthetic," says Alias' Gareth Hague.
19&20. Hal album and single sleeves by Blue Source. "The band pulled out a few montage references and old Harry Nillson sleeves. They were after something a little nonsensical and 'nondesigned'," says Blue Source's Andrew Flack. "On each of the sleeves there is a little interplay with how the source material interacts to relate to each title." Art Direction: Pete Richardson, Blue Source. Client: Claire Britt, Rough Trade Records. 21. Kitsuné is a fashion label, design studio and a record label based in Paris. Kitsuné X is their third compilation release and the sleeve and vinyl label design incorporates photography by Tom Davis and illustrations by Walther Rothschild and Eric Gill

12

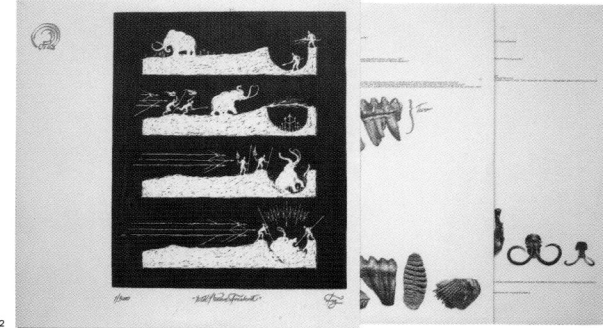

13

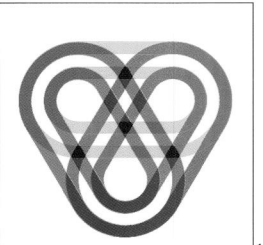

14

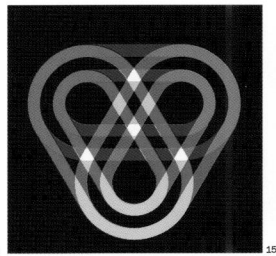

15

16

17

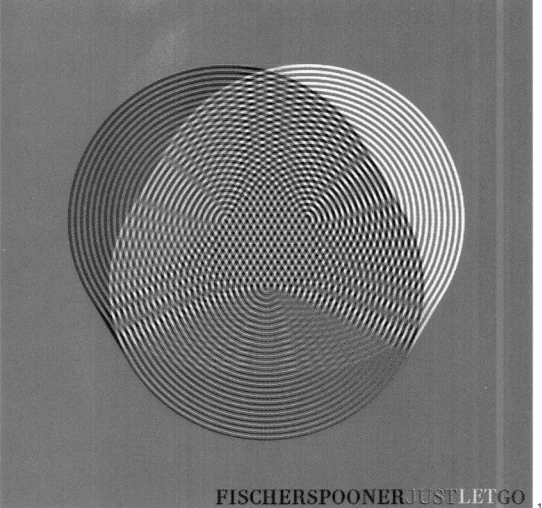

FISCHERSPOONER JUST LET GO

18

19

20

21

The Upper Cuts is a collection of tracks which French musician and producer Alan Braxe has worked on over the last few years – including Music Sounds Better With You by Stardust. Shown, 1, is the disc itself. Design by Bertrand Largros de Langeron and Xavier Dulong de Rosnay at Death Squad. Label: PIAS. 2. CD from a special promotional box-set version of Kaiser Chiefs' album, Employment. The box-set, designed by Cally, has a retro game theme, hence this number spinner image. 3. This well-populated CD is for the Big City Loser EP by Chok Rock on Warp records. Designed by Check Morris. 4. Patrick Duffy created stripey packaging for Basement Jaxx's singles compilation called, er, The Singles. The disc enclosed, however, isn't stripey

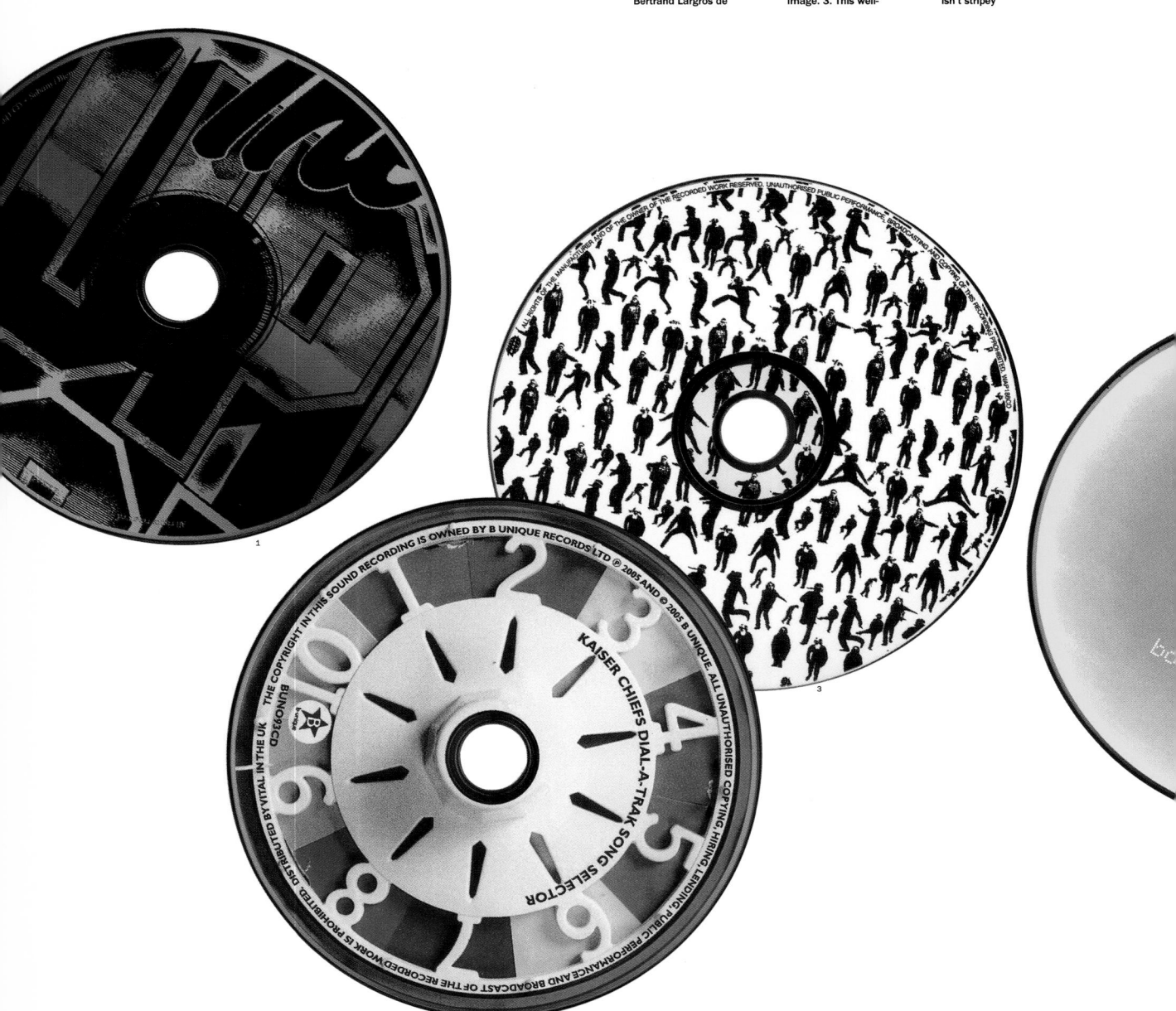

5. The CD of David Jack's Iron Out San Francisco album on KFM Records is adorned with this very delicate print. Illustration: Suzi Q. Design: Lucy Reeves. 6. The Debt Collection is the debut album by The Shortwave Set and is described by the band themselves as "a collection of shonky hangover songs". It's out soon on Independiente. "The birds in a vacuum jar on the CD were drawn by Chris Graham, my long-time collaborator," explains art director of the packaging, Patrick Duffy. 7. Another delicate CD print, this time for Danish Radio Big Band & Eivør Pálsdóttir's album entitled Trøllabundin

1. The Abandon Music sleeve for Electronic Music Composer took its cues from the album's title. Says designer Ben Curzon: "The idea was to illustrate the moment in a night club when a toilet cubicle becomes the only means of escape from the spinning in your head." Record Label: Planet Mu Records.
2. Text free sleeve of the vinyl-only album sampler of The White Stripes' forthcoming new album, Get Behind Me Satan. Photography: Ewen Spencer. Label: XL Recordings. 3. The Stealing Air EP by Huron on Como Park Music features a die-cut outer sleeve, hinting at the multi-layered nature of the band's music. Designed by Stylorouge/ T&CP. 4&5. Covers for The Departure's singles, All Mapped Out and Lump In My Throat, designed by Tappin Gofton.
Photos by Nadav Kander pick up on the horizontal line running through the band's logo. "We projected narrow bands of different coloured light into empty anonymous spaces into which we could photograph the band individually and as a group for singles and album respectively," explains designer Simon Gofton. Record label: Parlophone.
6. This sleeve of album YES! by band Do Me Bad Things was created by the band's bass player Adam Mallett in collaboration with label manager Ian Johnsen.
Label: Must Destroy / Atlantic. 7-11. This is the first issue of new quarterly music magazine, Dummy, the brainchild of John Burgess (ex-Jockey Slut editor), Paul Benney (co-founder of club night Bugged Out!), ex-art director of The Face, Craig Tilford, and writer Chris Cottingham, the new publication's editor. Issue 1 includes photographs of synthesizers by Christopher Griffith (9) and a Billy Childish interview (10).

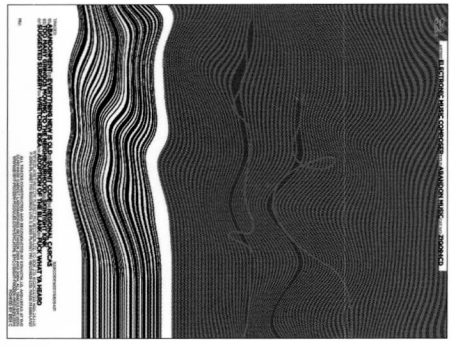

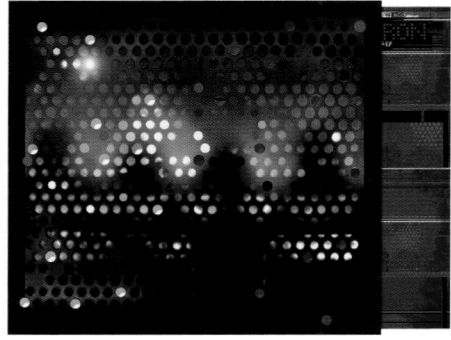

12. The debut album from South African musician Nodern features packaging by French designer Laurent Fetis. The CD includes four interchangeable covercards with imagery by Mikhail Straat, Flore Bottaro and, most strikingly, Ries Straver and Federica Palmarin.

13. Diefenbach's album Set & Drift on label Wall of Sound. Sleeve design by Tom Hingston Studio. Photo: David Hughes.

14. Autechre's latest album, Untitled. Designed by Alexander Rutterford.

15. Jamiroquai, Feels Just Like It Should Single promo: a 12" Perspex laser-cut version of the artist's Buffaloman logo was dropped onto sheets of mirror. Photographer Jason Tozer used a sound trigger to activate the shutter and a high-speed flash to capture the impact. Says art director Richard Bull of

Yacht Associates, "We had 60 sheets of mirror and got the shot on sheet 54. A total of 378 years bad luck." 16-18. Sound Track Sector Nine are, says Dave Bailey of The Designers Republic, "something of an institution on the alt, post/rock scene" in their

native Athens, Georgia. For the band's Artifact album, TDR was asked to interpret "moments", "memories", "exploration" and "possibilities". The package was produced on a pulp board digipak, printed in silver foil. 19. Matthew Herbert's Plat du Jour

explores the complexities of food politics. The album includes tracks based on the sounds made by a grain of sugar and 30,000 chickens. Artist Stanley Donwood developed the sleeve, which explores the hidden horrors in food dyes. Donwood made the images

by dripping food dyes onto chromatographic paper. Images are annotated with information about content in the dyes. The album, packaged like a hardback book, will contain further images plus text on food production and distribution

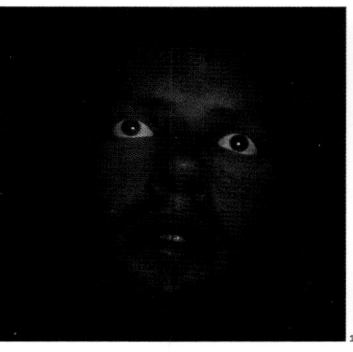
12

13

14

15

16

17

18

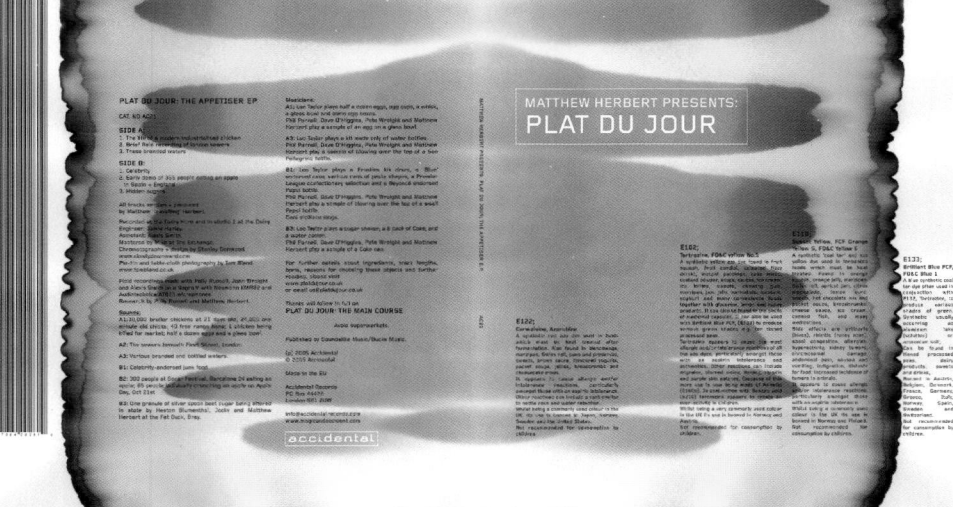
19

1. The video for the first single from Nitin Sawhney's new album, Philtre, was created using antique film footage. Taking track, Koyal, as the soundtrack, director Tim Pearce used footage from 1929 film, Prapancha Pash (A Throw of the Dice) by Franz Osten.

The source film used over 10,000 extras, 1000 horses and, we're reliably informed, 50 elephants. 2-5. CD sleeve and films made to accompany chill out DJ Chris Coco's album, Heavy Mellow. Malcolm Goldie and Anthony Burrill worked on the sleeve,

which is based on a photograph taken by Chris Coco in St Petersburg. Among filmmakers who developed work to accompany tracks are: PAM, Stuart Hilton, Gary Smith, James Goggin, Kate Rogers and Kevin Meredith. Label: Distinctive Records.

6. Design agency Holler have created the new website for the UK band, Hope Of The States. In collaboration with designers, Type2Error (who completed the artwork for the band's latest single) the concept for the new site, www.hopeofthestates.com,

is based on constellations. The horizontally-scrolling navigation and intricate diagrammatic animations make for an innovative approach to a band site. 7. Campaign promoting hard rock music channel and magazine, Kerrang. Produced by Emap TV

Design in collaboration with Up Creative and animation production house Conkerco, the ads ape government warning commercials from the 1970s, and include a loud, violent take on everyone's favourite road safety squirrel, Tufty. The aim of the ads? To remind

us that life in the real world isn't a bed of roses, in fact, "life is loud". Creative director/director: Jamie Balliu @ Up Creative

1

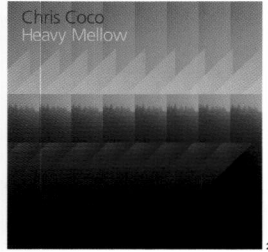  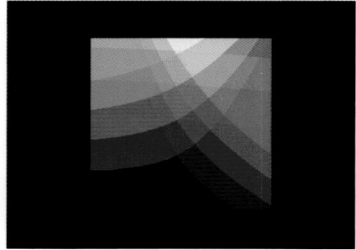 

Chris Coco
Heavy Mellow

2   3   4   5

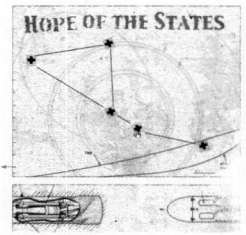 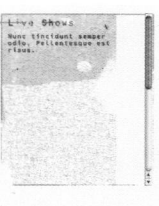 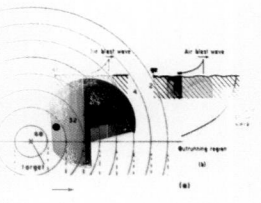 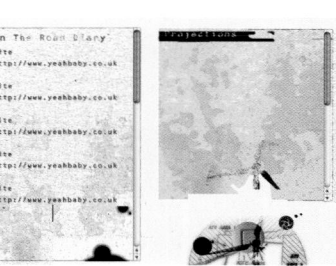

6

8. Ralfe Band have a very idiosyncratic sound, which is why this video to track, Women of Japan, looks so bizarre. Directed by Nigel Coan and Ivana Zorn, and based on drawings by the band's frontman Oly Ralfe, this animated adventure follows the journey of a strange-looking man across the ocean to a far away land and back again. (Subscribers can watch the video on the DVD that came bundled with this issue.) Ralfe also hand-illustrated the sleeves of 200 promo CD copies of his debut single, Albatross Waltz (9-11). Label: Skint. 12. Singer Emiliana Torrini stars in this promo for her track, Heartstopper, which mixes live action with puppetry to charming effect. Production company: Passion Pictures. Director: David Lea. 13. Fuzzy felt and screeching rock make a winning combination in this opening sequence for VH1 show Matzo & Metal. Director: Aaron Stewart. Production company: Hornet Inc. Animator: Efrain Cintron. 14&15. To promote MTV Japan's annual Music Video Awards, Kessels Kramer created the campaign, Discovery Hunt, a scavenger search where participants can win tickets to the show if they find one of 200 EyeDolls (15) that are hidden in secret locations around Tokyo. TV spots and idents (14) give clues as to where to find the dolls. Illustrator Jakob Westman and Swedish animators Fido brought the EyeDolls to life. Project team: Masahiko Otake and Megumi Kuwasaki at MTV Japan; Engin Celikbas, Marc Wesseling, Nils-Petter Lövgren, Tyler Whisnand and Pieter Leendertse at KesselsKramer. Character design: Jakob Westman and Arno Peters

  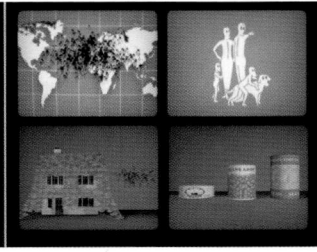 

7

8   9   10   11

12

13

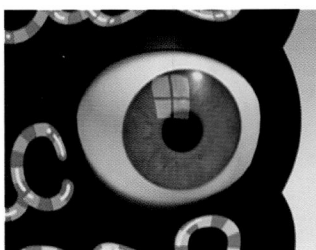   

14   15

Julian House of design studio Intro has launched his own independent record label. Ghost Box is for artists who, the intro page at ghostbox.co.uk says, "find inspiration in library music albums, folklore, vintage electronics and the school music room." House designed the website (shown, 7-9) and, for the discernably esoteric roster of musicians, a range of book-like record sleeves including: Belbury Poly's Farmer's Angle EP (1) and The Willows album (4); The Focus Group's Sketches and Spells album (2) and Hey Let Loose Your Love mini-album (5); and Eric Zann's Ouroborindra album (3, CD shown, 6). Each release carries a number on the front cover so that it has the feel of a text book documenting the current work of each artist

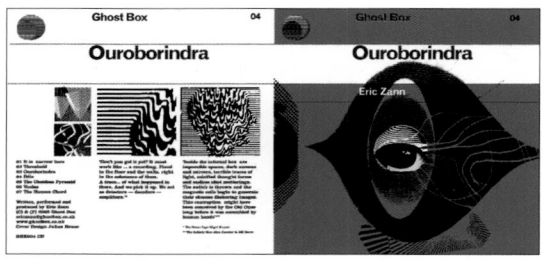

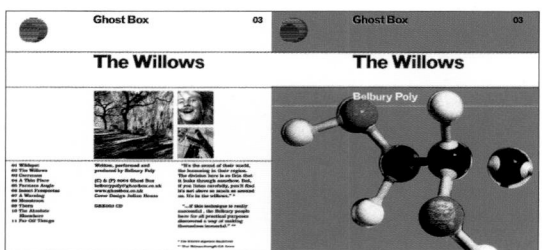

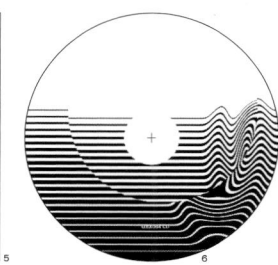

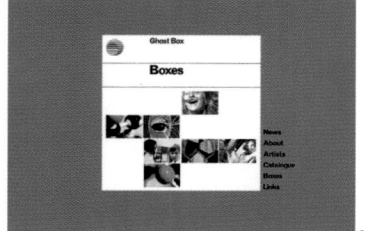

1

Home

These beautifully illustrated images are stills from two spots for Nippon Paint by Leo Burnett, Singapore. Three commercials make up the campaign, each one recounting an ancient Chinese story to highlight a different functional quality of the paint. Yu (shown 1), focuses on the story of Tai Yu, a man entrusted by the Imperial government to prevent the Yellow River from flooding. In ancient China Tai Yu became a shining example of commitment and sacrifice. During floods he never once went to check on his own family home. In the ad, Yu is asked by a colleague why he never returns to check his own home after seeing such devastation. He replies confidently "My house is painted with Nippon Paint 3 in 1 Star, it's highly water proof – there is no need to worry." In another spot (2), the ancient story of Nv Wa is recounted. Nv Wa purportedly fixed a hole in the sky by filling it with beautiful gems. In the ad, she returns from saving the world to find another god (who lives in the flat above) has been doing some DIY drilling, causing a crack to appear in her ceiling. Luckily a can of Nippon Paint is at hand... In the third spot (3), the owner of a tea house on the border between two warring states easily displays shifting allegiance (in order to survive) thanks to the washability of his Nippon painted walls which make overpainting a doddle.
Senior art director: Clara Suc.
Copywriter: Sam Su.
Production company: Da Joint, Hong Kong. Directed and illustrated by Chan Ka Hing

4&5. Afro hair and lava lamps: retro puns galore in a campaign for an interior design handbook by The Guardian. The campaign, from agency BMP DDB, was written by Andrew Fraser and Leslie Ali. The photographer for Afrobush was Wayne Parker, the photographer for Lava Level, Jason Tozer.

6&7. Sound men and special effects teams turn up personally to thank households for appreciating their skills (via the Sony Wega theatre system) in a campaign, from Fallon. Written by Dave Masterman and Ed Edwards. Director: Ringan Ledwidge. Production company: Harry Nash

8&9. Gorgeous photography from Giles Revell for a print campaign for furniture store Heal's, again from BMP DDB, created by Mark Reddy

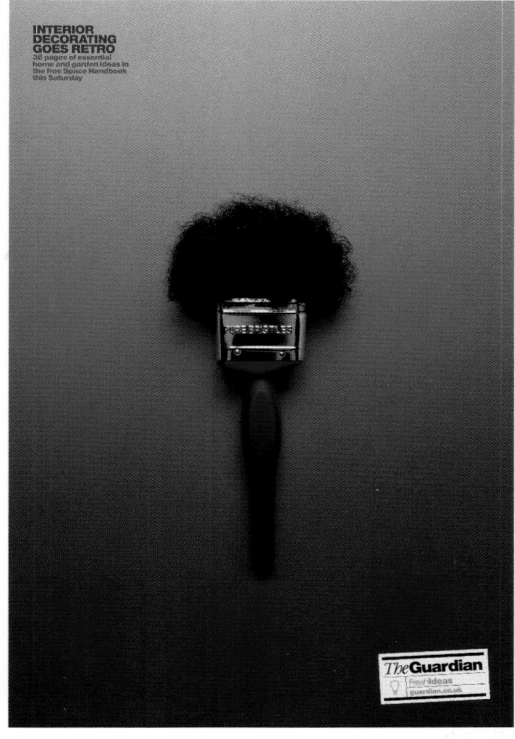

BOWWOW

innovative materials...
...traditionally crafted

HOME   PROFILE   FURNITURE   WORKSHOP   CONTACT   PRESS   1

ISOKON PLUS
CLASSIC & CONTEMPORARY FURNITURE

HISTORY   FURNITURE   LINKS   CONTACT   STOCKISTS   2

1. Website for furniture designers BOWWOW by Alex Lampe at Lewis Moberly. Neutral colours echo the natural materials used in the furniture, as do the site's simple, clean lines. www.bowwow.co.uk

2. Designer Steve Price of London-based multidisciplinary agency, Plan-B Studio, created this website for British furniture company, Isokon Plus. www.isokonplus.com

3-5. Catalogue for American furniture company DWR (Design Within Reach), created by Pentagram's San Francisco studio. Art Direction: Kit Hinrichs. Design: David Asari. Photography: Bill Acheson and Russell Abraham.

6. Tomato's Dirk Van Dooren made this film for London bar and restaurant Sketch. The idea was to develop wallpaper for a room and project it onto all four walls. On entering the room, the viewer was completely surrounded by images.

7. Sydney-based Wishart Design created this identity and mail shot for local furniture designers Norman and Quaine, now N+Q. The poster folds to make a mailable brochure.

8. This Pepe Jeans boutique is decked out using second-hand furniture and found objects. Clothes are displayed on tabletops. Concept developed by Pure Sang

WORKBOOK
DWR PROFILE

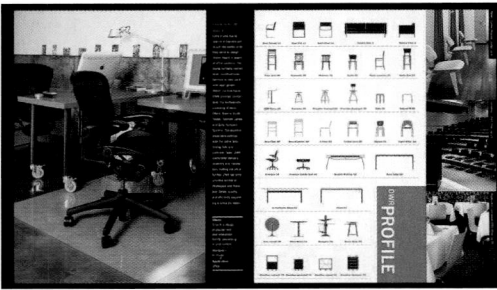

Six Reasons to Join Profile.

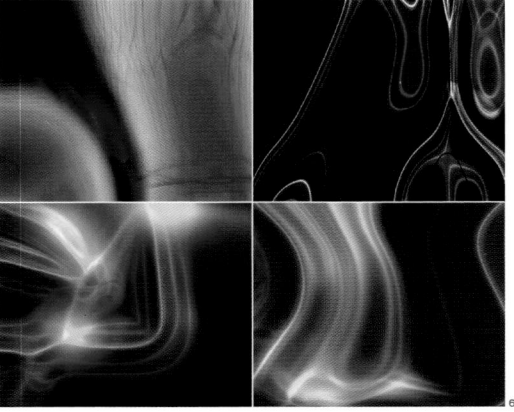

DWR PROFILE

9

10

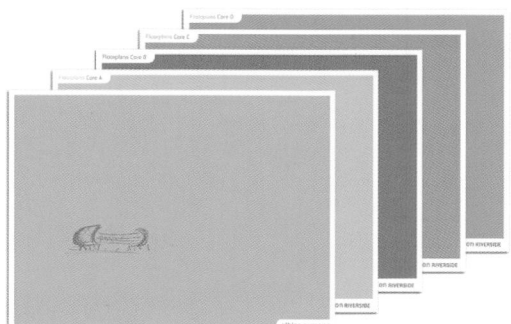

11

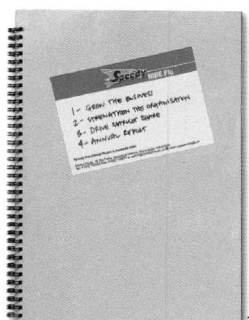

12

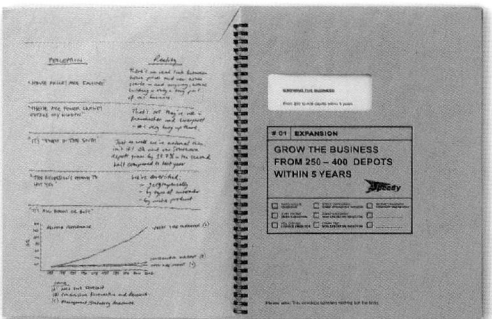

13

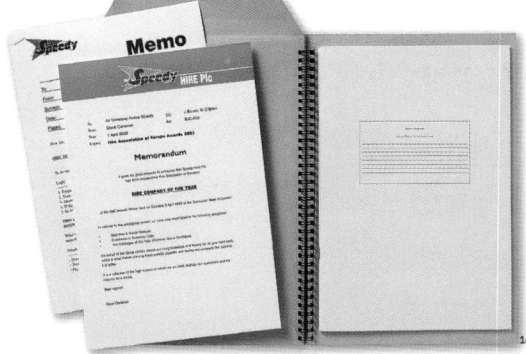

14

15

16

9. Studio Myerscough designed the graphics for the British Council's Hometime: Eight Rooms exhibition. Interior designers including Ben Kelly and Tom Dixon each created a different room for the event which will tour China.

10. New corporate identity for Italian domestic appliance manufacturer, Ariston, by Wolff Olins. Responding to research suggesting that Ariston customers like to spend more time together at home rather than go out, it attempts to avoid the clinical and sterile approach of its competitors.

Creative director: Angelo Ferrara.

11. Brochure covers for Albion Riverside, the Norman Foster development on the river front at Battersea. Designed by Identity.

12-14. Annual report for UK plant

hire provider, Speedy Hire, by NB:Studio. The information inside is printed on sheets placed inside a variety of typical office envelopes.

15. Pentagram New York partner Abbott Miller designed this current exhibition, Do It Yourself: Home

Improvement in 20th-Century America, for the National Building Museum in Washington.

16. Habitat Autumn/Winter 2003 press pack poster, concept by DV. Photography: Maria Moore. Illustration: Annabel Milne

**THE BRINDLEY ESTATE
PUBLIC WORKS PROGRAMME**

FLOWER BED?

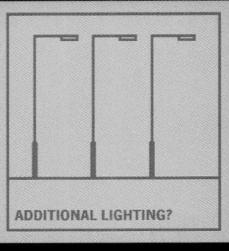

ADDITIONAL LIGHTING?

COMMUNAL CAR?

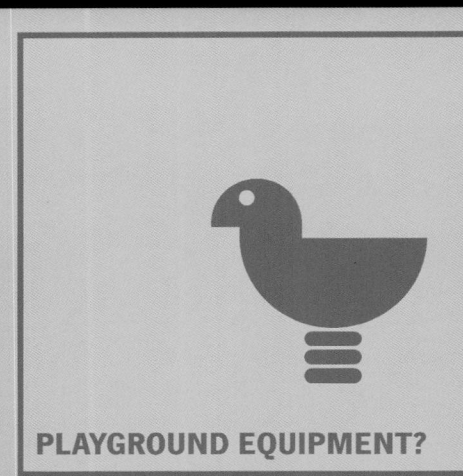

PLAYGROUND EQUIPMENT?

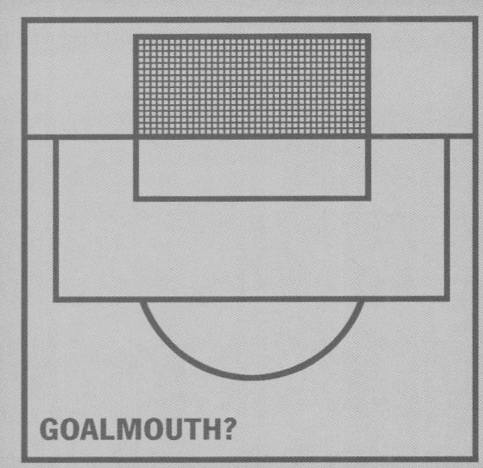

GOALMOUTH?

This catalogue developed by architects FAT, and designed by Anthony Burrill, is for the Brindley Estate Public Works Programme: an art project for the Brindley council estate in north-west London. The idea is that residents choose how the money for the project is spent. The catalogue lists a number of possibilities including commissioning a formal sculpture, buying in playground equipment, installing more park benches or even just using the budget to make some general repairs. On each page of the red and pink booklet is a new suggestion, simply illustrated by Burrill, the idea being that residents tick the suggestions they favour and post them back to FAT. "The estate has quite a multicultural population so it had to communicate to the widest possible audience," explains Burrill of his illustrations. The front runner at the moment, he informs us, is a fountain surrounded by flower beds. The colour scheme for the catalogue was chosen to comply with FAT's intention to make whatever the residents choose to have in pink. The project was commissioned by SPACE Studios for Stadium Housing Association

NEW SECURITY GATES?

ADDITIONAL
PARKING SPACES?

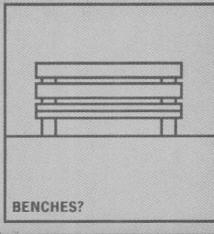

BENCHES?

viaduct

dining chairs
1

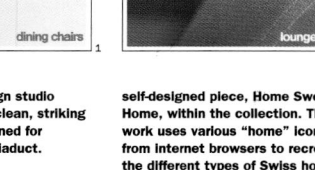

viaduct

lounge chairs
2

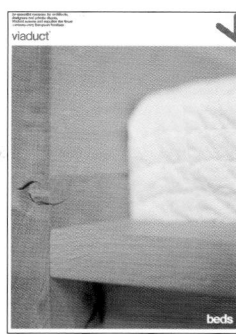

viaduct

beds
3

viaduct

stools
benches
4

viaduct

tables
5

1-5: From London design studio Made Thought, these clean, striking catalogues were designed for furniture specialists, Viaduct.

6. Happypets in Switzerland curated the book Pathfinder: A Way Through Swiss Graphics and included this

self-designed piece, Home Sweet Home, within the collection. The work uses various "home" icons from internet browsers to recreate the different types of Swiss houses that feature in each canton within the country (the areas that Switzerland is divided up into).

7. Bill Amberg is known for his leather bags but also specialises in interiors (leather doors, floors, bespoke furniture etc). In order that Amberg hide samples can be clearly distinguished from those of his competitors, BOB Design developed this amusing animal-shaped solution:

each one corresponds with the animal that it came from.

8. Wonderwall in Japan created the look of Tokyo's flagship Q store by employing the theme "casa" – home. Each room references an area of a modern house and acts as a display

space for the store's products.

9. Waltrose Washing Up Gel packs by Carter Wong Tomlin. There are seven variants, each of which has a special valve that stops clogging. Senior designer: Neil Hedger

6

7

8

9

1-3. Small Houses features 37 illustrated case studies compiled by architect Nicolas Pople that, apparently, represent some of the best examples of small homes built worldwide within the past five years. Published by Laurence King. Designed by Rose Design.

4-6. This beautiful book, Home, was co-published by Steidl Publishers and the Hasselblad Centre, Göteborg to accompany an exhibition by Swedish photographer, Lars Tunbjörk. The series was shot across Sweden and is the final part of a trilogy by the photographer. Distributed by Thames & Hudson in the UK, £20.

7&8. These striking pictures by Jenny van Sommers (originally intended for publication in Casa Vogue) are actually interiors of dolls houses that were styled to scale.

9. US photographer Todd Hido reverses the sense of the home as a place of comfort and security, revealing a more isolated side to suburbia in his atmospheric shots of homes at night.

10&11. Shot for Rear Window, from the July/August issue of Wallpaper*. The story continues the newly re-designed magazine's policy of bringing in fresh photographers and using them in unexpected areas as still-life specialists Coppi Barbieri shoot an interiors feature. Creative director: Tony Chambers. Interiors editor: Leila Latchin

9

10

11

1

2

3

4

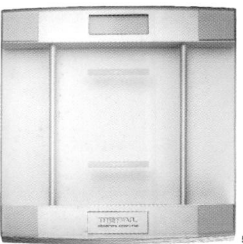

5

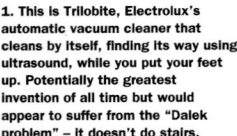

6

7

8

9

1. This is Trilobite, Electrolux's automatic vacuum cleaner that cleans by itself, finding its way using ultrasound, while you put your feet up. Potentially the greatest invention of all time but would appear to suffer from the "Dalek problem" – it doesn't do stairs.

2,3&4. Notime, Nightime and Finetime, a stylish set of clocks from Farrow Design for furniture company SCP. This is the first time that Farrow Design has developed products. Markings on the Nightime version glow in the dark.

5. Artiss glass-topped scales which digitally record your weight, from Seymour Powell for client Tefal.

6. Designer Simon Heijdens' moving wallpaper: the pattern shifts from a floral motif to the outline of a car and back again by virtue of thermo-sensitive ink that is heated using several layers of screenprinted silver circuitry. Dutch design company Droog exhibited Heijdens' work at the Milan Fair in April.

Sweden Graphics have created a series of wallpaper designs (7) and are currently looking for a producer and manufacturer. The company also designed this ceramic ceiling tile (8) for a private residence in Stockholm. The design can be oriented to create a range of different patterns (9)

11

12

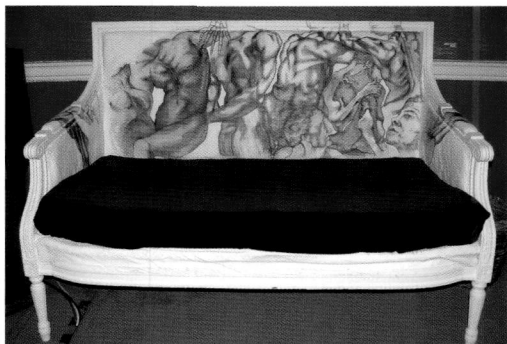

13

15

14

10. Hand-flocked wallpaper from London-based designers, HG Colours. The paper was produced by Cole & Son using blocks that date back to the Edwardian and Victorian periods.

11. Standing almost 17 inches high, this sculptural object made from poplar wood and MDF has been created by House Industries and is based on an illustration from their forthcoming Shag font collection. Only 100 were made and all are signed and numbered.

12. These bizarre-looking speakers from Bang & Olufsen are the most technically advanced around, apparently. They read a room's acoustic response and adapt to it, to produce pure, perfectly balanced sound with a whopping 2500 watts per channel. A snip at £10,000.

13. Customised furniture from Daniel Cohen of Finktank. Cohen decided the office couch needed livening up, so decided to give it a bit of a Renaissance twist. It is currently being exhibited at Square Art in Golden Square, London W1.

14. MiniSkool by Philippe Starck. This cool children's plastic desk and chair is still only a prototype but will be available to buy next year.

15. Alexander Gelman of New York agency Design Machine is producing a series of rugs based on his posters and other graphic design projects. See www.designmachine.net

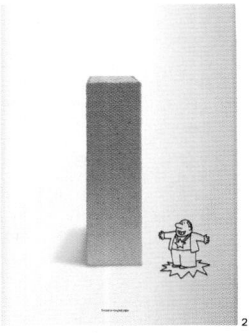

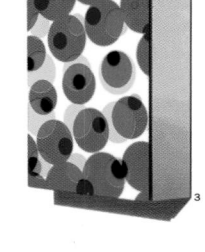

1&2. The front and back cover, respectively, of a book published by build-it-yourself furniture merchants, MFI. The book, by Rose Design, was created to encourage MFI employees to be proactive with problem–solving ideas: it draws on an example of a match factory worker who suggested saving money by only putting a sandpaper strip on one side of matchboxes.

3&4. Thin, flat Artcoustic speakers hang on the wall like picture frames. Customers can choose a fabric and design for the front panel to complement their decor. Prices start from £695 per pair. More info at www.artcoustic.com

5. For designer children (or childish designers): Kozmos building blocks by Karim Rashid, available at SCP in London, £105.

6. Matt and Austin of graphic design agency NEW were commissioned by Redwood Publishing to decorate the walls of their office with imagery reflecting the company's range of domestic lifestyle magazines

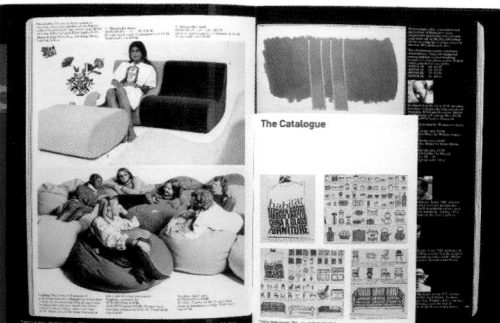

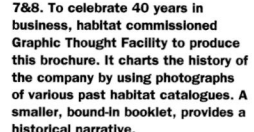

7&8. To celebrate 40 years in business, habitat commissioned Graphic Thought Facility to produce this brochure. It charts the history of the company by using photographs of various past habitat catalogues. A smaller, bound-in booklet, provides a historical narrative.

9. Oregon Scientific alarm clock, designed by Phillipe Starck. Includes easy-to-read weather forecast and a display of the moon's phases. Available at SCP, from £50.

10,11&12. Weird and wonderful household products from the Alessi Spring/Summer collection 2004. Objects include a rather natty stainless steel "citrus basket" (fruit bowl to the rest of us) from the Campana brothers (10). These sleek electronic kitchen scales with LCD (11) are by Stefano Giovannoni. Also shown, Din-don glassware (12) designed by Alessandro Mendini.

13&14. Agenda Design created the identity and marketing material for new venture GuestInvest, which offers individuals the chance to buy hotel rooms to stay in when they're in town and rent out when they're not. Guesthouse West, in London's Westbourne Grove, is the pilot property for the scheme

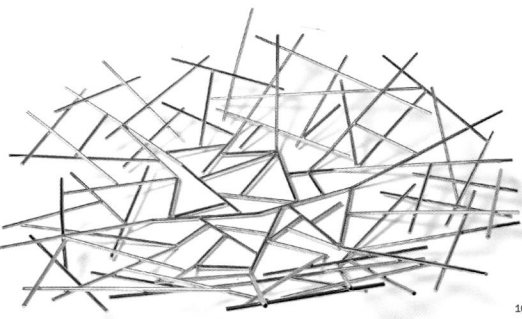

1

2

3

4

5

6

7

1-7. Emer O'Brien is a member of the photodebut collective, a new organisation that aims to connect and support talented photographers. The group recently worked on a project themed on the home: O'Brien's piece, The Fridge Films, was based on an archive of 30 rolls of undeveloped film that she found at the bottom of her parents' fridge. The earliest rolls are 25 years old and, overall, the collection spans the period 1979 to 1989. O'Brien decided to process the films this year: the house that features in many of the pictures is her childhood home in Toronto. "The building is fragmented in my mind, a room here, another there, a bit of corridor that does not connect them," says O'Brien. "I can see this home now as I did with my child's eye: the whole building is scattered about and dissolved inside me." Further details of the group's artistic and commercial projects are available at www.photodebut.org

Background: Ringo wallpaper by Graham & Brown, more info at www.grahambrown.com

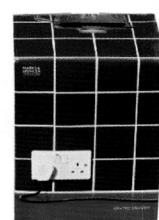

8

9

Marks & Spencer's first Lifestore opened in Gateshead at the end of February. Boasting an architectural centrepiece created by John Pawson (a two-storey house which shows off the wares of the store) this is M&S as you've never seen it before. Concentrating on products for the home, the concept store's wares are grouped, not in departments, but in nine different areas based on everyday rituals: relax, rest, renew, alfresco, cook, organise, escape, play and celebrate. Tyler Brûlé's Winkreative studio was commissioned to design the accompanying Design Directory (cover shown 12) which is essentially a catalogue for Lifestore products. Michael Nash Associates devised the logo (10) and also the carrier bag's distinctive pattern (11), while designer Ilse Crawford was commissioned to create the poster/invite to the Lifestore launch, shown 13. Lifestore packaging (including that for toasters, shown 8 and kettles, shown 9) was designed in-house at M&S under the guidance of former Interbrand creative director, Rodney Mylius who is now M&S head of brand design and delivery

10

11

12

13

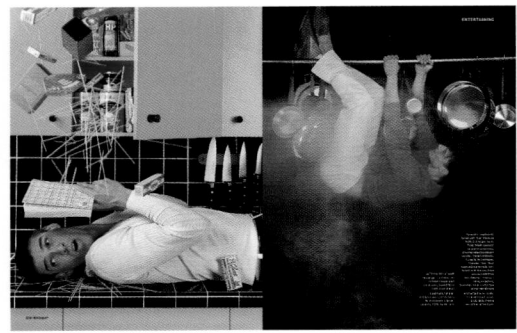

1&2. Cooking Up A Storm story from the May 04 issue of Wallpaper* magazine. Creative director: Tony Chambers. Entertaining editor: Charles Mellersh. Photographer: Kim Andreolli. Design: Meirion Pritchard.

3-5. Point Blank's redesign of art photography magazine Next Level includes this moving series of images of a housing project in Toulouse from photographer Luc Delahaye's publication, Une Ville.

6&7. DayFour is a magazine devoted to showing photographers' personal work. The theme for the latest issue is "Home Is Where…" The spreads shown are from photographers Lina Ikse Bergman (Home Is A Warm Feeling) and Jan von Holleben (Dreams Of Flying). Copies of the magazine can be purchased from The Photographers' Gallery, Whitechapel Gallery, Shipleys and other specialist outlets. Art director/editor: Fiona Hayes

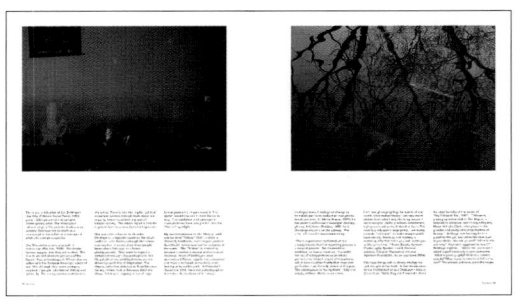

8

9

8&9. djøf Bladet is a weekly magazine published by The Association of Danish Lawyers and Economists. Design studio The Hort were commissioned to produce these illustrations for a feature about working from home.

10. One of a series of photographs of garages by Jenny van Sommers, commissioned for Intersection magazine but never published. Stylist: Katherine Mackenzie Dodds

10

1. This shot of an Aberdeen council block was taken by photographer Morgan Silk, who recently signed to the Rebecca Valentine agency in London. "I spotted this as I was walking into the city from the coast. The thing that struck me about the small block was the shadow on the wall and the bicycle inner tube in the tree." For more details, go to www.rebeccavalentine.com.

2&3. Servite Houses are a not-for-profit housing organisation. Earlier this year CDT designed their new corporate identity, which had its first public outing in this annual report. Servite Houses was keen to show that it was moving forward while not forgetting that people are the most important aspect of what they do. This idea of looking forward and looking back inspired the flip-book approach to the report, showing photography when flicked forward, and figures when flicked back.

Design by Gene Cooke, Alistair Hall, Catherine McArdle and Neil Walker at CDT Design. Photography by Christine Donnier Valentin. Copy by Servite Houses.

4. Mailer for Nick Doddy, a photographer specialising in abstract prints for use by housing developers in show apartments etc. Removable business cards slot into its surfaces as if they were pictures on the wall. Designed by Harriet Devoy at The Chase, London.

5&6. To announce their recent move to St John Street in London, design studio Intro sent out these change of address cards along with a red, green or yellow T-shirt. The work celebrating their "nuevo casa" was designed by Mat Cook

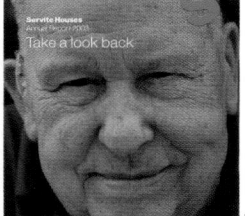

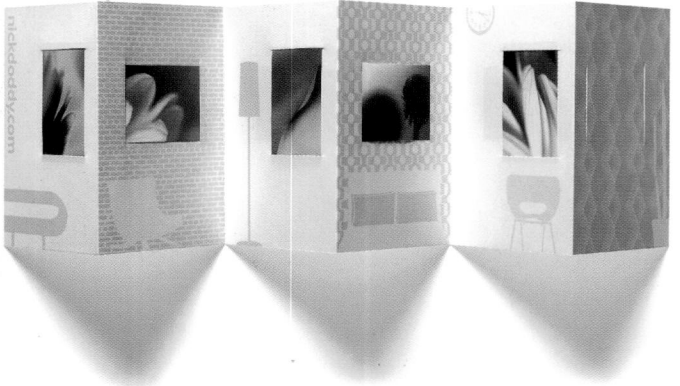

Shelter

h
is for
Shelter

7

8

constituencies · hypothetically · theoretically · objectified · ergo · alma maters · intrinsically · stakeholders · fundamentally · mutuality · dichotomous · paradoxically

interdependence · notionally · perceptionally · holistically · 360 degrees · imagineering · bilateral · reciprocity · evolutionary · conjoined · applicability · opportunistically

simple   readable

It's not just how we look

It's how we talk as well.

Everything we write should be as positive, authoritative and intrusive as possible.

That's difficult if we use jargon, use impossibly long sentences (or use badly thought through ideas in brackets, like this, for example).

If you're writing for Shelter, keep it short. And make sure it keeps to the new copy-checking guidelines, coming soon.

Keep reminding yourself that words like 'stakeholder' or 'constituency' remind normal people of either Dracula movies or politicians. Or both.

Read it through. If it's difficult to read aloud, redo it.

9

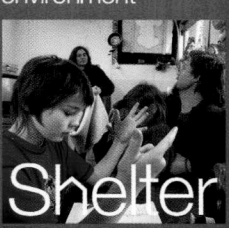

Perhaps this isn't the ideal homework environment

Shelter

10

Imagine if this were parked outside your house. You'd do something about it then, wouldn't you?

Shelter

11

12

home
hope
here
have
hideaway

13

A Shelter Guide
Private tenants
right to fire safety

A Shelter Guide
Private tenants
paying a deposit

A Shelter Guide
Homeless?
Read this now

A Shelter Guide
Housing benefit

14

7-14. Shelter launches a new corporate identity this month created by johnson banks. The new logotype makes the "h" in Shelter into a roof, reflecting the charity's desire to shift perceptions away from the idea that is is purely about the homeless and remind the public that its main focus is on housing.

"We were brought in initially by the ad agency Hooper Galton," explains johnson banks' Michael Johnson. "They were helping Shelter work out a new positioning: most people associate them with the homeless but their work is mainly to do with poor housing." Hence new slogan: "bad housing wrecks lives".

"The old identity [in a typewriter font] was quite cumbersome," claims Johnson. "It had an agitprop, angry feel to it but the organisation has moved on. You can't make an angry scheme neutral but, with this, you can turn the volume up or down. You can be angry but you can also use it on an 80-page legal document. This is formidably simple: it says 'we're now about housing'."

Johnson banks worked for around eight months on the scheme. "We've given them a proper house style," Johnson says. The charity will use Helvetica as its main typeface with Arial used for letters and internal reports. The logotype will appear in red primarily but can also be used in black, white or grey. There is a secondary colour palette of warm brown, blue, pink and green.

Johnson has also helped the charity develop its tone of voice, avoiding jargon and aiming to be as positive and authoritative as possible, and has devised guidelines on image use. He hopes that, within six months, there should be a clearly recognisable "Shelter style" to all its communications – so much so that a reader could tell something is from the charity even if they cover up the logo with their thumb.

"It's a very clean, simple, grown-up scheme," Johnson claims, with the distinctive, roof-shaped "h" at its heart. "In three years' time you should be able to use just the 'h' and have people know it's Shelter"

Clumsy people bemoan lack of DIY skills in this spot for ACE Hardware stores. Agency: Goodby Silverstein & Partners. Creatives: Mike Sweeney, Jack Woodworth. Director: Bennett Miller, Hungry Man

Colour's emotional impact is explored in ad for Crown Paint via a sneaky peek at people's homes. Agency: BDH/TBWA. Creatives: Danny Brooke-Taylor, Gary Hulme. Director: Kevin Thomas, Thomas Thomas

Unpopular man's life changes when he discovers Rags In A Box. Agency: Howard, Merrell & Partners. Creatives: Scott Crawford, Billy Barnes, Scott Ballew. Director: Scott Vincent, Hungry Man

Domestic bliss for odd couple David Hasselhoff and Mike Reid in these funny ads for Sky+. Agency: HHCL/Red Cell. Creatives: Steve Henry, Billy Faithful, Ross Neil. Director: Allen Coulter, Hungry Man

2 days earlier

2 days earlier

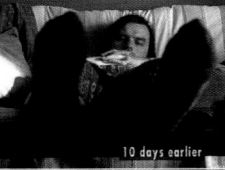

10 days earlier

10 days earlier

15 days earlier

One minimalist vase turns a messy man's life up-side down in this clever spot for Ikea. Agency: *S,C,P,F... Barcelona. Creatives: Patricia Luján, Carlitos. Director: Julio del Alamo, Alamo Films

2 days earlier

5 days earlier

28 days earlier

Woman gets both a tan and a man thanks to Ikea and its comfy-looking sunloungers. Agency: *S,C,P,F... Barcelona. Creatives: Patricia Luján, Carlitos. Director: Julio del Alamo, Alamo Films

Different ways that colour can affect or change our lives... from Nippon Paint. Agency: Leo Burnett Singapore. Creatives: Tay Guan Hin, Ng Tian It, Karl Dunn. Director: Jess Bluck, The Sweet Shop

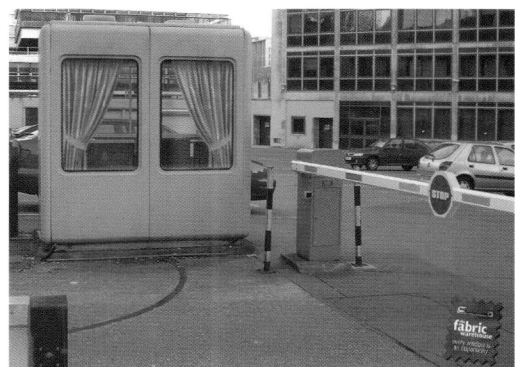

1&2. Print campaign developed by Leo Burnett India, geared at illustrating the unusual speed and power of Bajaj ceiling fans. Witty images include a set of scales that keeps registering the pounds (the power of the fan is pushing the scales down) and a doll (that shouldn't be able to topple over) lying on its side. Developed by creative team KV Sridhar, Agnello Dias, Santosh Padhi, Ramakrishan Hariharan, Kiran Chandorkar. Photographer: Kiran Owal.

3&4. Funny campaign exploring the lure of Fabric Warehouse. Seemingly, after a trip there, shoppers will feel compelled to deck out even the humblest of windows. Agency: CheethambellJWT, Manchester. Art director: Roger Leebody. Copywriter: Gill Glendinning.

5&6. Recipe instructions wittily double as interior design tips in these stylish ads for the new Sainsbury's home range. "Cover with caramel and chill" refers to the caramel-coloured cushions on a white sofa in a minimalist apartment with stunning city views. "Place on middle shelf" refers to the prospective placement of a clock in a wood-panelled apartment. Agency: Abbott Mead Vickers.BBDO. Creatives: Diane Leaver, Simon Rice. Photographer: Henrik Knudsen.

7. Ad for Matelsom.com, an online mattress and bed supplier based in France. London-based design studio FI@33, who created the ad, have been working with the company since September 2001, helping them develop communications solutions and devising a new identity.

Wallpaper manufacturers Cole & Son's new Contemporary Collection includes work by interior designer David Hicks (Hicks's Moghul shown, following page) who died in 1998 after a long and distinguished career. See www.cole-and-son.com to view the entire collection and to order samples from the range

Degree Shows

"What does it mean?" asked Charlotte, who had never used soap flakes in her life.

1

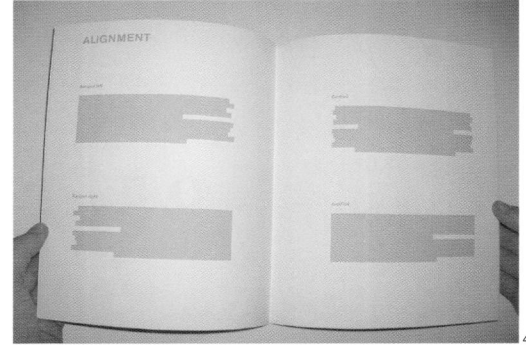

ALIGNMENT

4

"Thank you for contributing"

1. Illustration for EB White's popular children's book, Charlotte's Web. By Mooks Hanifiah of the RCA.

2&3. Alison Puyaoan studied Graphic Design at the University of Brighton. Her re-design of magazine The Face rigorously follows RNIB guidelines for partially-sighted

readers (see also CR January).

4. Michael de la Lama, also from the University of Brighton designed this book exploring typographic techniques. This section expresses different types of alignment.

5. RCA students Kirsty Carter and

Emma Thomas' project The Grey Blanket comprises a series of messages made by rubbing away the dirt on city walls. In another project, the pair set themselves the task of sending a bit of New York back to the UK: this they did by faxing back, piece-by-piece, this full-size image of a street scene to Emma's dad (6).

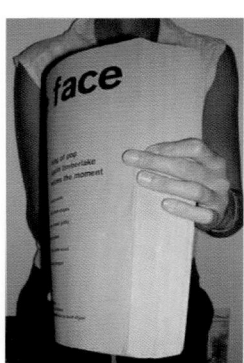

face

2

up
moschino

down
moshpits

3

New York

6

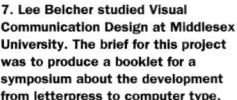

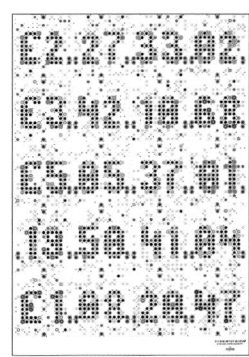

7

8

9

7. Lee Belcher studied Visual Communication Design at Middlesex University. The brief for this project was to produce a booklet for a symposium about the development from letterpress to computer type.

8. Poi Ein Wong of LCP's Graphic and Media Design course created

these stamps. Red dots signify decimal places after pound values and before pence values, allowing users to see the total value of stamps on a package at a glance. The dots also refer to the perforations on the edges of stamps.

9. RCA Communication Art and

Design MA graduates Sebastian Helling and Ellen Jacoby created this poster for a sound seminar at the RCA entitled Cellular Activity. The lettering is made from 7253 stickers representing different types of cells found in the human body.

10&11. Also from the RCA MA,

Mildred Djupvik's project documents meteorological data for London over a year, sampled at two-hour intervals and reflecting the precipitation and tonal value of the sky. The piece consists of 365 small collages, made from strips of colour made using thread, mounted in 12 rows and measuring 200cm x 120cm.

12&13. Antigone Charalambous from the LCP's Graphic and Media Design course attempted to convey the scale of World War Two using a series of postcards. Each card, divided into seven columns, describes the events of one week in the conflict: each day is colour-coded depending on its importance

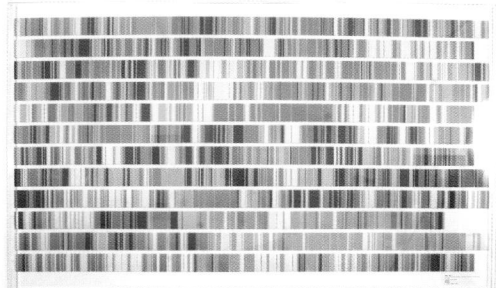

10

11

12

13

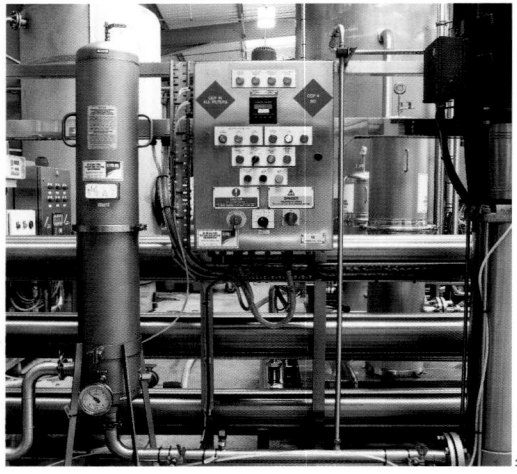

1

1. One of a series of highly detailed industrial interiors by Lee Hickman of the University of Plymouth.

2. Ly Tran took this shot on Hampstead Heath and then, responding to a poem by Nazim Hikmet about preserving landscape and memories, peeled apart a C-type print of the image (having soaked it in water) and set the layer containing the image in ice. This is the beautiful result of the project.

3. Tom Fearn and Chris Smith's series on north London took them to Alexandra Palace to shoot this piece, Ice Rink Staff. Both studied Graphic Design at St Martins.

4. For Joss McKinley's project, The End, the St Martins Graphic Design graduate documented the lives of the official London darts team. Shown here are their supporters watching them in competition at Tottenham social club, The Edge. McKinley has recently launched www.andsobegins.co.uk, a portfolio he shares with three other students.

5. Sarah Eastwood of the University of Westminster took this shot of brother and sister James and Clare as one of a series of double portraits of siblings called Born to Love You.

6. This untitled piece, by Torill Øye at Kent Institute, was taken in the Norwegian countryside.

3

2

4

5

6

7. Graduating from the University of Brighton's Editorial Photography BA course, Tony Ellwood took this brooding shot of sky and sea at Shoreham-by-Sea with his back to a power station. One of a series of shots of the sea looking out over a sewage outlet. "I think a lot of the colours in the water may be caused by the waste being constantly pumped into it," he comments, "and yet it's incredibly peaceful there. The place has an end-of-the-world quality to it."

8. For her Photography MA at the University of Westminster, Cinnamon Heathcote-Drury created this piece entitled Heterotaxy-A. The title refers to a condition in which major internal organs are misaligned. The piece is part of a series which reacts to misogynist portraiture by placing men in typical female poses with deliberately androgynous results.

9. University of Brighton's Lewis Allen took this photograph in the summer of 2002 in Nagoya, Japan's fourth largest city, whilst he was living there and working on a photographic project of which this image is a part. Influenced by futurist Marinetti's idea of the global megalopolis, Lewis explains his project: "I work mainly at night and concentrate on man-made structures and modern living space whether it be within large Utopian complexes, street spaces or, in this case, an underpass of a Japanese highway."

7

8

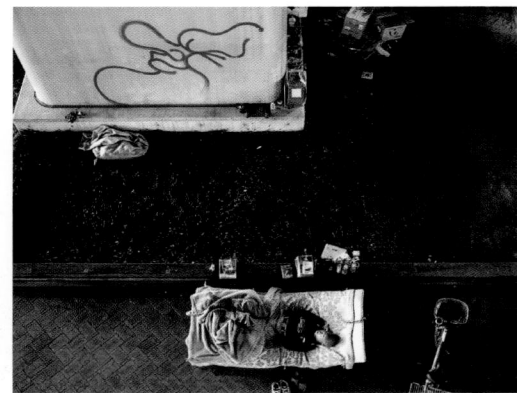

9

Word on the Street

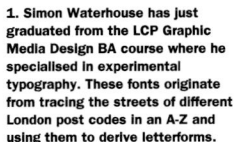

1. Simon Waterhouse has just graduated from the LCP Graphic Media Design BA course where he specialised in experimental typography. These fonts originate from tracing the streets of different London post codes in an A–Z and using them to derive letterforms.

2. RCA student Mark Hopkins' brief from the Communication Art and Design department was to produce a self-portrait. Hopkins' response is this ingenious letterpress piece. He weighed metal type, selected an amount of characters equal to his body weight and then printed them.

3. For his Illustration course at the London College of Printing, Henrik Andersson created the Blam typeface using various guns and rifles. It was then used on the cover of his book Nowhere Fast.

4. Terry Stephens, Lee Asher, Mikkel Lehne, Harvey Coxell and Emma Barratt of the Southampton Institute, created a book on famous graphic designers (cover shown).

5. Matthew Falla of St Martins' Graphic Design course designed this typeface entitled Celebrity Status.

6&7. Rin Quang Chau of Middlesex University decided to tackle the D&AD brief to design a series of mailers for Creative Review. "My idea was to form the words within their literal context," explains Chau

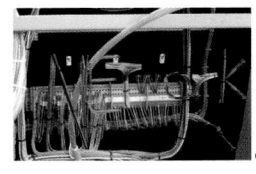

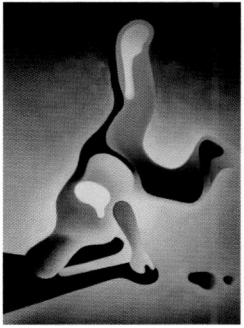

1&3. Graduating from the Central Saint Martin's BA course in Art and Design, Tom Gavin has produced a series of paintings of breakdancers, created using oil paint on board. Says Gavin on the series: "My main concern was to try to represent space and movement by altering the human form to the point of complete abstraction".

2. Also by Tom Gavin, this image was created by adding sketches of breakdancers onto an urban photograph (also shot by Gavin) using Photoshop.

4. This illustration formed part of Henrik Andersson's book Nowhere Fast (see 3, previous page).

5. This brilliant illustration of a crowd scene was created by Central Saint Martins BA Graphic Design graduate Rob Farquhar.

6. Unique and fun, this stencil portrait was created by LCP BA Graphic and Media Design graduate Borja Martinez who used melted chocolate instead of ink.

7. RCA communication art and design MA graduate Yuko Kondo has created a comic book based on the story of Romeo and Juliet entitled Mask. Shown here are 3D toys of the characters and wallpaper featuring frames from the comic. They are available for sale directly from Kondo himself at junboyuko@hotmail.com

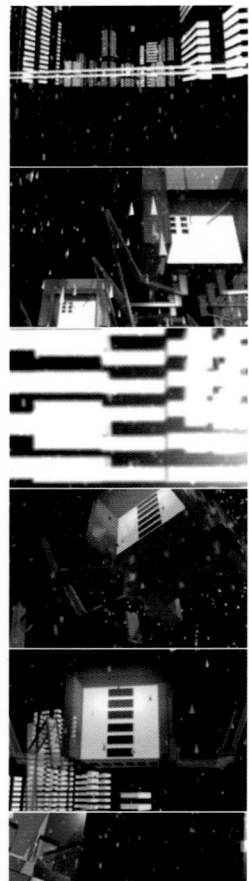

Jason Gregory of Bath Spa University's Graphic Design course created this charming would-be Channel 4 ident in which a spider-like machine walks among tower blocks through an urban nightscape

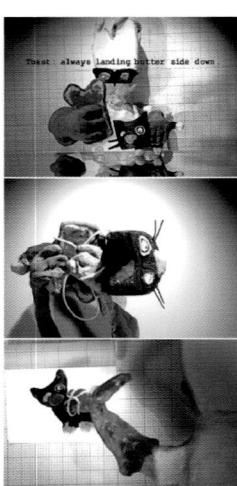

The scientist in Katharina Koall's Merry Science film, for St Martins' Graphic Design course, tests the theory that toast always lands butter-side-down by taping a slice to a cat who is flung out of the window

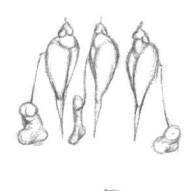

Emily Mantell's RCA film, To Have and to Hold, is a pencil-drawn animation featuring several female figures of various sizes and a selection of subordinate penises

The Amazing, Mysterious and True Story of Mary Anning and her Monsters tells of Anning's struggle to get her prehistoric discoveries accepted by her fellow scientists. By Laura Heit at the RCA

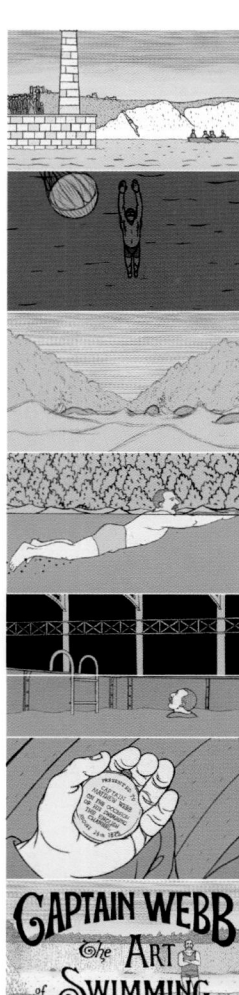

Robert Milne's beautiful RCA animation, Captain Webb: The Art of Swimming, charts the sad tale of Webb's fateful attempt to swim the rapids of Niagara Falls in 1893

Tina Mansuwan made her film, Ode to Winter, for the St Martins Graphic Design course. Animated in Flash, the piece follows the romantic adventures of two foxes in a snowy fairytale landscape

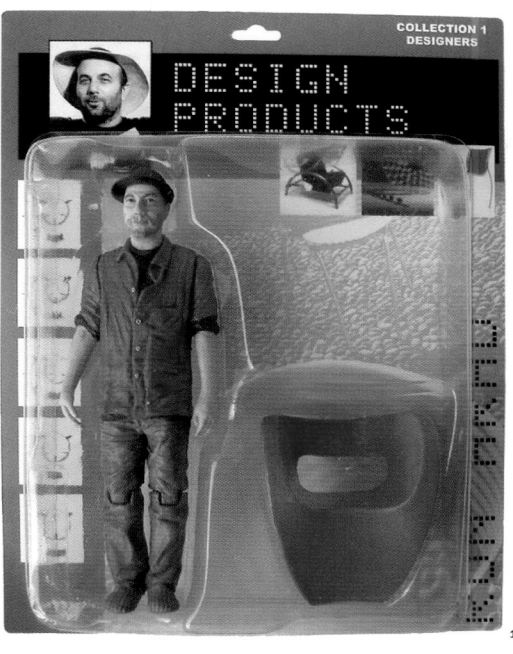

1. Playing on the trendiness of collectable designer dolls, RCA Product Design graduate Khashayar Naimanan has gone one step further: the designer as a doll. This moulded and cast, hand-painted Ron Arad toy comes complete with a to-scale Ron Arad chair and is the first of a planned series of designers as action figures.

2. Also from the RCA's Product Design course, Murat Konar exhibited what appeared to be lights. Silent and emitting a steady glow when not being played with, the Loopqoobs come to life when picked up. They generate loops of music depending what side they're resting on. One cube triggers drum loops, the second bass loops and the third electronic blips. All are sequenced so that all the sounds are in synch

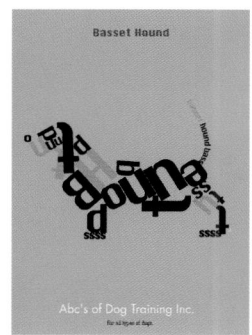

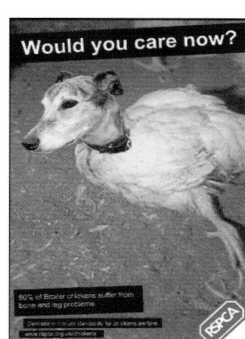

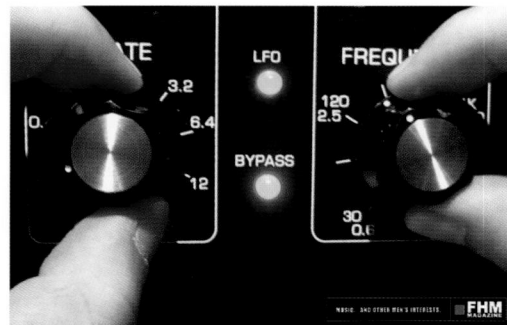

3. One of three executions for a Listerine brief by Miami Ad School's Santiago Mussfeldt (art director) and Chad Williamson (copywriter). Each ad suggests the nasty effects on your breath of eating without following up with a mouth wash.

4. One of a series of typographical ads for a dog training centre that caters for all types of dogs. Each traces the shape of a different breed using the letters of its name. By Steve Timana, also from the MAS.

5. Nick Dellanno and Will Thacker of the Surrey Institute of Art & Design developed this campaign which highlights cruelty to animals issues for the RSPCA. Playing on the Brits' reputation for loving their pets, a chicken's head has been replaced with that of a dog to show how abysmal conditions generally are for mass-bred broiler chickens.

6. One of several clever executions for a suitably smutty FHM campaign by Miami Ad School graduates,

Marjorieth SanMartin and Jinho Kim, both of whom are art directors.

7. Teabow Braine and Thanh Chu of Central St Martin's Graphic and Communication Design course came up with this simple and witty ad for Hovis. Anyone for toast on beans?

From this year's D&AD Student Awards: 1. Esther Alcaide from Barnet College won first prize in the Ambient Media category with this inscribed bench – the brief was to "build the Pret a Manger brand to new customers" and keep it "fresh and relevant". 2. First prize in TV Graphics went to Tim Smyllie of Chelsea College of Art and Design for his on-screen identity for a personalised TV channel. 3. The brief for the Information Design category was to "design a fundamental improvement in the way information for a familiar medication is communicated". Debbie McKay of Duncan of Jordanstone College of Art won first with this packaging solution for Warfarin (3), a drug which prevents the recurrence of blood clots. 4. "A new and desirable whisky concept for a younger audience", created by Ben Cox of Somerset College of Art and Technology who won first prize in the Brand Identity and Development category. 5&6. In the Graphic Design category, students were asked to create a campaign that "introduces Adobe Acrobat to the finance, government or manufacturing industries". The first prize went to Taikee Chan of Middlesex University

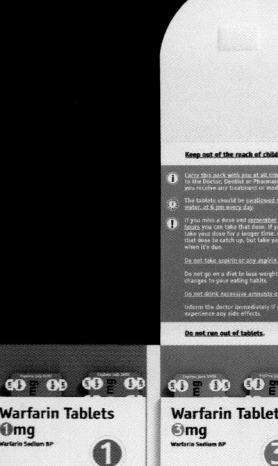

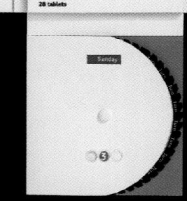

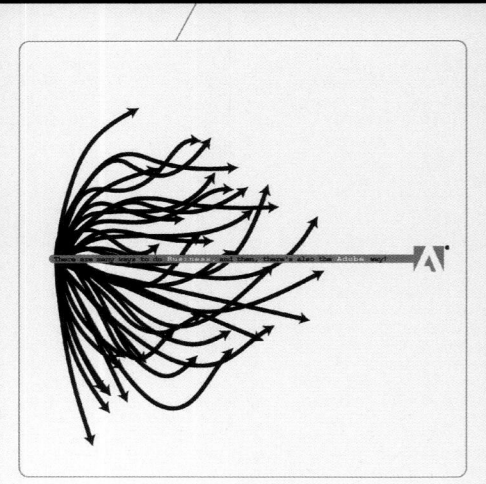

Front Cover

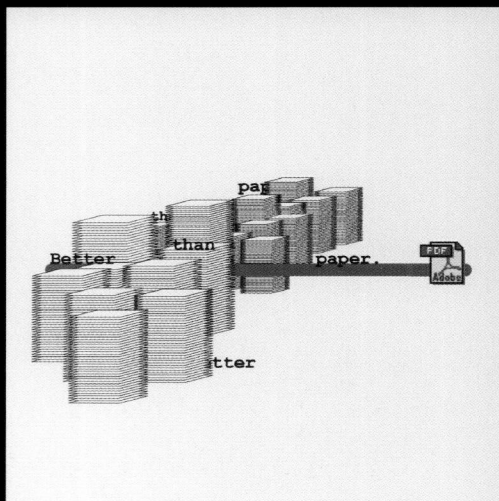

7

9

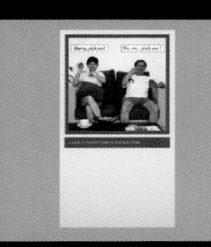

10

11

Billboard

13

For the Typography category, students were asked to design subscription mailers for Creative Review using expressive letterforms. There were no first prizes but Pie Lee-Mun of Birmingham Institute of Art and Design won second prize (7, bitter? Us?) as did Anna Hjertqvist (8) of Central Saint Martins. 9-12. David Leisinger Zhirong of Temasek Polytechnic in Singapore won first prize in the Website Design category with his site demonstrating the benefits of texting to the over-40s. 13. The first prize in Advertising Campaign – Open Brief went to Kathrina Hahn and Stephen Howell of Buckinghamshire Chilterns University College for their campaign launching the Peugeot 206 GTI 180, which was supposed to position the car as the "new hot-hatch benchmark". 14. Alex Braxton and Mark Ward of Central Saint Martins won first prize in the Advertising Transport Media category for a series of bus-sides aiming to get younger people to read Good Housekeeping magazine. For more on the awards, see www.dandad.org

159 Tips for making your garden splendid

Good Housekeeping

61 I killed my husband

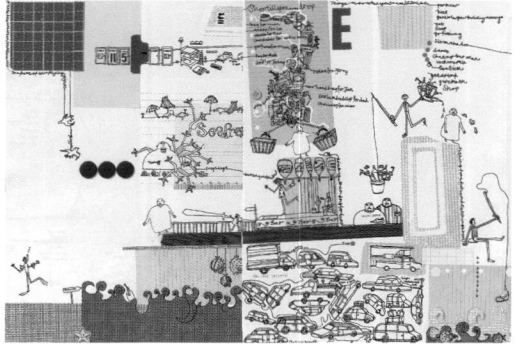

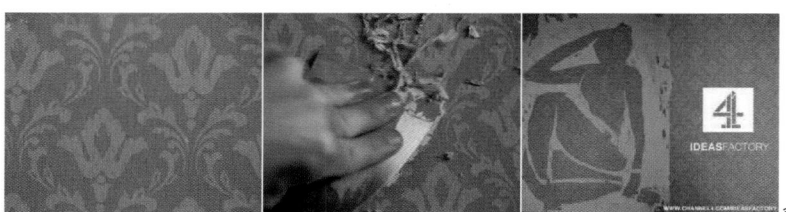

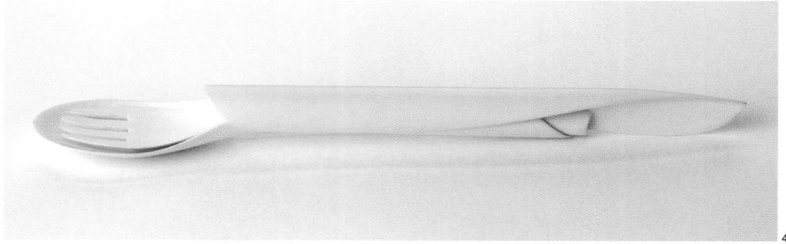

Work from the winners and finalists of this year's D&AD Student Awards. 1. Image illustrating 22 miles (the distance of the channel crossing from Dover to Calais) for ferry company SeaFrance. The brief asked that illustrations be appropriate for use in local press, brochures and direct mail. This is student Ella Sparkes of Birmingham Institute of Art and Design's response.

2. Jan Lun Lee of Glasgow School of Art won the Environmental Design category with this airport departure lounge concept for Virgin Atlantic.

3. Neil Andrews of the University of Portsmouth responded to a brief from Channel 4's Ideasfactory. The challenge was to create a 60 second on-air promotional trailer.

4. D&AD Student of the Year Marta Lago Arenas of the Royal College of Art developed this beautiful Global Food Concept cutlery. She shared the Student of the Year honour with John Threlfall, of Blackpool & the Fylde College who brings the country to city-dwellers' doorsteps via his ambient media campaign for National Magazine Company title Country Living (5&6).

7. Those split ends never looked better: a clever ambient campaign adhered to mirrors in women's toilets, encouraging them to catch up on the beauty tips available to Cosmopolitan readers. Part of an ambient campaign developed by Simon Au of Ontario College of Art & Design in Canada

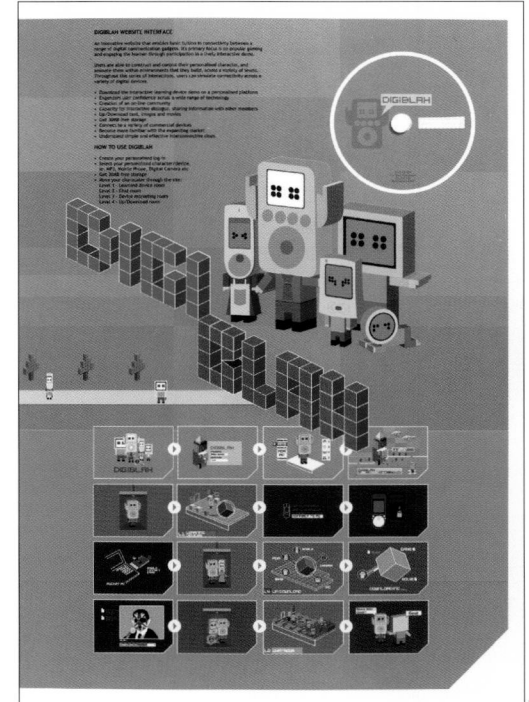

8. We think it's a blue bird... again, it's in response to the SeaFrance brief to illustrate the distance of the Channel crossing from Dover to Calais. Drawn by James Nelson of Southampton Institute.

9. Ka Yan Leung Perry of Chelsea College of Art & Design developed this website interface engendering connectivity between various digital communication devices.

10. This was one of a series of posters by Mark Palmer of Ravensbourne College of Design & Communication. The brief from organisation Witness was to raise awareness on human rights issues.

11&12. In-store concept for Pret A Manger, communicating the launch of new products. Designed by Katie Schofield at University of Salford.

13. This information pack for Durex was intended to help raise awareness about the importance of safe sex to students, particularly during Freshers' Week. This glow-in-the-dark pillow case has a pocket on the back for keeping condoms in. The luminous text serves as a constant reminder. Designed by Eugene Ng Wing Kin of London College of Communication.

14. Tesco.com ad campaign aimed at selling the store's online service to busy young professionals. It was developed by students Kelly McDonald and Andrew O'Sullivan of Buckinghamshire Chilterns University College

1

1. This image by Ellie Tobin of a road with tyre marks was part of a project about disused or reclaimed spaces: she took it as part of her BA Photography course at Camberwell College of Arts.

2. Shot by Joe Humphrys, taken from his book project A Point of View/A Viewpoint exhibited at the Surrey Institute BA Photography degree

show. The book contains images of a person viewing a landscape upside down and also images taken from that person's upside down perspective.

3&4. "As isolated fragments seeking to represent the loss of the individual within the office space, these quiet melancholic images stand as intimate observations of

the passing of existence," says Lucy Atkinson of these images. They formed part of her degree show with The Arts Institute of Bournemouth.

5. Ian Hayman of the University of Portsmouth took this image of the Millennium Stadium, which explores the multi-faceted way in which the structure is used by the public

3

4

6

7

More work from The Arts Institute at Bournemouth. The photography produced this year by the students was of an extremely high standard and the images on this page are just a few highlights. Einar Horsberg shot these beautiful pictures of trees, (6&7) explaining: "My goal is to create spaces where the haunting characteristics of the night are passed on to the audience, allowing them to get lost in their own imagination."

8&9. "My work discusses notions of the sublime and control within nature and the self," explains Thomas Brown of his pictures. "They depict very powerful masculine environments containing details of control and intervention. The work raises questions about the authenticity of natural environments and the stability of the concept of nature itself."

10. This striking image of a blow-up doll was taken by Hannah Bradburn. "My work represents the cultural objectification of women, using a surrogate to explore and deconstruct the issue," she comments

8

9

10

1

2

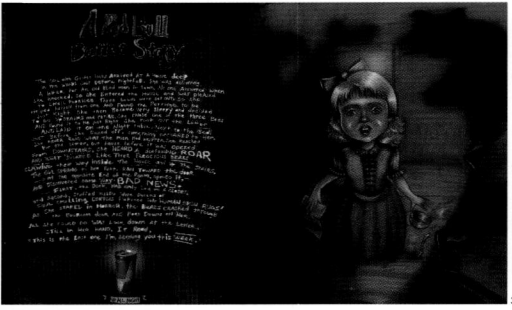

3

4

5

1. Erin Petson of Liverpool John Moores University's Graphic Arts course created this delicately illustrated ad for fashion label Chloé.

2. Also from John Moores, Natasha Jordan art directed and illustrated this ad for Selfridges.

3. Nicely art directed ads exploring different ways to stay up all night, be it terrifying bed time stories or cans of Red Bull. Creatives: Kevin Koller, Joel Guidry, Dan Hofstadter, Miami Ad School, Miami Beach.

4. This poster campaign for Consumer Reports magazine gets brutal with the truth. Created by art director Svetoslav Nikolov and copywriter Roberto Lastra of the MAS, San Francisco.

5. The Baby Einstein Company specialise in developmental products for babies and toddlers. This ad shows the potential side-effects of buying their products. Also by Kevin Koller, Joel Guidry and Dan Hofstadter, MAS, Miami Beach.

6. This witty ad for Dairy Crest Milk is by Hannah Tourle of Somerset College's BA in Design (Advertising).

7. Sharp campaign for Wustoff Knives: Svetoslav Nikolov and Roberto Lastra, MAS, San Francisco.

8. Chav-tastic campaign idea for fashion label Burberry. By Deborah Lyal of Glasgow School of Art.

9. "I used urban images to create the idea that the three stripes will see you through the toughest and roughest of urban environments," says Chris McClean of Cambridge Regional College of this adidas ad

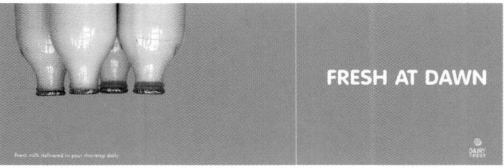

FRESH AT DAWN

6

7

8

9

10. Sandeep Channarayapatna of the RCA's Animation MA course created a touching tale of love and loss using the simplest of drawn lines and forms. The poetic nature of the narration complements the sparse animation beautifully.

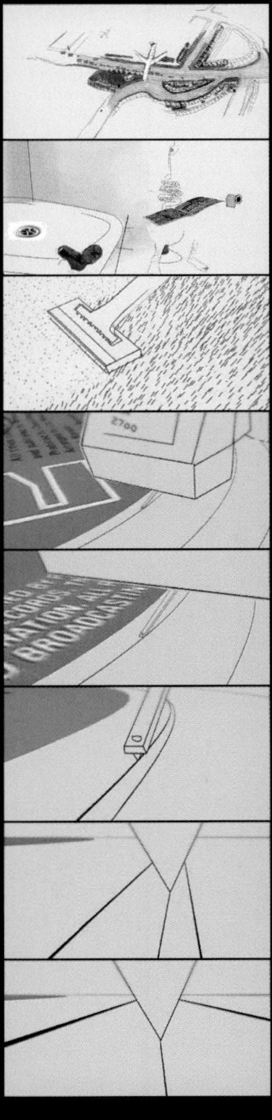

11. Video stills from Chris Cornish: "The degree show consisted of two pieces, 'Volume' and 'So it goes' which is a dual screen piece." explains Cornish. So it goes he describes as a "high resolution video depicting a desolate, haunting landscape environment. Abandoned concrete structures and atmospheric effects evoke a feeling of uncanny wonder in what could be an arena of war." Volume is a repeating video sequence "in which the camera circles the perimeter of a woodland clearing. Scorched concrete and an unexplained volume of light pay homage to both the painting of Friedrich and the writing of Ballard." The Slade School of Fine Art.

12. Barry Murphy of the RCA's MA Animation course creates the illusion of three dimensions using simple, clean lines in his film A Perfect Day.

13. Also from the RCA. Sumito Sakakibara's beautifully illustrated and directed film Kamiya's Correspondence sees a young girl writing a letter to her family with all her news

10

11

12

1

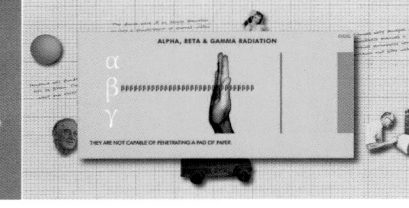

2

1. www.crew8.net showcases the graduate work from Sweden's new media college, Hyper Island. The project was conceived by students Nico Nuzzaci and Vinh Kha, with help from Adam Frankel, Daniel Carlsson and Mikael Wideström.

2. Interactive project by Tom Tribe of the University of Wales Institute, Cardiff. Entitled A Thousand Suns, it explores the science behind the first atomic bombs. "Emphasis is placed on making complex data both educational and entertaining," comments Tribe. This project was one of D&AD's Best New Blood. See www.athousandsuns.com

3. This site for Social Suicide, a clothing brand set up by Simon Waterfall and Matthew Grey, was designed by Hyper Island students Adam Frankel, Henrik Engdahl and Nico Nuzzaci. A book on the project (4&5) was also produced by the team. The online work was done at Poke in London and is set to replace www.socialsuicide.co.uk soon.

6. Michael Claque, University of Wales Institute, Cardiff was another winner of this year's D&AD Best New Blood. "Because new technology is seen by many as merely a production tool, it has been overlooked as a means of evoking emotions and experiences. AOOA is a place where users can experience these emotions and interact with the computer on a personal level," he explains. See www.aooa.co.uk.

7. Charlie Koolhaas and Olie Sylvester's MA show at Goldsmith College, University of London was entitled Phonebrainz. Sponsored by Orange, it features mobile phones, which are displayed in sculpted heads, "talking" to each other via animations displayed on the phones' screens (example shown, 8). The project aims to examine picture messaging as a new form of communication

3

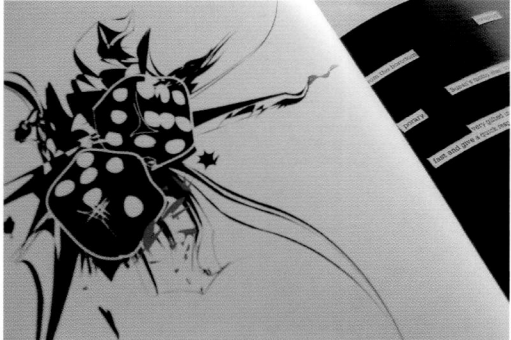

4

5

6

7

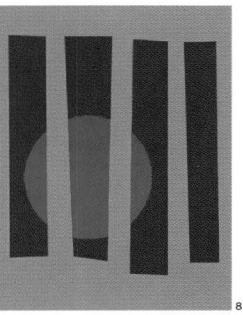

8

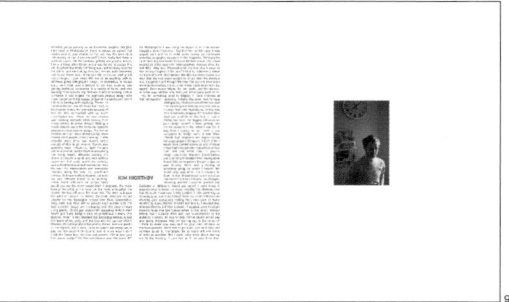

9

10

11

12

13

14

9&10. S Book 2 contains interviews with 24 leading record sleeve designers (spreads for Kim Hiorthøy and Stefan Sagmeister shown), put together by Southampton Institute graphics students Richard Spencer, Janine Singh, Daniel Sillifant, Lindsay Burdekin and Craig Toomey. Edited and art directed by Nick Long. Published by Art Books International.

11. Dominic Witter of Liverpool John Moores designed this logo for the Forestry Commission.

12. Poster design by Luke Helliwell, also of John Moores, for a talk at Urbis in Manchester regarding the future of record sleeve design.

13. Responding to a brief set by John Brown Citrus Publishing

through The Young Creatives Network, John Moores' Emily Alston created this magazine concept called Beware of Fluff.

14. Abby Rampling designed covers, endpapers and slipcases for five children's novels (Treasure Island cover shown) as part of Stockport College's BA Design and Visual Arts course.

15&16. Stuart Rittschoff from Kingston's BA Graphics course answered the open-ended brief, Package 100 with this direct mail piece where recipients could place £1 into a slot, seal up the package and post it off to the charity UNICEF. Rittschoff's work formed part of D&AD's New Blood exhibition and was also shortlisted for their John Gillard Award.

17. Wordsworth: a project by Antima Nahar and Kruti Saraiya, typography students at the London College of Communication. Nahar and Saraiya spent three days in a room, writing down all the words said there: "If words were really tangible how saturated would you feel [by them]?" they ask. This is their attempt to bring this concept to life

15

16

17

1

2

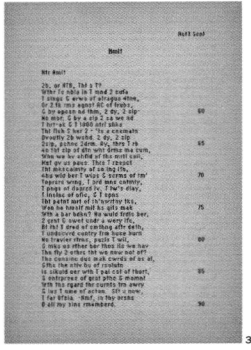

3

4

Jameel Gallery of Islamic Art

V&A

Victoria and Albert Museum
Cromwell Road
London SW7
020 7942 2000

Opening Times

5

1. To promote a lecture on sound and music by John Wozencroft, Gareth Holt and Daniel Mair at the RCA created a series of 20 musical instruments from tape and recycled materials. Each object included all the details for the talk and was also a functioning instrument.

2. Brilliantly executed typeface in the style of neon light signage by Joe Harries of Central Saint Martins.

3. As an exercise in bizarre modern formalism, John Moores student, Richard Bowater set Hamlet's famous 'To be or not to be' soliloquy in phone text abbreviations.

4. Neil Watts of University College Northampton created this poster to show the results of his investigation of non-computer related systems to develop pre-existing letter forms.

5. Graphic design student James White of Ravensbourne College of Design and Communication designed this merchandising for an Islamic Arts exhibition at the V&A. Geometric patterns are used throughout: "an important aspect of Islamic art," says White.

6. Muji lightbulb packaging based on a paper lampshade by Malcolm Fernandes, graduate of Loughborough University's Graphic Communication course.

7&8. Packaging design for Ski yoghurt and Asda own-brand pasta by Clare Stedman from Norwich School of Art & Design

6

7

8

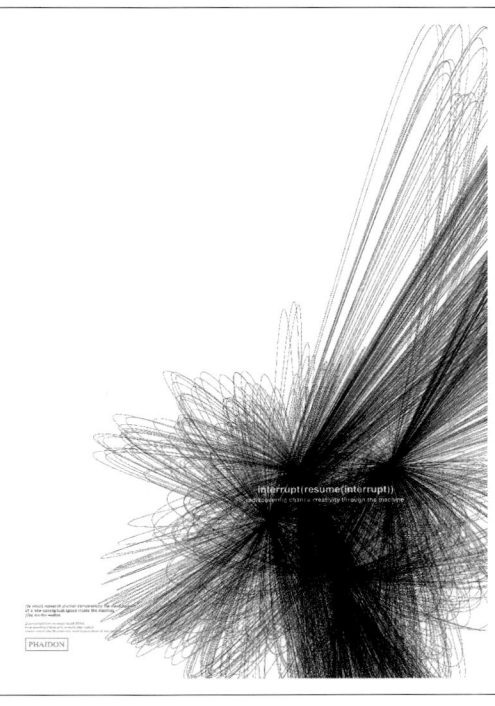

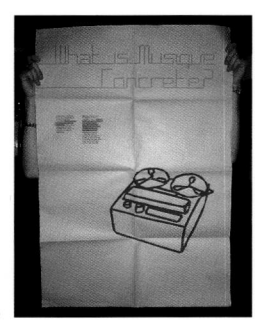

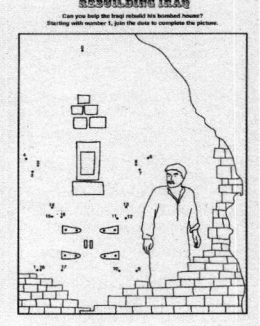

9. interrupt(resume(interrupt)) is a project by Martin Mains, graduating from the Graphic Communication course at University College Northampton. It seeks to exploit the way in which computers work in order to produce "chance creativity". Mains wrote "freethinking" programs which produced visuals, one of which appears on this poster.

10. This poster by Luke Pendrell of the RCA has been hand drawn and coloured and then covered with layers of newsprint soaked in glue to give an unusual varnished texture.

11. One of a set of seven posters by Si Dawson of Buckinghamshire Chilterns University on the theme of Musique Concrete – a movement from the 50s where music was composed from found sounds using tape. Thus, the image and type were made up by hand from audio tape.

12&13. Beautifully observed children's puzzle book in which all the games relate to the war in Iraq. By Izabella Bielawska of LCC.

14. Tesco Jelly packaging by Keely Jackman of Norwich School of Art & Design: the challenge was to appeal to both children and adults without forgetting that it's such a simple and silly product," she explains.

15. Different strengths of Superdrug cod liver oil have the required level of yuckiness in this packaging concept by Sarah Pidgeon, also from Norwich. Sarah designed these Extra Strong mint packs (16) as well

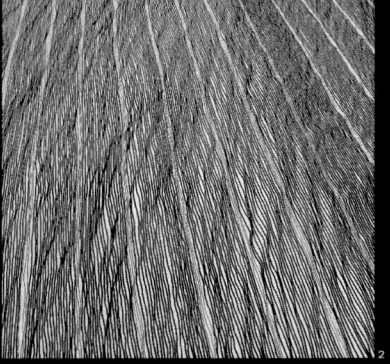

1. Anna Lundqvist's work examines gender roles in a capitalist society. These framed images form part of her illustrative portfolio from Camberwell College of Arts.

2. Jane Templeman, also of Camberwell, developed this visual examination of the passage of time. The lines are a private diary, a form of daily meditation; each line is drawn freehand with reference to the line above it, the lines coalesce to form a surface which represents time," Templeman explains. "Every day 5cm was added to each drawing, reaching a final length of 10m, and 1.5m wide," she adds.

3. This silkscreen print entitled Mrs Bixby in New York is by Leona Deger from Central Saint Martins.

4. One of three screenprinted posters by Claire Elliot of Leeds Metropolitan University. Each poster is based on a song lyric. They juxtapose nature scenes with images containing violent connotations. The latter are applied using a varnish, making the finished poster all the more ominous.

5. Spread from RCA student Astrid Chesney's textless but beautifully illustrated book entitled La Nuit.

6. By Monika Spahl, RCA. "I wanted to draw as quickly and emotionally with the thread as I do with ink and graphite," says Spahl. "I used a soft, thin thread to draw the soft shapes of the female body."

7. Julia Hutchinson from Bath Spa University's Fine Art degree course created this piece called Believer by handwriting text from the Bible.

8&9. Gary Dewar's illustrations of characters from the Wizard Of Oz reference the Frank L Baum novel, which is far darker in tone than the movie. Dewar has just graduated from the Visual Communcation course at Edinburgh College of Art

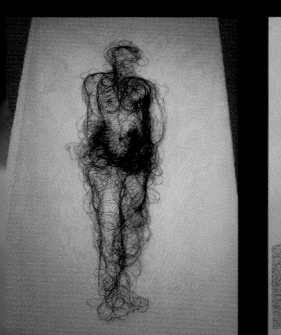

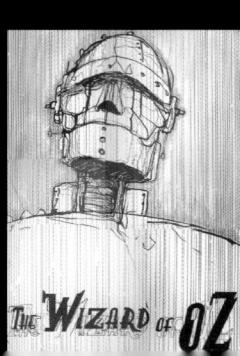

Charities & Not-For-Profit Organisations

1. Poster for Parisian park and cultural hub, La Villette, promoting a free firework display designed by famous pyrotechnic artists Groupe F (who also organised the millennium fireworks at the Eiffel Tower). Designed by Johnson Banks.

2. Leaflet for Deptford Design 03, an exhibition bringing together designers from London SE8. Designed by Cog Design, who also did the identity which is used on the cover as a background image in a spot varnish.

Since 1995, The Jerwood Foundation and the Crafts Council have collaborated on the UK's first major prize for applied arts. This year, NB:Studio were asked to design the print and marketing campaign for the Glass competition. NB:Studio commissioned photographer Martin Morrell to shoot a model behind safety glass to create a striking poster (4). The project also includes banners, an exhibition catalogue, and invitations (3)

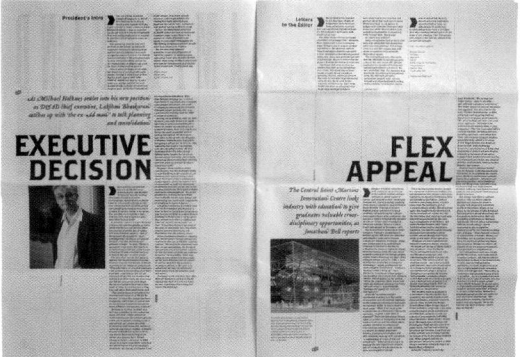

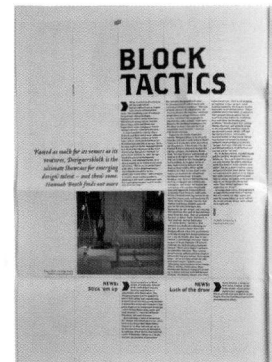

5-7. Editor Lakshmi Bhaskaran and Frost Design have turned the D&AD's members' publication, Ampersand, into an editorial design lab. Each issue is entirely different both in terms of layout and format. The latest is in the form of a one colour, 20 page newspaper, 345mm x 497mm. The fonts used are Woodtype Antique, Clarendon, Tribute, Brothers, Council and Helvetica Neue. Creative director: Vince Frost. Designer: Matt Willey.

8. Registered charity Cubitt is an artist-run gallery and series of studios based in Islington, London. Designers A2-GRAPHICS/SW/HK produce all promotional material for the organisation, including this elegant show invitation. Printed offset-litho onto a coated paper in an edition of 1000, the only limitation on this brief, we're told, was an extremely small budget.

9. NESTA, the National Endowment for Science, Technology and the Arts, funds and supports innovative ideas and projects in the three areas. London's Blast Design produce a tri-annual, "issue"-based journal for them. Each is themed around a subject which NESTA are actively involved with: the June 2003 issue looks at where creativity comes from and the barriers to it.

10&11. TypoGraphic is a journal published three times a year by the International Society of Typographic Designers. For TypoGraphic 60, designers A2-GRAPHICS/SW/HK addressed the theme "Primal Typography". The journal consists of eight, inter-leaved eight-page sections of coated and uncoated papers, printed off-set litho by FS Moore in London. It was then over-printed, letterpress, in both wood and metal by Stan Lane at Gloucester Typesetting Servies. A2 personally hand-folded the pages for each issue, wire-stitched the journals and hand-folded all the jackets. They also developed three typefaces specifically for the project. A real labour of love

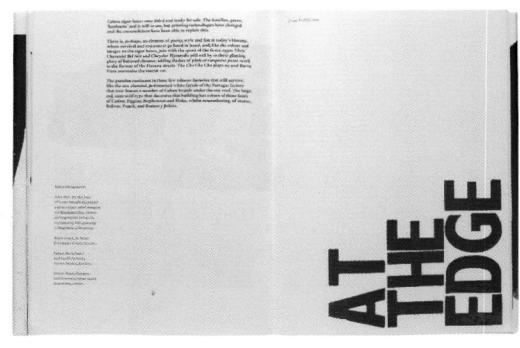

GÖR VÄRLDEN
LITE BÄTTRE.
WEBAID.SE

1   2

3

4

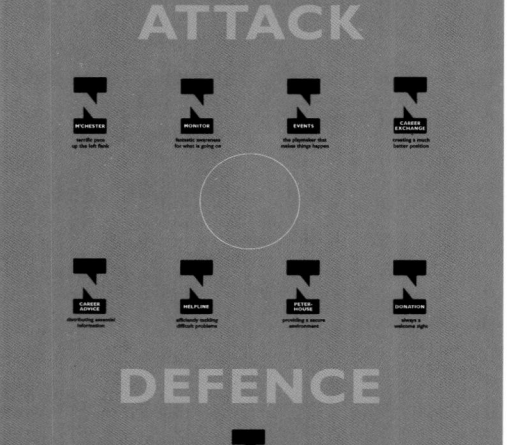

ATTACK

DEFENCE

5

1&2. Sweden Graphics have produced three short spots for a web-based charity, Webaid, which distributes money to projects initiated by other charities, reporting the developments on their website. The films, which all end with the tagline, "Make the world a little bit better" aim to get people to visit the site and see how they can help to contribute. The "helping hand" of the charity brings much needed water to victims in the Volcano spot (1) and bends the barrel of a tank's

gun backwards in Bang (2). Sweden worked on the project with intern Sakari Paananen and the music is by Kalle Baccman.

3&4. Before and after poster for Fairbridge, a charity set up to help inner city youth. The concept ties in with the charity's new annual report and is based on the effect that its work can have on young people. Copy reads, before, "I really couldn't face another day", after, "This year I've seen I'm worth something".

Designed by hat-trick, photography by Christine Donnier-Valentin.

5. Poster for NABS, the National Advertising Benevolent Society using the analogy of a football team to demonstrate the positions and strategy of the charity and its staff. Design consultancy: Lewis Moberly. Art director: Mary Lewis. Designer: Paul Cilia La Corte.

6. In Oxfam's Make Trade Fair spot a woman points and screams at a

man harmlessly ignoring a keep off the grass sign, the point being she could be using that finger to text and join a fair trade petition. Written by Simon Manchip, HHCL/Red Cell. Director: Tom Geens at Harry Nash.

7. Action Aid annual review, designed by Ranch. The charity fights to create a world without poverty. Its report features full-colour images of Action Aid's work. Included are scenes shot in the notorious City of God in Brazil

6

7

8. Poster for New Yorkers For Parks 2003 benefit gala by Michael Bierut at Pentagram, NY.

9&10. Neasden Control Centre created the images in this ActionAid booklet which explains the charity's work combating world poverty. Photographic images were inlaid with symbols and patterns to give the subject matter an emotional and personal context.

11. New logo for the Prince's Trust from Wolff Olins. The consultancy was also asked to help the charity to communicate with an audience who have reading and writing difficulties. A series of icons was devised (one shown, 12) challenging people to do something with their lives through the organisation. They are used across all Prince's Trust communications. Creative director: John Besford. Designers: Craig Hadley and Dave Shenton.

13. Identity for the Jewish Community Centre in Manhattan by Pentagram's Paula Scher who also devised a signage programme for the Centre's new building.

14. Pentagram partner John McConnell was appointed by The

Council for the Protection of Rural England (CPRE) to design a new symbol that would revamp their image. The redesigned symbol was launched this year to coincide with the organisation's new name: Campaign to Protect Rural England.

15. Print ad by FCB Melbourne for St Kilda Mission. It ran in local papers and encourages readers to donate blankets to the homeless. Creatives: Scott Lambert, Mark Ringer, Ben Couzens and Jim Ingram. Photography: Garth Oriander.

16. Simple, effective posters from Spirit Advertising for Trees For London, illustrating how planting trees can benefit the environment. Creatives: Tony Hector, Chris Hubert, Phil Ramage.

17. East Sussex County Council commissioned London's root to create an ad campaign for its Fostering Service. Root's aim was to bring humour and personality to the service and make it more friendly and approachable to potential foster parents. By interviewing parents of people who share the same name as someone famous they touched on the country's fascination with celebrity. Photography: Dave Young

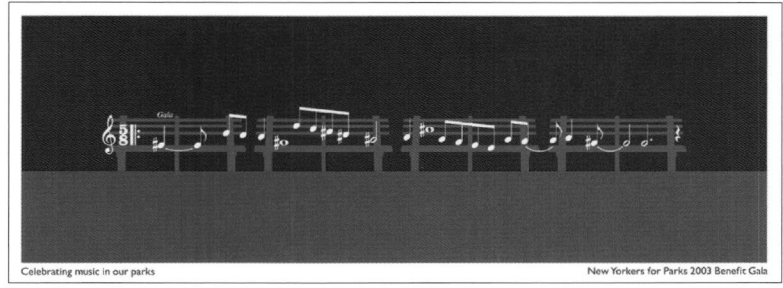

Celebrating music in our parks

New Yorkers for Parks 2003 Benefit Gala 8

9

10

Prince's Trust 11

get out of your box 12

JCC manhattan 13

Campaign to Protect Rural England 14

15

AIR FRESHENER

Trees absorb harmful gases like carbon monoxide through their leaves

Trees for London 16

We really care about Julia Roberts

take a starring role in a child's life
01323 747499

the fostering service 17

MEET
FRANK

0800 77 66 00 talktofrank.com
1

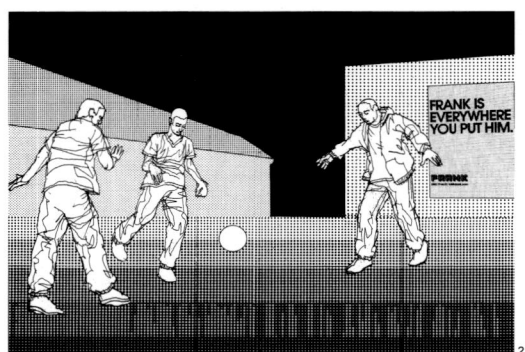

FRANK IS
EVERYWHERE
YOU PUT HIM.

FRANK
2

WHO MIGHT WORK WITH FRANK?

FRANK will work with anyone who can help. FRANK get in touch with FRANK's target audience. Some examples could include...

A fast food chain. This is one place where a teenager, a drug user and a worried parent would all go to regularly.

Or football clubs. Again somewhere that all our target audiences gather. Perhaps all clubs and their regular sponsors could be persuaded to replace their sponsors' logos with FRANK's name & number for a week.

Or how about FRANK teams up with after-school activities, or youth clubs? Maybe even a FRANK week takes place, where drugs are the main focus within each activity.

FRANK
0800 77 66 00 talktofrank.com
3

WHAT ELSE DOES FRANK GET UP TO?

Once established, there's no limit to where FRANK could go and what FRANK could do, as long as everything FRANK does is aimed at reducing the harm caused by the use of drugs.

And now you've got to know FRANK, you have the potential to use FRANK to do just that. Whoever you help, whatever drug they need help with, FRANK will help you help them.

Thank you for reading! Enjoy FRANK...

FRANK CAN
BE WHEREVER
YOU WANT
HIM TO BE.

FRANK
4

YOUR FRANK PACK

FRANK can help you out by providing a whole host of templates so that you can create your own local resources such as posters, stickers and business cards.

However, please remember that while FRANK can be anywhere and everywhere, FRANK only reflects Government drugs policy. So please use FRANK sensibly. If you are unsure about anything, go to drugs.gov.uk.

COCAINE
HEROIN,
WILL SORT YOU
OUT WITH ALL
OF THEM

FRANK
0800 77 66 00 talktofrank.com
5

FRANK
0800 77 66 00 talktofrank.com
6

FRANK
0800 77 66 00 talktofrank.com
7

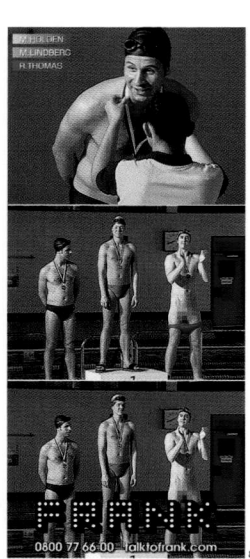

FRANK
0800 77 66 00 talktofrank.com
8

Calls to drug helpline FRANK almost doubled the week Mother's promotional campaign was launched. Commissioned for the COI, on behalf of the Home Office and Department of Health, the aim was to reduce the use of class A drugs in the UK. The campaign needed to communicate in different ways, to an extremely multifaceted audience including teenagers, parents, drug users and action workers. Copywriter Caroline Pay and art director Kim Gehrig realised that the best way to tailor this message to so many different people was to create "umbrella" brand FRANK, which could incorporate TV commercials, posters, radio ads, a website, a phoneline and action packs for individual drug workers across the country. "So FRANK can be a branded website, he can sponsor events, be a phone line at the end of a programme, he can bring out literature on drugs... he stands, very simply, for the whole thing," explains Pay. The name was chosen to lend a human element to the whole project: "We wanted it to be as human, non-judgmental and non-governmental as possible," adds Pay. "The brand has allowed us to talk to lots of different people in different tones of voice." Art director Gehrig worked with Peter Selberg, Richard Hart and illustrator Keith Watts on the overall identity. "We wanted a brand that was cool, friendly and approachable... we didn't want it to be seen as a crisis line," explains Gehrig. "The FRANK packs are used by local action groups (brochure cover and inside spreads shown, 1-5) so the whole look had to be cheap and easy to reproduce, which is why we went for the black and white: it can be replicated at very little cost." 6-8 shows examples of TV commercials highlighting the embarassment people feel about discussing drug issues, directed by Traktor. Gehrig and Pay deliberately went for a humorous tone: "You can't say 'Don't do it', or use shock tactics" says Pay of the work. "If you make people laugh, though, they'll listen to you." Creative directors: Jim Thornton and Robert Saville

New York-based Worldstudio Foundation is a non-profit organisation whose mission is to "stimulate, coalesce and channel social activism in the design and fine arts industries; to encourage discussion of the fields' ethical assumptions; to promote professional practices sensitive to ecological and humane issues; and to expand the global consciousness of individual artists, architects, designers, and the businesses they serve". It does this through a variety of scholarships, publications and mentoring programmes. One of the latter was the Create! Don't Hate, Tolerance poster project. Eleven design and illustration students were each partnered with a professional designer in order to produce a poster on the theme of tolerance. Sponsors Adobe provided InDesign software which was used to create each work. The final posters were published in Worldstudio's Sphere magazine and were recently exhibited at the Condé Nast building in New York. Shown are works by:

1. Tarek Atrissi of the School of Visual Arts and Paul Sahre, Office of Paul Sahre, New York, which proposes a universal hand gesture for the idea of tolerance.

2. Jenny Tran, Art Center and Karin Fong, Imaginary Forces, LA: a typographic treatment made up of hate messages posted on the web.

3. Wonravee Chavalit, Academy of Art College and Brett Wickens, MetaDesign, San Francisco: an anti-road rage message using an image of streaming headlights and type based on the visual language of car licence plates.

4. Michel Baptiste and freelance illustrator, Robert de Michiell: a comment on the labels others impose on us and the image that we ourselves project.

For more on Worldstudio Foundation, go to www.worldstudioinc.com

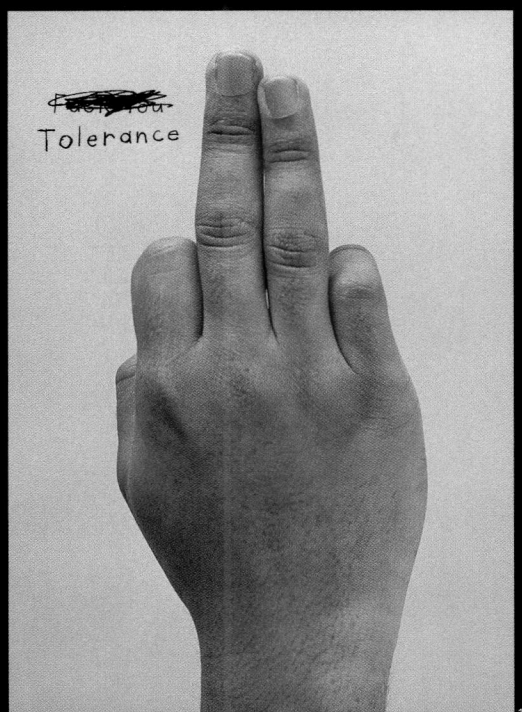

1

2

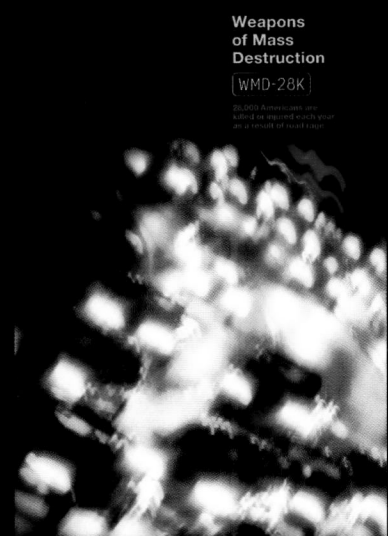

3

4

1&2. This consecutive page ad for online forum Asthma-Help neatly uses the red cross associated with first aid, to allude to an England football shirt. Copy points out that while footballer Paul Scholes has asthma, it hasn't stopped him playing for his national team. Creatives: Tony Bradbourne, Dominic Corp, Murray White. Typographer: Richard Bateman.

3. A prod to the conscience is used in this campaign for the NHS Gateway to Leadership programme, which aims to recruit and develop the next generation of leaders for the service. The concept was developed by Adrian Talbot at Intro and applied to press and website www.gatewaytoleadership.nhs.uk.

4. The latest spot from St Luke's Gremlins campaign for the COI/DfES. The ads highlight the humiliation suffered by people with literacy or numeracy problems via various evil gremlins who taunt the subjects. Each one is resolved by the main character seeking adult learning help, leading to the gremlin packing his/her bags. Creatives: Seyoan Vela, Colin Lamberton. Director: Chris Dada @ Academy.

5. Cardiff-based Golley Slater has produced a hard-hitting campaign aimed at raising awareness of problems caused by binge drinking in the Army. One is set in a nightclub, the other in a barracks. Both show soldiers vomiting into a toilet. As they do so, symbols representing their career are also shown going down the pan. Creative director and copywriter: Kerry Lloyd. Director: Mark Wordley, Wordley Productions

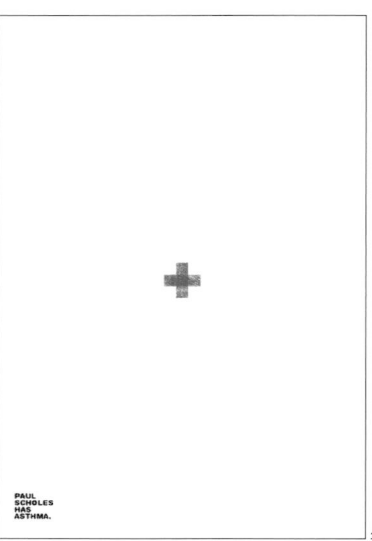

PAUL SCHOLES HAS ASTHMA.

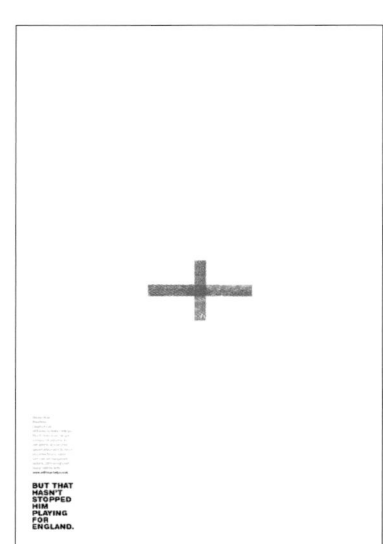

BUT THAT HASN'T STOPPED HIM PLAYING FOR ENGLAND.

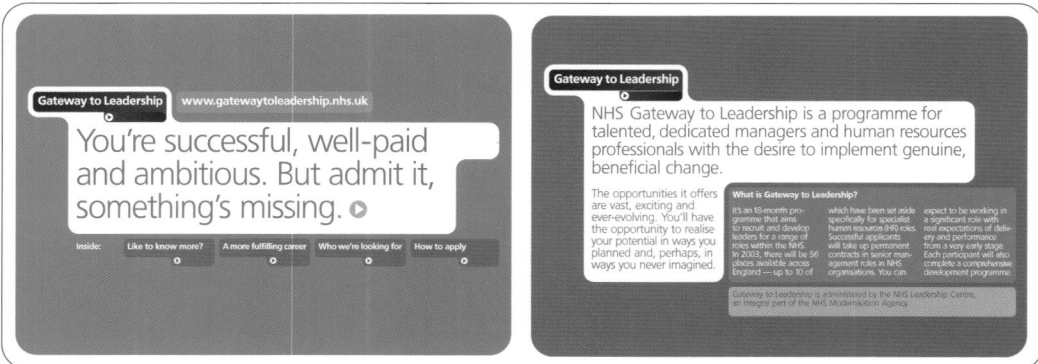

Gateway to Leadership | www.gatewaytoleadership.nhs.uk

You're successful, well-paid and ambitious. But admit it, something's missing. ●

Inside: | Like to know more? | A more fulfilling career | Who we're looking for | How to apply

Gateway to Leadership

NHS Gateway to Leadership is a programme for talented, dedicated managers and human resources professionals with the desire to implement genuine, beneficial change.

The opportunities it offers are vast, exciting and ever-evolving. You'll have the opportunity to realise your potential in ways you planned and, perhaps, in ways you never imagined.

What is Gateway to Leadership?

It's an 18-month programme that aims to recruit and develop leaders for a range of roles within the NHS. In 2003, there will be 56 places available across England — up to 10 of which have been set aside specifically for specialist human resources (HR) roles. Successful applicants will take up permanent contracts in senior management roles in NHS organisations. You can expect to be working in a significant role with real expectations of delivery and performance from a very early stage. Each participant will also complete a comprehensive development programme.

Gateway to Leadership is administered by the NHS Leadership Centre, an integral part of the NHS Modernisation Agency.

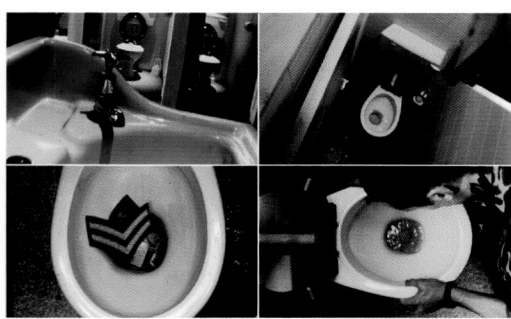

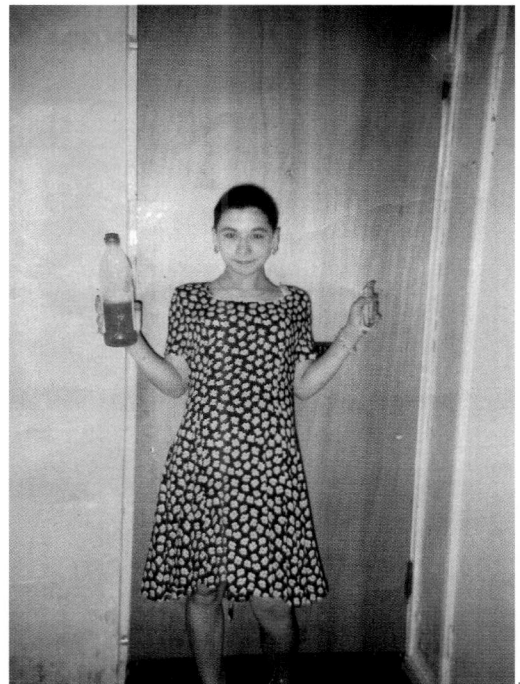

6,7&8. Useful Photography # 003 is a collaboration between the creators of Useful Photography Magazine and the National Missing Persons Helpline. Published by Artimo, it presents a series of images used to help search for people that have gone missing in the UK. The various photographs were collected and edited by Hans Aarsman, Claudie De Cleen, Julian Germain, Erik Kessels and Hans Van Der Meer.

9. Lighthearted, but nonetheless effective, ad for The Experience Corps. In the spot a voiceover urges Eric a jobless, isolated man in his 50s, to call and enquire about doing some skilled voluntary work.
Agency: Saatchi & Saatchi.
Creatives: Andy Clarke, Paul Ewen.
Director: Tom Norcliffe, Bikini Films.

10. In this cinema ad from the fpa (formerly the Family Planning Association), actress Lisa Faulkner asks couples in the audience to hold hands before asking each other searching questions about their sexual history. Written by Angus Macadam and Paul Jordan at Leo Burnett. Directed by Patrick Bergh from Partizan

www.onetermpresident.org

LETTER TO VAN GOGH
FROM HELL

1&2. DM pack for Amnesty International's Urgent Action campaign by James Victore. A mailer opens out to form a poster on one side (2). On the other (1) is information about how the programme works – members are asked to write or email a number of appeals regarding prisoners to the authorities each month – plus a cut-out coupon. Notepaper and stickers are also included.

3. Downloadable poster from www.onetermpresident.org. Stencils are also available from the site.

4-6. Letter to Van Gogh From Hell is the personal testimony of Iraqi artist, Saad Hirri, who suffered torture in the 1980s at the hands of

Saddam Hussein's regime before escaping to Scotland. As part of Scottish Refugee Week, Glasgow-based Freight designed the book and published it under its own imprint on behalf of the Scottish Refugee Council. Thirty-seven of Hirri's drawings and paintings are included.

7. Future Forests aims to reduce the world's carbon levels. To raise awareness and funds, Brandhouse WTS devised a gift idea whereby a newly-planted tree would be named in the recipient's honour. Creative director Dave Beard designed this series of tree-like cardboard tubes, with different "barks" to brand different types of gift. The tubes open to reveal specially-designed certificates authenticating the gift

8

9

8. Teaser for a Greenpeace anti-GM maize campaign by Airside. The ads have been put up along roadsides encouraging consumers to return their milk to supermarkets that do not guarantee that their milk comes from cows fed on GM-free feed. Airside have also produced banners, badges and stickers to promote the campaign. In addition, activists in milkman uniforms will be distributing leaflets which have a postcard

included in order for people to complain to supermarkets.

9. T-shirt designed for Medecins Du Monde by Airside. Available at www.airsideshop.com, £20, all profits to Medecins Du Monde.

10. The Shopper's Guide To GM is a Greenpeace website designed by Bureau for Visual Affairs (see p22). It features a database whereby users

can enter the name of a food product and find out its manufacturer's position on GM issues. www.www.greenpeace. org.uk/Products/GM/index.cfm

11. Maudlin people looking for a bit of perspective on life should check out the Global Rich List website. Tap in your income, and you'll probably find you're among the richest on the planet. "In a simple, truly interactive

and shamelessly action-driven piece of persuasion we're aiming to build on that moment of realisation and get individuals to make a donation to CARE International," explain Poke who developed the site. Check it out at: www.globalrichlist.com

10

11

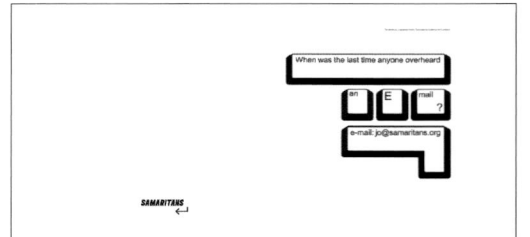

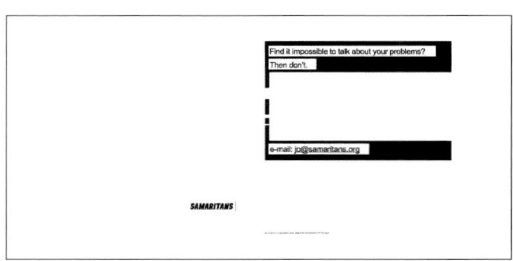

1-4. AMV.BBDO produced these posters for the RSPCA to show the distress fireworks cause animals. Launched to coincide with Bonfire Night, the work emphasises the sensitivity of animals' hearing to excessively noisy fireworks. Creatives: Paul Belford, Christian Sewell, Nigel Roberts, Andy McAnaney.

5. Illustrators and designers Kai and Sunny created this anti-war poster for CND. Also printed on T-shirts.

Also from AMV is a campaign for the Samaritans' recently launched email service (6&7). Picking up the phone is still an obstacle to some people who need to get in touch with the organisation; now they're able to email them in total confidence too. Creatives: Ian Heartfield and Matt Doman. Typographer: Steve Davies.

8-10. Land Registry posters from North: part of a campaign about its ongoing mapping of the country. "The Land Registry is re-engineering the physical landscape into a digital one," says North's Jeremy Coysten. Turning grid references into bytes of data allows The Land Registry to build a comprehensive land and property ownership database, which is why they dominate these posters.

11. The historic town of Bam, situated in eastern Iran, was destroyed by an earthquake on 26 December 2003. The World Monuments Fund, a non-profit organisation dedicated to the preservation of historic art and architecture, asked photographer Richard Mosse to document the devastation of the town's famous citadel and surrounding area. "They were interested in getting shots of the famous fortress, the Arg-e-Bam, which is an enormous World Heritage Site that was almost levelled by the quake," explains Mosse. Armed with his camera and a letter of endorsement from the WMF (enabling him to enter the town without attracting the attention of the police) Mosse also documented the daily struggle in the modern part of the town. A member of the ever-exciting Photodebut collective, whose recent show It Went Dark and I Saw featured his photographs from Iran, more of Mosse's work can be seen at www.richardmosse.com

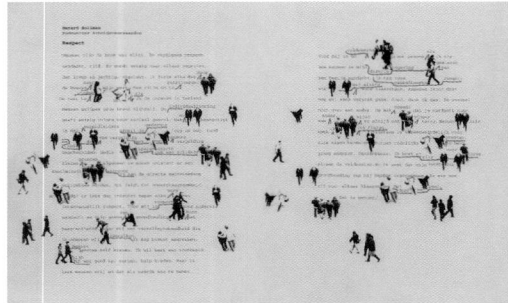

1&2. Amsterdam-based design agency Koeweiden Postma designed this annual report for Politie Gooi en Vechstreek – the police department of an Amsterdam district – and commissioned Marion Deuchars to provide illustrations and doodles.

3&4. In aid of the Greater Manchester Music Action Zone charity, Eg.G created this book with the cooperation of several year 10 students from Newall Green High School in Wythenshawe. Dom Raban and Paul Hemmingfield from the studio ran a course on "cyantyping" (a process that makes simple contact prints by placing acetate over coated paper and exposing it to sunlight) which made the illustrations for the book – a collection of the students' efforts at writing and performing Hip Hop.

5. The Commission for Architecture and the Built Environment aims to inspire people to demand more from their buildings and spaces. The Chase's London studio designed a new document that will be sent to the park rangers and groundspeople responsible for maintaining parkland. The step-by-step guide is based on photography of flipcharts shot in park environments. Designers: Harriet Devoy and Marc Atkinson

6. Press ad for The Global Fund to Fight AIDS, Tuberculosis & Malaria, by Publicis Conseil in Paris. Art director: Benoit Blumberger. Photographer: Jean Marie Vive. The copyline reads "Big problems require big solutions". As part of the same campaign, Publicis Zurich produced a special stamp bearing the Global Fund logo (7), designed by Lucas Vetsch, which was issued by the French post office.

8. Think London's task is to encourage inward investment in London. Johnson Banks created its identity and publicity materials in conjunction with Circus, who worked on the strategy. Creative director Michael Johnson says "It's a city identity that doesn't try to distil 8 million people down into one picture. It's a 'new' skyline based on all the things London has to offer." Principal designers: Michael Johnson and Julia Woollams. Photography: Chris Steele-Perkins, Magnum

9

10

Pippi-Dagen is a yearly event celebrating the birthday of The Astrid Lindgren Children's Hospital in Stockholm – an institution which relies on economic support from private beneficiaries and local companies. Shown (9) is the poster for this year's event designed, as it is every year, by Markus Moström and Jonas Bergstrand who also design all aspects of promotion and branding for the event.

10. You need to squint to read the text in this ad for the Royal National Institute for the Blind. "Every day," it points out, "over one hundred people in the UK start to lose their sight." Agency: J Walter Thompson, London. Creatives: Ian Gabaldoni, Richard Baynham. Typographer: Sefton Quest.

11. Annual report for Witness, designed by Lippa Pearce. Witness-trained partners produce videos that help expose human rights violations throughout the world. The report was designed to the same size as a video tape, and printed on recycled stock using soy-based inks.

12. Posters for Pilotlight which recruits high-fliers from business and industry and matches them with charities who need their skills. The A0 posters were produced by Lippa Pearce for a party to attract new recruits: the idea was to play on the mutual dependence of charity and high-flyer.

Disgusted with the logo visible from his own house, graphic designer Mark Brown of studio Honkshoo got in touch with Greenwich Peninsula Ecology Park and offered to design a decent one for them (shown 13). While he was at it, he also designed the Wildlife Watch Club logo for them too (14)

11

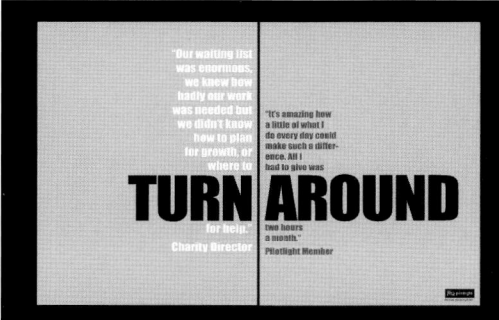

"Our waiting list was enormous, we knew how badly our work was needed but we didn't know how to plan for growth, or where to
"It's amazing how a little of what I do every day could make such a difference. All I had to give was
TURN AROUND
for help."
Charity Director
two hours a month."
Pilotlight Member

12

GREENWICH PENINSULA
ECOLOGY PARK

13

wildlife watch club

GREENWICH PENINSULA ECOLOGY PARK

14

Will you remember today forever? You read the news. You learnt that someone on TV had an affair. House prices went up. A celebrity had a boob job – or did she? A revolutionary diet raised health fears. A politician launched an initiative. A footballer had a haircut. But will you remember today forever? An ad on the tube changed your life. You remembered what really matters, and you decided to do something about it. You offered your professional experience to VSO. You volunteered to go and live and work in the world's poorest countries. You didn't wait to read that the world had changed. You went and took part in it. This is the ad. This is the website: www.vso.org.uk. This is the number: 020 8780 7500. This is the day.

VSO
Sharing skills
Changing lives

Will you remember this ad forever? You read one like it a while ago. It didn't offer you anything cheaper, cooler, with less fat or another one free. All it offered was the chance to do something about the state of the world. Then you got off the train, and on with your life, as usual. But will you remember this ad forever? This time you decided you wanted more than life as usual. And not for you alone, either. You have professional experience and unique talents. You volunteered to share them with people in the world's poorest countries. To go and live and work with them. To change your life, and theirs. And maybe the world. Remember this ad. Go to this website: www.vso.org.uk. Call this number: 020 8780 7500. Today.

VSO
Sharing skills
Changing lives

Veterinary

Preventative medicine

Highly contagious and potentially serious, kennel cough has been endemic here for as long as anyone can remember. Running in parallel with the Royal Veterinary College (RVC) investigation, we started a trial whereby dogs being brought into the Home by their owners were immediately isolated on the third floor of the Kent kennels building.

It sounds straightforward, but it has involved a huge amount of work and team effort between all departments, as kennel cough is so contagious that even a tiny mistake could lead to infection and we'd be back to square one. Kennel staff working in these areas could not go anywhere else or handle any other dogs in the Home and any other essential staff had to wear protective suits and footwear. Dogs rehomed from this area left the Home via a different route – they even had their own special exercise run.

Over 70% of dogs rehomed from the clean area never contract the cough at all, so during 2003 the kennel-cough 'trial' was made permanent policy. Seeing so many dogs leaving the Home without so much as a splutter makes all the hard work worthwhile.

How are you feeling?

Ruff

twelve

What effect has the Crypt had on your life over the past year? We asked twelve people.

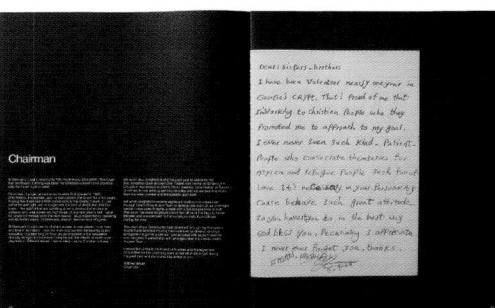

Chairman

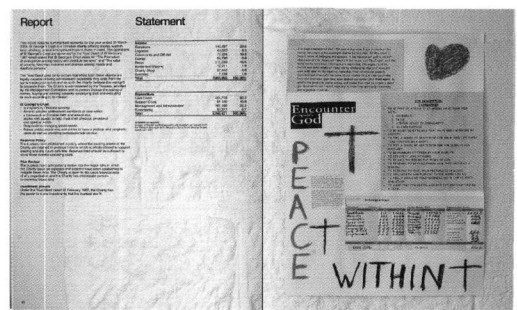

Report   Statement

PEACE WITHIN

1&2. VSO tube ads by Kitcatt Nohr Alexander Shaw. Copy: Paul Kitcatt. Art director: Jamie Tierney. Typographer: Bryan Riddle.

3&4. Annual report for Battersea Dogs Home by Imagination. Animal and people photography by Jo Sax.

5-7. Annual report for St George's Crypt, the Leeds-based Christian charity for the homeless. As the report also acts as the charity's main marketing collateral and communication for fundraising, designers Brahm tried to make it a celebration of The Crypt and its work. Twelve features the stories of 12 individuals and a review of the past 12 months. Packs containing pens, crayons, paper, pencils, disposable cameras and a creative brief were sent out to the 12 participants who were asked to respond in words and pictures to the brief "What effect has the crypt had on your life over the past year?"

8&9. Clever campaign by FPP for the British Chiropractic Association, which helps people who are flat out with back problems (hence the shots of ceilings) get back on their feet. Creatives: Simon Storey, Mick McCabe. Photography: Alex Telfer

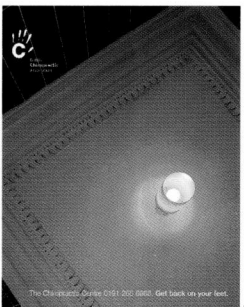

10-15. Design group Hat-trick were asked to "emphasise the themes of transparency, internationalism, and evangelism," when developing these eye-catching building graphics for The Salvation Army's new International Headquarters, near London's Millennium Bridge.

The brief from the client was to make the building itself "interact more directly with anybody near or in it". Reflecting the charity's global activities (few know that the Salvation Army is actually active in 109 different countries) international faces and costumes were used to form backdrops and partitions. "Quotes from the Bible wrap around facades and meeting rooms, and simple religious icons such as the 'five loaves' are used to bring life to the cafe and link the secular with the religious," comments Hat-trick's Jim Sutherland.

Text decorating the building is set in Gill Sans, with the "t" redrawn to become a perfect cross.

"The inspiration really came from stained glass, as all the signs and lettering are coloured and transparent," Sutherland explains. Hat-Trick have also created a signage system and exhibition graphics for the charity

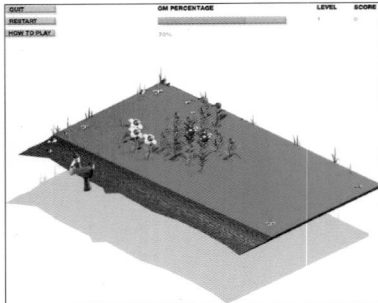

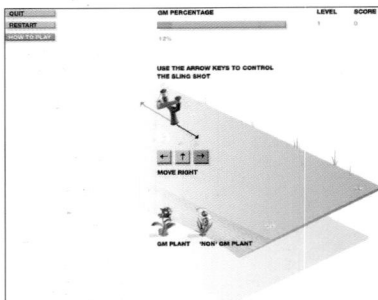

USE THE ARROW KEYS TO CONTROL
THE SLING SHOT

MOVE RIGHT

GM PLANT   'NON' GM PLANT

GREENPEACE
GM WARRIOR
BECOME A GM WARRIOR
STOP GM PLANTS
CONTAMINATING OUR
ENVIRONMENT

PLAY   HIGHSCORE   HOW TO PLAY

WHAT IS GM

WIND FARM
LEVEL 1
GET READY
START

GREENPEACE DIGITAL

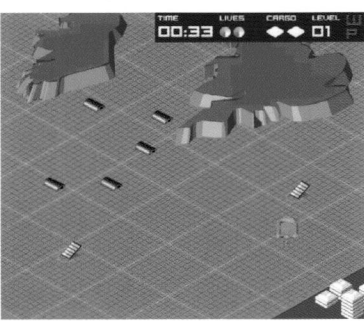

The latest work from Saatchi
& Saatchi's for the NSPCC's Full
Stop campaign, is a chilling
spot that illustrates how child
abusers control their victims.
Directed by Daniel Kleinman,
the spot shows the eight-year-
old victim as a ventriloquist's
dummy; emphasising the
powerlessness of an abused
child. The charity asserts that
there are thousands of children
across the UK who have no-
one to turn to in cases of
abuse. The spot communicates
how, controlled by her abuser,
the child is unable to pay
attention at school, make
friends, or tell the truth to her
family. Art director: Jan
Jacobs. Writer: Leo Premutico

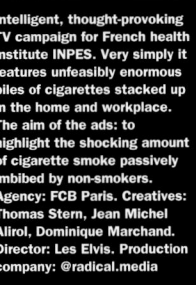

Intelligent, thought-provoking
TV campaign for French health
institute INPES. Very simply it
features unfeasibly enormous
piles of cigarettes stacked up
in the home and workplace.
The aim of the ads: to
highlight the shocking amount
of cigarette smoke passively
imbibed by non-smokers.
Agency: FCB Paris. Creatives:
Thomas Stern, Jean Michel
Alirol, Dominique Marchand.
Director: Les Elvis. Production
company: @radical.media

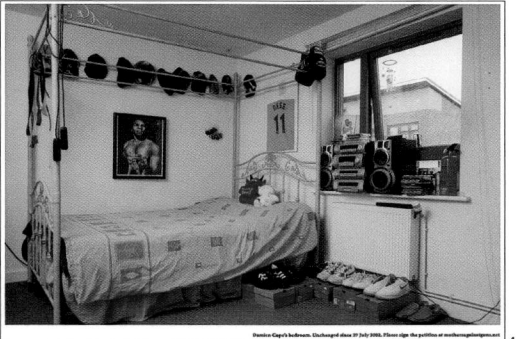

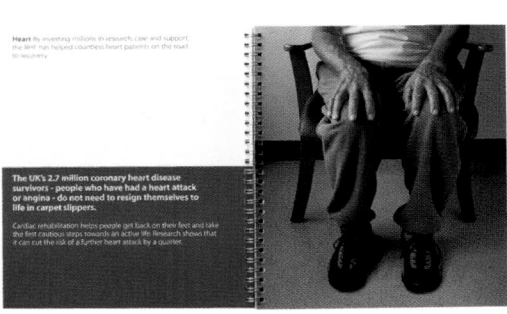

1. Poster for a series of research books for Edinburgh College of Art, designed by Paul Sudron, Elmwood. A dot-to-dot theme was chosen to encourage readers to interact with the publications as well as acting as signposting to the college's website.

2&3. Annual review for Fairbridge, a charity that helps young people into work. Photography: Christine Donnier-Valentin. Design: Hat-trick.

4. This ad for Mothers Against Guns features Damien Cope's bedroom: his mother has kept it exactly the way 22 year-old Damien left it before he was shot and killed outside a night club in 2002. Agency: Grey, London. Creatives: James Dive, Sam Hibbard. Photographers: Adam Broomberg, Oliver Chanarin.

5&6. Touching the State is the first publication to come out of RED, the new R&D unit of the Design Council. RED's aim is to spark debate on social and economic issues: Touching the State explores the meaning of citizenship. Designer Gary Cook of Cook Design used a red square throughout to refer to the Design Council logo. Magazine-style visual language is used in order to break away from an institutional feel. Cook also used fonts Scala and Base instead of the Design Council's Helvetica to reinforce the publication's separate identity.

7&8. British Heart Foundation annual report by Radford Wallis Design. Using half-page reveals, the report illustrates the impact that the BHF's activities have on people's lives, eg educating children to improve diet. To illustrate this, the cover image is of a boy eating a burger: however, when the half page is turned over, he is eating an apple instead. Creative directors: Stuart Radford and Andrew Wallis. Designers: Phil Bold and Mark Wood. Main photography: Jean-Philippe Defaut

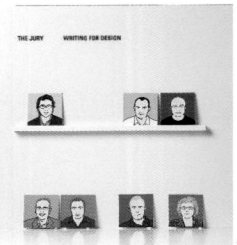

INTERACTIVE &
DIGITAL MEDIA [2004]
THE JURY

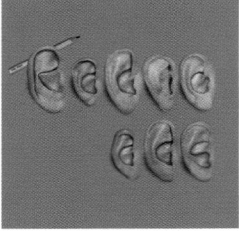

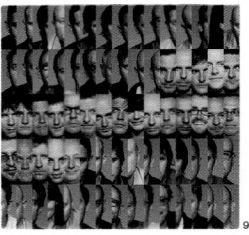

This year's D&AD Annual, under the guidance of CDD's Dave Dye, celebrates the (possibly) dying art of the record cover. The Annual is titled Now That's What I Call Design/ Advertising 42! and features a cover done in the style of the long-running series of compilation albums. Inside, a selection of leading creatives and designers were asked to portray each category jury from this year's D&AD Awards in the style of a record sleeve for the chapter dividers. Shown here are:

1&2. Writing for Design jury by Nick Bell of UNA (London) designers.
3&4. Interactive & Digital Media by Adrian Shaughnessy.
5&6. Radio Ads by Ben Casey of The Chase. 7&8. Music Video by Vince Frost of Frost Design/ EmeryFrost. 9&10. Television & Cinema Advertising by Michele Januzzi of Januzzi Smith.

11. Age Concern challenges age discrimination head on in this poster campaign from Reg Starkey, Pete

Matthews and Max Doyle.
Photography: Peter Rand.

12. Genuine police shots chart the gradual decline of a heroin addict in this press and poster campaign for the Metropolitan Police. In the final shot, the woman, an American called Roseanne Holland, was only 38 years old. Agency: MCBD.
Creative: Jeremy Carr.

Sport

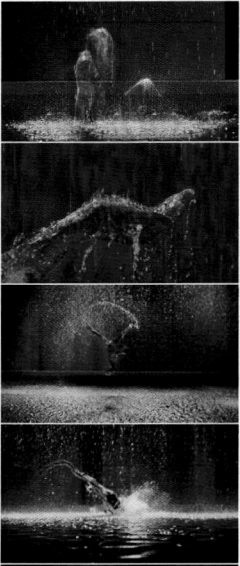

A woman made of water stars in this spot for Lucozade Sport Hydro Active. Written by Colleen Philips and Kit Dayram at M&C Saatchi. Directed by Philippe André. Production company: Harry Nash

Written and directed by Peter Arnell of US agency Arnell Group, this Reebok spot features rappers 50 Cent and Jay-Z waxing lyrical about new clothing and footwear range, G-Unit Collection by Rbk

Footballer David Beckham and rugby player Jonny Wilkinson try their toes at penalties and free kicks in ads from 180. Creatives: Richard Bullock, Andy Fackrell. Director: Chris Palmer, Gorgeous Enterprises

International stars play urban rugby in this lively Nike spot. Written by Steve Jackson and Christy Peacock at Mojo Partners Melbourne, Australia. Directed by Steve Rogers at Rose Hackney Barber

Promotional films by Why Not Associates for the launch of the Nike Total 90 football and airzoom boot. "The boot's thus called because you can play for 90 minutes without noticing – it's apparently that comfortable," comments Why Not's Andy Altmann. The films feature footage of world-class players such as Roberto Carlos and Ronaldinho, as well as scenes with the products themselves. These promotional pieces were sent to retailers around Europe and were made in collaboration with Nike Europe

Motion Theory created this spot for Fox Sports' coverage of the NFC season. Creative directors: Matt Reinhard and Brian Bacino at Foote Cone & Belding. MT creative directors: Mathew Cullen and Grady Hall

BBC Radio Five Live's ad apes the MC battle scenes from Eminem film 8Mile as sports commentators describe goals to a rapturous crowd. Written and directed by Ron Scalpello at BBC Broadcast

1&2. These images of battered boxers are from New York-based photographer Ben Watts' forthcoming book, Big Up, to be published by Princeton Architectural Press this month. Australian-born Watts (brother of actress Naomi) worked as a nightclub doorman and trained and competed in amateur boxing tournaments while studying photography at Sydney College of the Arts in the late 80s. Intrigued by American Hip Hop culture, he went to New York in 1990 and began to photograph urban youth while also spending time at the Times Square boxing club. A selection of oversized prints of some of his work and proof pages of the book will be exhibited for the first time in the UK at Hoxton's Scout Gallery in London from 5 December to 31 January 2004. See www.scoutgallery.com

3-6. Takeshi Hamada, the designer behind tigermagazine.com, created these images as part of a media presentation pack for Japan's only international football magazine, World Soccer Graphic. Creative director: Takuya Harayama. Art director: Takeshi Hamada. Copy writer: Takashi Yamada

Savvy sports brands have been exploiting the fashion crossover of their wares for several years but the recent collaboration between adidas and über-trendy Japanese label, A Bathing Ape, takes the idea to a whole new level. The brands decided to work together after adidas' head of non-athletic promotions, Gary Aspden, met with Bape in Japan last year. "It wasn't really born out of 'big brand seeks small independent cult label', adidas has enough kudos of its own. It was like-minded individuals from different cultures getting together and saying that it might be fun to work on a project," he says. Bape came over to adidas' head office in Germany to meet the design team. They chose two shoes to produce in their own style in very limited runs. The first range, based on the Superstar, was released at the end of August. Four styles of Super Ape Stars were produced, three of them in runs of 500 pairs each worldwide costing £150 a pair, one in a run of only 100 pairs which were not sold but given away to "friends" of the brands. In London, the shoes were exclusively sold in the Bape shop in Upper James Street, Soho where trainer fetishists queued all night to buy them (they were only allowed to buy one pair each). In October, the second range will be released – the Super Ape Skate. "For us this is a brand marketing exercise not a profit-making one," says Aspden. "I see that brand cross-fertilisation is going to happen more and more in the future. We have a part of our customer base that is very knowledgeable about product and we have to respond to them in an appropriate way."

As with all Bape products, the attraction of the project lies in the design details:

1. Both the Super Ape Stars and the Super Ape Skates come in a specially designed, origami-inspired box created by Bape bearing the adidas logo and "with a bathing ape" added below. The adidas three stripes are rendered in camo pattern and the apehead logo with three stripes is also used. Tissue paper inside also bears both logos.

2. Each pair of Super Ape Stars is supplied with four pairs of laces: plain, black apehead logo on white and two styles of BAPE-camo.

3. T-shirt shrink-wrapped into the form of the apehead logo.

4. Ape medal – a stamped, black and white leather tab bearing the three striped apehead and the motto "the respect is mutual".

5. In-soles with full camo print plus apehead and adidas logos.

6. The lace jewel was introduced in the late 90s – original Superstars didn't have them. This one is in gold with an apehead embossed detail.

To win an exclusive Bape/adidas display model, see Gallery p111

5

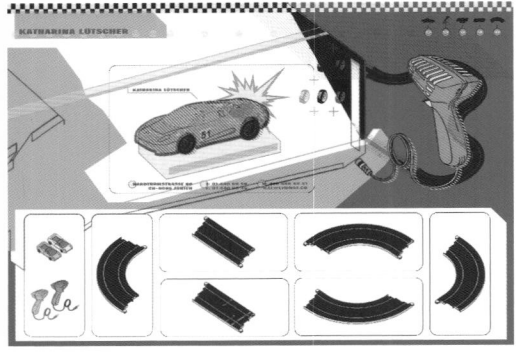

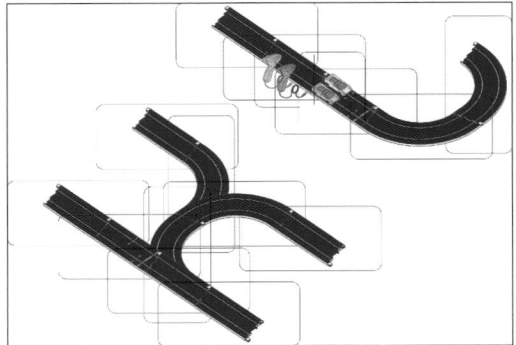

Martin Woodtli designed this graphic identity for sports photographer Katharina Lütscher. The car image defined by the central rectangle (1) forms her business card while Scalextric-style lettering is used to spell out Lütscher's initials (2).

3&4. Crispin Porter + Bogusky in Miami developed this clever campaign for Shimano, makers of hard-wearing components for mountain and racing bikes. The emphasis of the Improving the Human Machine campaign for the new XTR gadgetry is on the control and power behind the designs. Art director: Tony Calcao. Copywriter: Rob Strasberg. Photographer: Sebastian Gray. Technical Illustrations: Pudik Graphics. Medical illustrations: Fluke, Inc.

5. Happypets in Switzerland created this image as part of a series of illustrations for the Levant newspaper's sports issue. Designed by Patrick Monnier and Violène Pont, the work is supposed to convey the effects of doping as a kind of "supernatural aura" that seeps out of sportsmen and women during and after playing sport.

Facing page: Tinside Pool in Plymouth, photographed by Jason Orton before its recent renovation. From a series on coastal lido and tidal swimming pools in Britain

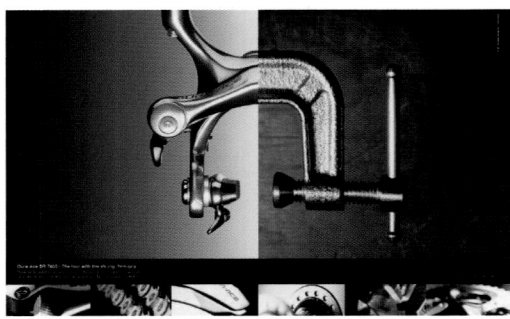

1

2

3

4

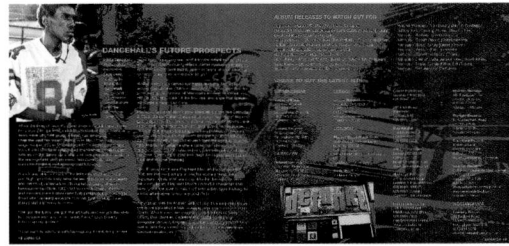

5

1. English & Pockett created the new identity for the 2003-2004 season of the UEFA Champions League. Implemented across both on and off-air applications, the brand is used on TV, stadium graphics, in print and publication design and digital media. The cover of the "brandbook" (1), which showcases the identity to media partners and sponsors, makes interesting use of some powerful floodlights. Creative director: Darrell Pockett. Senior designer: Michael Berthon. Designers: Alan Lo and Cristian Cook. Producer: Richard Wallman.

2. Communications consultancy Clinic created Reg the Ref, the mascot for Littlewoods' interactive gaming experience, Game On. Clinic worked with branding agency Heavenly on the campaign.

3. Not anti-sport but anti-celebrity, these T-shirts were designed by Ded Ass. and are available to buy from www.boredofthebeckhams.com.

Cover (4) and spread (5) from In

Celebration of Jamaica, a magazine produced by Puma as part of a collaboration with trainer shop size? celebrating Jamaican culture. The project ties in with Puma's sponsorship of the Jamaican athletics team and also includes a range of shoes and clothing, photography exhibitions and live events. Executive producer: Helen Sweeney Dougan, Puma. Creative agency: Espionage. Project director: Adam Dewhurst. Project managers: Dave Chase and Lex Sommer.

6. Bobby Charlton prepares to take a corner kick for Manchester United versus Ipswich Town circa 1970, from Football Days, Classic Football Photographs by Peter Robinson, published by Mitchell Beazley, £30

6

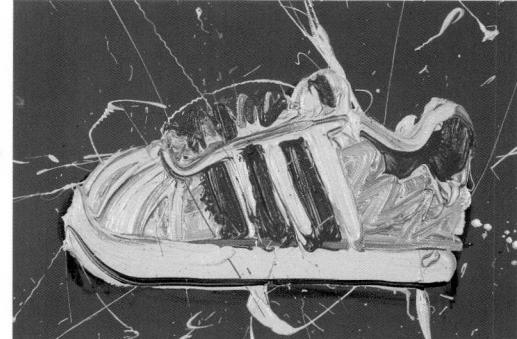

7-10. A trainer fanatic, Liverpudlian artist Dave White's collection of trainer paintings (and trainers, no doubt) grew when approached and sponsored by trainer shop size? to produce and exhibit paintings of classic adidas and Nike designs. The resulting exhibition, Clash Of The Titans, was due to hang in the exhibition space in the newly refurbished and enlarged size? flagship store on London's Carnaby Street. Behind-schedule building work meant that the exhibition actually hung throughout September in the foyer of creative agency Exposure in central London. Another, more extensive exhibition is planned when the new store is complete. Trainer anoraks will recognise White's oil-on-canvas renderings of the Nike Dunk Hi (7), the adidas Superstar (8), Nike Air Max 97 and adidas Micropacer (10). To see more of White's work, go to www.davewhite.me.uk

11&12. Under the art direction of Markus Kiersztan at MP Creative in New York, photographer Sølve Sundsbø created these stunning images for Nike global/Japan's Fall Winter 2003-04 campaign. Agency: Wieden + Kennedy New York. Creative Director: Todd Waterbury.

13. Kiersztan's art direction again features in this campaign for Nike Japan's Spring Summer 2003 collection, using a split image.

Agency: Wieden + Kennedy, Tokyo.
Photographer: Norbert Schoerner.
Creative director: John C Jay

In-store graphics for the Nou Camp Stadium superstore. The vast Nou Camp is the home ground for FC Barcelona, a football club kitted out by Nike. When the Nike Europe in-house team re-designed the store, they approached Why Not Associates to supply the graphics. "The brief was that some graphics include images of the Barcelona players," explains Why Not's Andy Altmann of the project. Nike passed on some graphics images to them

however, the size these images were supplied in wasn't big enough to create banners to the size Why Not required. "We got round that by building pictures out of type," says Altmann. "We found a way in Photoshop to use the names of the players as the dots of the image." In a neat reference to local artists Joan Miró and Antoni Tàpies, two of the walls, one made from sections of Perspex, feature flowing, hand-written texts. They have a really

strong history of mark-making, so we decided to paint everything… We got brushes and rollers and splattered paint around here in the studio, the aim being to create a kind of Catalan feel I guess." adds Altmann. Apparently, it was more difficult than it looks to make it appear as though the text was drawn with the sort of abandon that the team wanted to achieve: "So I worked out this special method, where you do it left handed with your

eyes closed. You get this wonderful lettering you couldn't possibly draw if you were looking," he laughs. "It was nice to do something so loose, to get on your hands and knees with a paintbrush." The lettering was scanned in and printed out, before being bolted onto the walls. The images of Barcelona players were also printed and displayed in the windows on lightboxes. "So it's kind of Pop Art meets Catalan art meets graphic. A nice," muses Altmann.

ATHENS 2004

1

Athenà Phèvos

2

Ξιφασκία
Fencing

3

Κανόε/Καγιάκ
Σπριντ
Canoe/Kayak
Flatwater

4

Καταδύσεις
Diving

5

Ποδηλασία
Cycling

6

Στίβος
Athletics

7

Πυγμαχία
Boxing

8

1. The emblem for the 2004 Athens Olympics was launched in September 1999. The design was picked from 690 entries to an international competition by 242 candidates in 14 countries. It was created by Greek-based Red Design in collaboration with Wolff Olins.

2. The overblown claims made on behalf of Olympic mascots are usually as ridiculous as their design (Mariscal's Cobi excepted). Athens doesn't disappoint. Created by Spyros Gogos of Athenian company Paragraph Design, Athena (goddess of wisdom and patron of Athens) and Phevos (aka Apollo, god of light and music) evoke "the brotherhood of man, equality of the sexes and participation irrespective of victory" apparently. They were inspired by an ancient Mycenaean terracotta doll, dating back to the seventh century.

3-8. Each of the 35 constituent sports at the games will be represented by a different pictogram based on the imagery of Ancient Greek vases.

9. A change of shirt manufacturer prompted this new badge for the Scottish football team by Curious Oranj of Glasgow. The design was developed around the existing crest. "Scotland" is written in a bespoke "celtic" font while a stylised Saltire sits below.

10&11. Comp slip featuring the new Lawn Tennis Association identity by Interbrand. Creative director: Jeremy Scholfield. Designers: Anne Wehebrink, Chris Thomas, Keith Tappin. Photo: Getty Images.

12. FA annual report and (13) match programme designed by Elmwood: part of a whole range of material produced by the consultancy for the FA, including the FA logo and logos for its various competitions

9

11

12

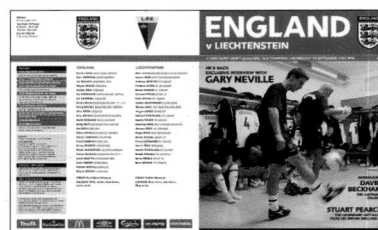

13

In 1963, Muhammad Ali was still known as Cassius Clay. Viewed by many as a lippy upstart who would soon get his comeuppance, he came to London to fight Henry Cooper at Wembley Stadium. In the fourth round, Cooper knocked Ali to the floor. With just 60 seconds to recover, it seemed likely that Ali would lose the fight: what happened next has entered into boxing folklore. Many believe that Ali's trainer, Angelo Dundee, deliberately tore open one of the boxer's gloves. The ensuing delay gave Ali enough time to recover: he went on to win the fight and become The Greatest. Over time, the gloves themselves have become holy sporting relics: to own them is to own at least part of the legend. Which presumably is why TBWA\London chairman and creative director Trevor Beattie paid £37,600 for the gloves at Christie's in 2001. They form part of an eclectic collection of around 20 iconic objects gathered by Beattie including Margot Fonteyn's ballet shoes, a signed Michael Jackson fedora and a burned copy of Salman Rushdie's Satanic Verses. Beattie says that the common link is that each piece has a particular cultural significance – hence his purchase of Alastair Campbell's copy of the Hutton Report in January. Beattie is currently putting together a book and exhibition of the collection, under the title One Previous Owner. He has commissioned photographer John Rensten to shoot the pieces, including Ali's gloves (shown 1), boots (2) and robe (3). Retouching by Dave Jewell at Propaganda. Rensten is represented by the Rebecca Valentine Agency. More of his work can be seen online at www.rebeccavalentine.com and www.johnrensten.com

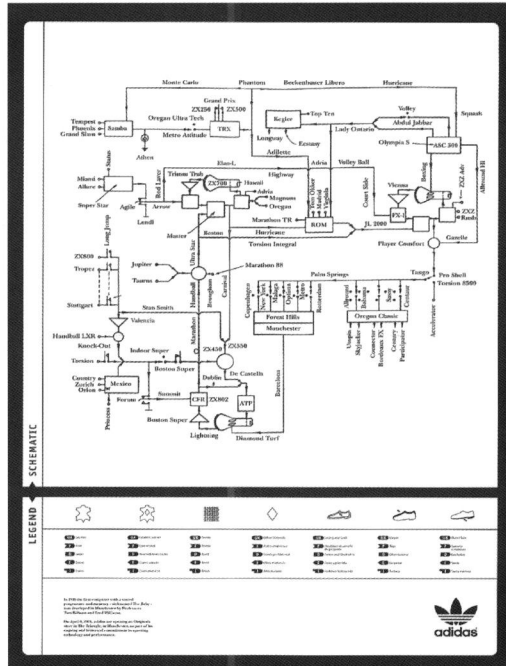

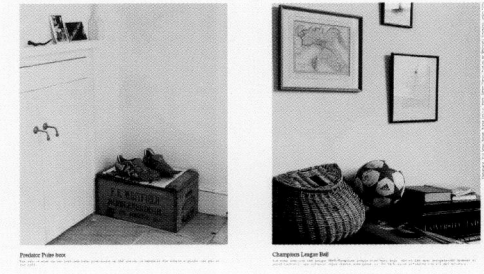

Predator Polar boxx

Champions League Ball

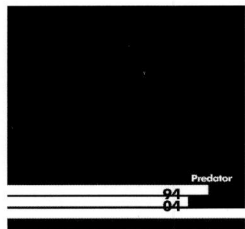

94/04
Predator

4-7. Promotional activities for the launch of the Manchester adidas originals store. This poster (4&5) announcing the opening was inserted into Flux and City Life and was designed by graphics team Four23. On one side, an illustration explores the technological superiority of original trefoil shoe designs. Continuing the originals/Manchester theme, on the reverse is a circuit diagram (in case you didn't know, the first computer, The Baby, was developed in Manchester). All references to The Baby are removed from the diagram and replaced with the names of historical adidas shoes. Other launch activity included the production of a limited edition booklet (6) by ink tank. Printed by John Walsh, the booklet was given to attendees on the opening night. Within is artwork from ink tank's contributors, which again explores the concept of Manchester "firsts". The evening was meant to feel more like a gallery event than the launch of a store. A giant shoe box (7) created by company Potential Development was deposited at key places such as The Lowry and Jodrell Bank. Footage of the box in-situ was projected at the opening. The whole project was managed by Mike Chetcuti for adidas UK through his company Magic Bag. The originals store, he tells us, is the first of its kind in the UK, another opens in London this August.

8. This adidas supplement was distributed in The Guardian. It features reportage-style photography by Tara Darby of used, dirty adidas products such as balls and trainers, lying casually around people's homes. "It's about showing the product in a way that portrays it as a constant in people's lives," explains producer/commissioner Jethro Marshall of JJ Marshall Associates. Designer: Damien Poulain.

9&10. Spread/cover from Predator 94-04 a visual retrospective of the innovative boot which will be ten years old this year. Apparel is reproduced to scale in the limited edition booklet, which accompanies an exhibition in the shop oki-ni. It was designed by Bibliothèque and produced/commissioned by Jethro Marshall for the trend marketing department of adidas international

1&2. TV show titles from the 1970s are coupled with shots of England players in an adulatory campaign for UEFA Euro 2004 from agency Bartle Bogle Hegarty. Creatives: Kevin Stark, Nick Kidney.

3. Martial arts coat, created through Puma's collaboration with London-based fashion designers Vexed Generation.

4. Logo for the British Golf Museum at St Andrew's, created by Tayburn who were tasked with rebranding the Museum to increase its appeal to golf followers of all ages.

5. Logo for the London Velodrome by Carter Wong Tomlin. The coloured stripes used take their cue from the different colours of the individual lanes on the track.

6. Pentagram designed this visual identity for Truce International, a charity patronised by Sven-Goran Eriksson which aims to use football to raise funds for the provision of football fields and sport therapy programmes for children whose lives have been devastated by trauma. Designed by Fernando Gutiérrez. Design assistant: Chris Duggan.

7. Peloton Design created this logo for The Tour of Britain cycle race.

For the latest campaign for Sky Media, London-based Clinic created these leaflets (8) which were sent to media buyers to generate awareness of www.skysports.com. The leaflet also transformed into a nifty little football game

10

11

12

13

14

9. Invitation from Elmwood to watch the England Switzerland game at their design studio.

Colors magazine recently returned to New York under the direction of Kurt Andersen, co-founder of Spy magazine and former editor-in-chief of New York Magazine. The Fan issue, number 61, suggests that often it matters little what the object of devotion is, but rather it's the devotion itself that counts. Try telling that to Patrick McQuade whose portrait of Beckham (10) is the crown jewel in the Fans Gallery section of the magazine.

11&12. Autumn/Winter 2004 print ads for Puma's 96 Hours and Nuala ranges respectively, by Base Design. This season, the 96 Hours range which, Puma says, fuses fashion and performance, was designed by Neil Barrett and based on football. The campaign attempts to reference the periods before and after a game. Photographer: Alex Cayley. The Nuala range of luxury yoga clothing was designed and previously fronted by Christy Turlington. The challenge this time was to develop the brand without the model's distinctive presence in the ads. Photographer: Yelena Yemchuck.

13&14. Illustrations on a sporting theme from the 2004 D&AD Student Awards Annual. Designed by Airside

The official on-screen branding for the UEFA Euro 2004 tournament shows stars like Zidane and Owen in action as a golden trail follows their movements. Created by sports branding specialists Markell:ID

Nike film, Run, depicts a girl running around her neighbourhood, and will show in Nike stores around the world. Written by Bas Van Koll at Nike EMEA. Director: Simon Cracknell @ Large

Thierry Henry battles imaginary footie opponents in a new spot for Nike. Director: Tom Carty, Gorgeous Enterprises. Creatives: Ollie Watson, Sebastian Wilhelm. Agency: Wieden + Kennedy Amsterdam

Michael Owen's mum recounts her son's life-long commitment to football (and a clean, Persil-washed kit). Agency: J Walter Thompson. Creatives: Tom Carty, Nick Bell. Director: Tom Carty, Gorgeous Enterprises

This spot for official sponsors of Euro 2004, T-Mobile, shows a football's view of a match. Agency: Saatchi & Saatchi Frankfurt. Creatives: Alexander Priebs, Nicole Grözinger. Director: Ben & Joe Dempsey. Production company: Rose Hackney Barber. Post: Finish

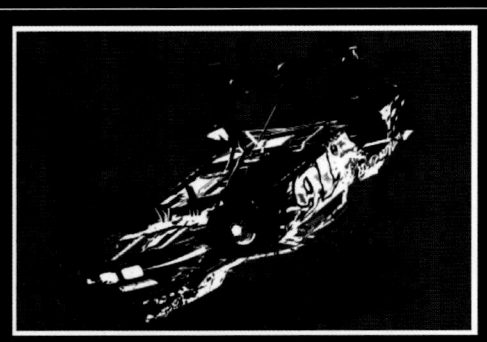

The language of the graphic novel provides the inspiration for this dynamic, animated ad campaign for Fox Sports, for their 2004 NASCAR coverage. The black and white commercials feature a towering, dark, dangerous Nascar driver embarking on the race of his life. The action is punctuated with bolts of animated lightning and the occasional bellowed "Aaarrgh". Production company: Psyop. Fox Sports creative director: Mark Denyer-Simmons

For ESPN's broadcast of the NBA finals in the US, ad agency Wieden + Kennedy New York and director Brian Beletic teamed up with The Black Eyed Peas for TV campaign 24 Seconds to Live. EyeballNYC provided additional graphic elements to complement the theme of a clock running down. EyeballNYC creative directors: Limore Shur and Julian Bevan. Designer: Daniel Garcia. Producers: Mike Eastwood and Eve Ehrich

In Road To Lisbon, adidas-sponsored footballers ride their scooters to Euro 2004 and have a little fun on the way. Written by Andy Fackrell at 180 Amsterdam. Directed by Ringan Ledwidge

Renault F1 drivers share their passion for racing in this people-oriented spot for the brand. Creatives: Gavin Kellett, Nik Studzinski @ Publicis. Director: Andrew Douglas, Anonymous Content

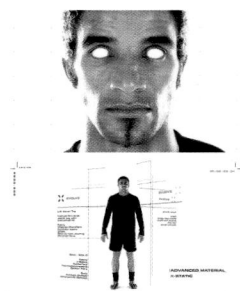

New TV spot for Umbro's performance football concept, Evolution X, features David James, Michael Owen and John Terry transformed into superhumans. Created by Code. Director: Richard Oliver

Live action and animation are married together in this clever campaign promoting the BBC's coverage of UEFA Euro 2004. Creatives: Paul Grubb, Dave Waters @ DFGW. Director: Martyn Pick, Bermuda Shorts

1

2

1. One of Julian Germain's Subbuteo Superheroes: the photographer's work appears alongside that of Marcus Coates, Ravi Deepres and Julie Henry in Only A Game?, a football-themed exhibition at the Impressions Gallery in York, open until 3 July.

2. From a 16-page Nike advertorial in the May 2004 issue of Dazed &

Confused intended to present the new Nike Total 90 collection and to reflect the national identity of each country at Euro 2004 in a humorous and playful way. Art direction and set design by Damien Poulain. Photography: Jean PacÙme Dedieu.

3. From a campaign promoting this year's Paralympics in Athens, by Leo Burnett, Amsterdam. Creatives: Stan

van Zon and Gido van der Vlies. Photographer: Jan Holtslag. Modelmaker: Rob's Propshop.

4&5. First issue of the redesigned Ace Tennis magazine, published by an offshoot of the Lawn Tennis Association. Design by Esterson Associates.

6. Basic Refereeing is one of a

series of six books recently launched by the educational division of the FA, FA Learning. Books cost £8.99 each. Publisher: Hodder Arnold.

7-9. Print campaign for 180 Amsterdam's Road To Lisbon spot for adidas (see p33). Creatives: Andy Fackrell, Stuart Brown. Photographer: Jake Chessum

3

4

5

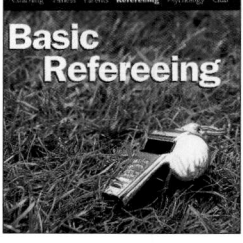

6

7

8

9

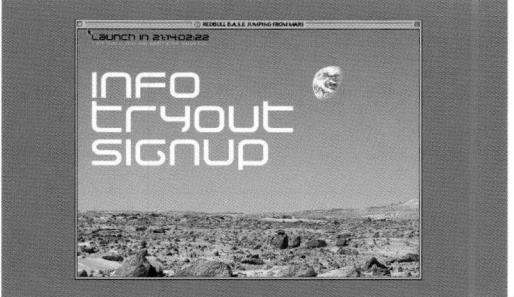

10

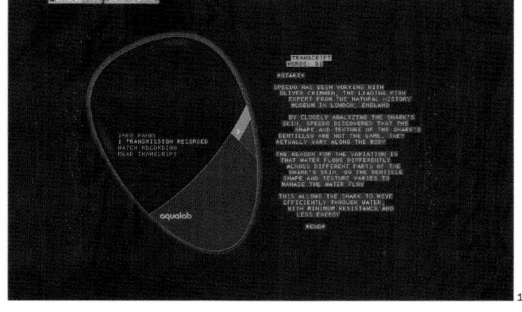

11

10. Less Rain have developed redbullbasejumpingfrommars.com, a teaser site for an online, virtual base jumping event. "It lasts half an hour and includes two intermediate stops for resting your fingers and 'energising' yourself," explains Less Rain's Vassilios Alexiou.

11. Speedoaqualab.com, a stylish minisite for Speedo, has been created to promote the Fastskin FSII swimsuit. Hopefully it should banish the company's reputation for producing unpleasant, skin-tight trunks forever. Concept/design/illustration/development: un.titled

12&13. Miami-based agency Crispin Porter + Bogusky created this campaign, Masks, for Bell BMX. Each poster tells of the magical protective powers invested in their tough helmets (as worn by bikers Allan Cooke, Steve McCann and Jamie Bestwick) that can banish "unseen forces" and "evil spirits". Creative directors: Alex Bogusky and Tony Calcao. Art directors: Alex Burnard and Mike del Marmol. Copywriter: Dave Schiff. Photographer: Sebastian Gray.

14. The loneliness of the long distance runner is spelt out, literally, in this press ad for adidas. It appeared around the London Marathon and relates the imagined thoughts of runners as they negotiate the course. Agency: TBWA\London. Copywriters: Paul Silburn, Kerry Gooden, Stuart Harkness. Art director: Paul Silburn. Typographer: Dan Beckett

12

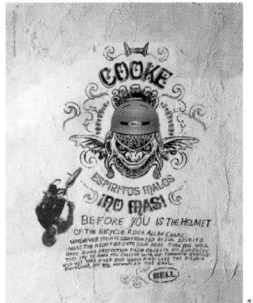

13

14

1. One of several funny press and poster ads for gymnasium Fitness Unlimited in Sheffield. The ads depict bizarre, impractical ways to reduce weight, and then suggest the gym as a healthier, saner alternative. Written by David Sedgwick and Warren Standring @ RACE International. Photography: Andy Greenwood.

2. Bath School of Art & Design put their puny fine art promotional budget on a horse called Joe's Edge

which romped home enabling the commission of this poster from designer and alumnus Darren Wall.

3. New press and poster campaign for Land Rover's Freelander Sport model includes this execution showing a road marker who has lovingly painted a penalty box around a parked Freelander Sport. Agency: Rainey Kelly Campbell Roalfe/Y&R. Art director: Jerry Hollens. Copywriter: Mike Boles. Photographer: Nick Georghiou.

4. HarrimanSteel designed these window displays for Nike in the run up to the European Championships. Appearing in specialist sports stores around the UK, they feature a football that floats in mid-air and oscillates from side to side within the window space. The ball, apparently, is kept in play by a vortex created by a blower installed at the bottom of each window. Production: Arno Fords

5&6. Goodbye Hoof Hello Nutmeg is

a new single edition Nike magazine conceived by Wieden + Kennedy to coincide with the Euro 2004 championships. The mag can be ordered online at www.nikefootballuk.com. Creatives: Chris Groom, Ben Walker. Editor: Scott Morgan. Publisher: Haymarket.

7&8. Amateur football players from around the world show off their favourite moves in this neat microsite for Nikefootball.com. Designed by AKQA.

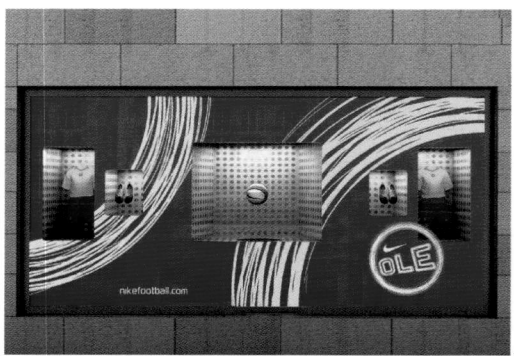

Food &
Drink

The big purple one is back. *Quality Street*

1

The big green triangle is back. *Quality Street*

2

Reason 29
Over 110 choices of fresh fish

More reasons to shop at **M** MORRISONS

3

Reason 14
Over 100 wines for under £3 each

More reasons to shop at **M** MORRISONS

4

1&2. Oversized sweet wrappers turn up all over the place in these posters for Quality Street. Written and art directed by Ed Morris at Lowe. Photography by David Stewart.

3&4. Gorgeous photography and matter-of-fact text: suitably no-nonsense posters for supermarket Morrison's. Agency: BDH\TBWA, Manchester. Creatives Doug Laird, Chris Lear, Danny Brooke-Taylor.

Photographer: Jess Koppel.

5. Don't Do Drunk, a viral campaign commissioned by The Portman Group to promote alcohol awareness in the 18-25 age group and warn of the dangers of binge-drinking. Films show young adults attempting, unsuccesfully, to deal with being very drunk in a toilet cubicle. Writer/director: Michael Keillor of Iodine, Scotland.

6. "Chin Up" is the sweet endline to this commercial for McCain from TBWA\London, which illuminates the restorative effects of the humble chip. Creatives: Trevor Beattie, Bil Bungay. Director: Daniel Barber, Rose Hackney Barber.

7. Bonkers spot for Wrigley's showing office workers trying to get their hands on new flavours of Juicy Fruit gum. Agency: BBDO, Chicago.

Creatives: Todd Hoffman, Al Wyatt, Jim Hyman. Directors: Blue Source. Production company: Blink, USA.

8. Subtly observed continuation of the Kellogg's Special K campaign in which women's true inner thoughts are revealed. Agency: Leo Burnett, Chicago. Creatives: Mark Tutssel, Stephanie Crippen, Reed Collins. Director: Tom Carty, Gorgeous Enterprises

5

6

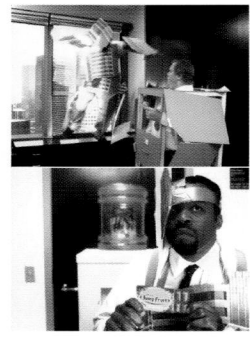

7

8

9

10

11

12

9. A cushion of air inside an Adshel site pushes the little balls of Maltesers around in this literal interpretation of the long-running strapline "the lighter way to enjoy chocolate". Creatives: Warwick Delmonte, Quentin Pfiszter. Agency: Colenso BBDO, New Zealand.

10. Stylish, aspirational ad that hints at the innately superior taste and intellectual prowess of Macallan

Whisky drinkers. Agency: CDD, London. Creatives: Sean Doyle, Dave Dye, Helen Board, Matt Lever. Photographer: Giles Revell.

11. BMP DDB created this press ad suggesting that Rosenborg is mild enough to be suitable for a newcomer to the blue cheese experience. Art director: Lovisa Almgren. Copywriter: Ben Wade. Photographer: Giblin & James

12. The new Mars Kingsize is very big. Bite one and you'll feel like you come from Lilliput. Agency: Colenso BBDO New Zealand. Creatives: Natalie Knight, Darren Wong Kam. Photographer: Steven Roke.

13. The therapeutic powers of Lipton Tchae Tea are subtly alluded to in this print campaign from JWT Lisbon. Creatives: João Espírito, Marco Figueiredo, Vanessa Castelau.

Photographer: Francisco Prata. Typographer: Irene Bandeira.

14&15. Posters made the same way as Kiwi Bacon: by hand (although we presume pigs had something to do with it too – for the bacon, not the ads). Agency: Colenso BBDO, New Zealand. Creatives: Guy Rooke, Steve Cochran. Typographers: Lorenz Perry, Jacko Van Derventer

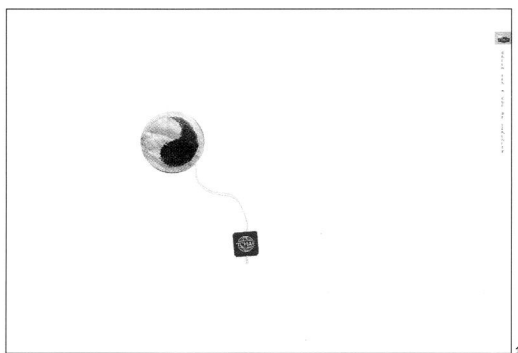

13

14

15

Inspiration can come from the unlikeliest sources: designer and artist Jake Tilson's latest book was inspired by the writing on a tin of tomatoes. 3. Found Fonts: An Exploration (Atlas, £14, cover shown, 1) is, as well as being an examination of graphic style, an evocative journey through Italian food and culture (spreads shown, 3-7). Tilson traces the origins of his tomato tin typeface (which he names Pomodori, 2) as well of those of two other found fonts, examining their context and influence on their surroundings. The book uses a rich variety of different papers, rubber stamped sheets and hand-glued illustrations. Tilson has created full versions of each font which are included on an accompanying CD-Rom which also features recipes, photographs, drawings and texts. The book is part of an exhibition entitled Ways of Saying which is at Loman Street Studios, London SE1 until 31 December and which also features work by David Blamey and Michael Marriott. Viewing is by appointment only: contact Liz Ruth on +44 (0)20 7202 2222

The startling interior graphics and identity of Belfast restaurant Cayenne rightly won a great deal of praise for Peter Anderson and his design studio, Interfield. The restaurant has been a big success and recently bought a space next door in which to expand. For this additional area, Anderson has created a series of new works based, as ever, in storytelling and rooting the design in its surroundings: the original menu designs for Cayenne, for example, featured all the surnames from the Northern Ireland phone book. The names were also cut into the 60-feet-long Moving Surnames wall which runs down one side of the restaurant interior and were arranged using elements from the Belfast street map – the significance being that Catholic names were placed next to Protestant ones in sectarian neighbourhoods. At one end of the new space, Anderson has created another wall, this time using 2000 miniature bottles of Bushmills Irish whiskey (shown, 1). The bottles spell out the words "Us + I". It is, says Anderson, "a romantic artwork which celebrates and questions aspects of our relationships". Strata

Kitchen meanwhile (2, 3 & 4) was made "as a little brother to the Moving Surnames wall". Again, it uses names but this time they are of people with which the restaurant's owners, Paul and Jeanne Rankin, have previously worked. The piece is made from 80,000 separate sheets of coloured paper. They were assembled as a block which was then digitally printed using a hi-tech version of screenprinting. "My job is in many ways to give the restaurant its character – what goes on the walls, the menus, signage – which is something that architects always used to do," says Anderson. "It moves away from the brand as a logo to be repeated, instead, it's a story which is made up by the individual artworks"

2

3

1. Addison's Madrid office designed the new identity for dark beer Mahou Negra, creating an elegant black bottle with type rendered in gold. Designer: Chema León. Creative Director: Luis Echánove. Client: Mahou-San Miguel.

2. Label design for Spanish winemaker, Compania de Vinos Telmo Rodriguez, part of a graphic identity by Fernando Gutiérrez of Pentagram.

3. David Davies and Stuart Baron's new design consultancy, D+B, created this identity for London-based organic food brand, Wild City.

4. Packaging design for organic pizza company What On Earth, part of an entire re-branding campaign from Albion Communications.

5. Packaging for Wistbray's range of Dragonfly Rooibos teas by David Hillman and Liza Enebeis from Pentagram. The photography is by Peter Wood.

6. Alessi's famous Anna G corkscrew now has a boyfriend: Sandro M. Also designed by Alessandro Mendini, Sandro M has a chrome-plated bowler hat and comes in a wide variety of polyamide outfits which will be renewed each season

7

8

7. Packaging for a range of chutneys from Mayfair Indian restaurant, Tamarind. The packs feature a new, lower case, Tamarind logo with a single red dot, a play on the traditional bindhi. The series of abstract shapes are derived from Jali screens. Brightly coloured type differentiates each product. Designer: Mary Lewis at Lewis Moberly.

8. Poppets are being re-positioned as "the ballsy little chocolates". The packaging has been re-designed by Turner Duckworth. As well as bold typography, there are little Japanese-style characters for each flavour, which are intended to represent Poppets with half the chocolate bitten off.

9. Lewis Moberly was asked to design the identity and packaging for Panini, an Italian café, bakery and patisserie at the ultra-exclusive Grand Hyatt hotel in Dubai. Designers Hideo Akiba and Fiona Verdon-Smith aimed for a fun, spontaneous style.

10. Packaging for Chai, a blend of tea, milk and spices. Albion Communications developed the containers for the product, as well as an ad campaign. Copy on the label reads: "Imagine if we all took ten minutes each day to think pure, kind thoughts, things would be different. Traffic jams would be a thing of the past and everyone would look good in sandals."

11. Babosh is a family-run café in Tooting, south London. The name comes from owner Aziz Hussein's

baby daughter, who used to refer to him as Babosh. Atelier Works designers, Ian Chilvers and Joseph Luffman, picked up on the family theme to create an identity that reflects Hussein's open and friendly personality. All typography is black and white with cheeky messages on menu cards and packaging.

12. Powell NY was charged with the task of developing everything for brand Cricket cola from design and packaging to positioning and marketing materials

9

10

11

12

DONALD J. MILLER
11-06-2000
(this image is half of a diptych)

STACY LAWTON
11-14-2000

LARRY WHITE
5-23-1997
(cigarette obtained, non-smoking facility)

JEFF SAMEY
4-16-1986

COME AND GET IT

LAST MEALS AND THE PEOPLE WHO EAT THEM
ESSAY BY CHARLES BOWDEN

PHOTOGRAPHS BY CELIA A. SHAPIRO

THE BILL OF FARE HERE
TOSSED BURGERS, POP, STEAK,
FRIED CHICKEN, LIVER AND ONIONS,
PLAIN FOOD FOR SLAVERERS,
APPETITES, LOOK OVER A HUNDRED
OR SO OF THESE, AND
THE IMPOVERISHED MENUS
TEAR THE BUREAUCRATIC SADNESS
JUNK-FOOD DEVOTION.

MARY FRANCES BAGGS
6-30-2000

From the current issue of American photography journal, Aperture, a feature on the last meals of condemned prisoners in the US. Celia A Shapiro's disturbing and hugely evocative photographs reconstruct the requested "last suppers" of Oklahoma bomber Timothy McVeigh (a giant tub of ice cream) and other death row inmates. She has been working on the series since 1999. "The tableware, except for the paper, are all high security dishes which I purchased from prison suppliers," Shapiro says. "I knew about them from having worked in a woman's prison in the early 80s (I created and taught a hands-on video programme)." Placing the food on a black background was, she explains, "influenced by a still-life painter named Juan Cotan who lived in the late 1500s- early 1600s. The nature of the light coming from the colour took a long time to perfect. My goal was to create the energy of colour that you see in church iconography." There are currently ten meals in the series. As Charles Bowden says in an accompanying essay, "the choices are not garden blow, perhaps because we generally fail to send many Harvard boys or gourmands to the death house". Words and pictures combine to bring home the full horror of this grisly ritual, the details of which are always published by the authorities: in one famous case, mentally ill Ricky Ray Rector even decided to set aside half of his pecan pie – so that he could finish it after his execution. Shapiro is currently working on a book of the Last Supper series

1. Food in its rawest state: Larry Dunstan's photograph is part of a personal project documenting life at the Church Crookham military base in Surrey.

2. This photograph of disgusting looking food is one of a series of images of edibles shot underwater by Jakob Straub. The images were run out as large format inkjet prints and put up in the Berlin Artschool to promote typefoundry, S-Fonts which Straub co-founded with Jan Sonntag when they were both students. "The series was about showing things in the wrong environment," says Straub. "Ess means eat in German, and S-Fonts sounds like a command to eat type. This project plays on that and forces the viewer to deal with the image."

3. Advertising photographer Gary Bryan, bored of seeing similar food photography for the last five or so years, took a series of decidedly different food shots for his portfolio in his London studio. Bryan enlisted the services of one of the UK's top home economists, Claire Ferguson and lit his subject matter with tungsten lights to cast very sharp shadows and "give the shots an outdoor, filmic quality", he explains. "I wanted to make the images look like landscapes." Hence this image of a head of garlic and a tomato which is strangely reminiscent of a gunslinger's stand-off from a Western

1

BRIOCHE BREAD PUDDING

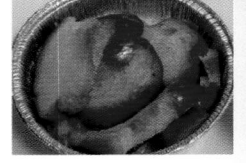

1 1/4	cups	heavy cream
1		egg
1		egg yolk
1 1/4	cups	sugar
1/4	tsp	vanilla extract
2	cups	brioche

DIRECTIONS

Position a rack in the center of an oven and preheat to 350°F. Butter two 10-oz. individual baking dishes and divide the brioche cubes between them. In a saucepan over medium heat, warm the cream until steam starts to rise, 3 to 5 minutes. Remove the pan from the heat and set aside.

In a bowl, whisk together the egg, egg yolk, sugar and vanilla until smooth. Whisking constantly, slowly pour the warm cream into the egg mixture. Divide the mixture between the prepared baking dishes and place them on a baking sheet. Bake until puffed and a toothpick inserted into the centers comes out clean, about 25 minutes. Let stand for 5 minutes before serving.

From William Sonoma

To make BREAD pudding, an oven is really necessary - you can't make it very well in a pot over a fire. And the oven needs to be in the home - and very few homes had ovens of any type until the 19th century. In cultures where bread was primarily baked by a professional bakery - as in France etc. - homes did not have 'ovens'. Puddings of all types were very popular in England. Bread pudding most likely originated there in the late 1600s.

2

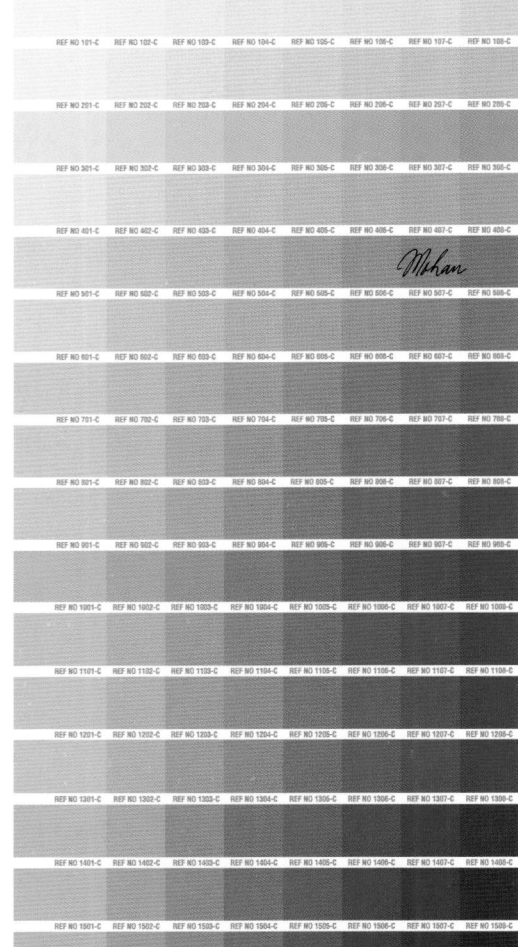

3

1-2. Starting life as a collection of in-house recipes designed to spice up the studio's lunchtimes, San Francisco design agency Noon's site www.lunch-at-noon.com has grown into "an opportunity to appreciate culinary art forms and food photography," says art director Cinthia Wen. Photography: Cinthia Wen. Web design: Claudia Fung. Copywriter: Craig Woodgate. Research: Amelie Wen.

3. Poster for Pantone Mugs, a project by Onkar Kular Singh in collaboration with A Practice for Everyday Life. The project explores the shared quest for perfection. Singh developed a series of mugs coloured to correspond with a drinker's ideal tea strength. A Practice For Everyday Life designed this chart, which people can use to approximate their ideal shade of tea. Users could then order a mug in the chosen colour, thus ensuring a perfect-strength cuppa every time.

Design For Freedom's Mug Shop produces limited edition coffee mugs from a selection of the best artists and designers around. Kozyndan (4), Phunk (5), and GHavisualagency (6) have contributed designs that should, say DFF, "bring happiness and joy to your desk, one beverage at a time". The three mugs featured here, and others, are available from www.designforfreedom.com

4

5

7. Trademark silliness from the inimitable James Jarvis: this image is from "James Jarvis' A3 Drawing", a series of illustrations featured in Japanese magazine, relax.

8-10. Cover and spreads from issue 15 of Japanese lifestyle and food culture magazine, Eat. Launched in 2000, Eat is bilingual (English and Japanese) with a circulation of 30,000. Creative director: Steve Martin. Photographers: Steve West (9) and Martin Richardson (10).

11. Eradicating "tea-making slaves or laggards" is the aim of this splendid website from Poke. Teabuddy allows those on the work tea roster to register preferences (sugar, milk, etc) allowing the person charged with brewing up to tick off affirmative respondents and print out a total order. Particularly handy for keeping an eye on tea-making slackers. Will be available from the Poke website from the new year. See www.pokelondon.com

1. Belu is a not-for-profit water brand: all net revenue will go to fund water projects worldwide. Packaging by Lewis Moberly features a glass bottle with a graphic of a spring on the back so that it sits behind the logo when viewed from the front. Client: Lifewater. Design director and copywriter: Mary Lewis. Designer and illustrator: Bryan Clark.

2. Thai wine-based drink, Sabai, asked Design Bridge to create a new label for export. Illustrated with hibiscus flowers (a key ingredient) plus animals, fish and other Thai associated imagery.

3. Packaging for Hill Station ice cream by Williams Murray Hamm.

4. Outdoor caterer, SOS OUT, commissioned bonbon London to create memorable packaging for Toast, a summer food festival held at London's Syon Park in mid-July. They produced this paper bag which unfolds flat to form a picnic mat on which to sit and scoff.

5. Tefal Jamie Oliver Professional Series pan packaging by Lewis Moberly. Design director: Ann Marshall. Designers: Ann Marshall and Alex Lampe

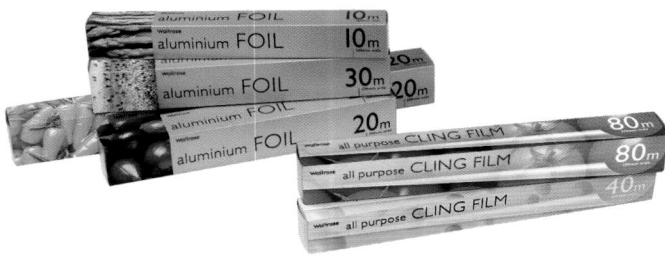

9

10

6. Jonathan Crisp range by Ziggurat, redesigned as a premium brand. "Our idea was to create 'Crisps for Snobs'," says creative director Allison Miguel. The eight flavours feature caricatures of the upper classes by Spitting Image artist Paul Baker. Designer: Hayley Bishop.

7. Typically understated Waitrose foil and cling film packaging by Carter Wong Tomlin. Designers: Nicola McClements, Neil Hedger. Photography by Mark Wragg.

8. Coley Porter Bell redesigned the entire packaging for the Wild Bean Café, the retail café within BP Connect service stations. The brief was to deliver "fresh quality food on the go" to target audience, the white van man. The packs play on greengrocer language and graphics because they represent freshness with a no-nonsense attitude. Creative director: Martin Grimer. Designers: Roberta Elliot and Paul Marsh.

9. Mangajo is a health drink brand

that produces a range of soya-based and tea-flavoured drinks. Stockists range from Sainsbury's to the Colette store in Paris. Packaging design by MadeThought.

10. The Carlsberg-sponsored man of the match awards at the Euro 2004 football championships took the form of a font – the bar-top objects from which draught beer is dispensed. Design by SiebertHead.

11-13. Shake Shack is a new food stand in New York's Madison

Square Park, which, we're told, is "the Dom Perignon of hotdog stands". Graphic designers: Paula Scher, Rion Byrd and Joe Marianek at Pentagram Design New York. Project architects: Denise MC Lee, James Wines at SITE. Client: Madison Square Park Conservancy

11

SHAKE SHACK

12

13

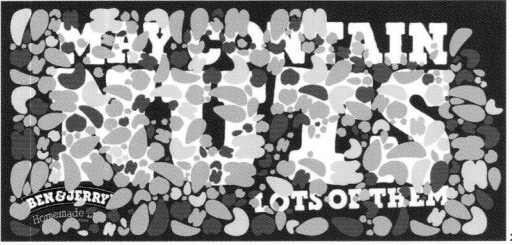

1&2. Fallon's Ben & Jerry's campaign continues with these posters and tube cards extolling the virtue of added cream and nuts in your ice-cream. We can only agree. Creatives: Glenn Gibbins, Simon Roseblade (Cream) Antony Nelson, Mike Sutherland (Nuts). Creative directors: Richard Flintham and Andy McLeod. Designer: Pieter Janssen.

3&4. Clinic were appointed in 2003 to work on the articulation of Brains Brewery's newly developed brand personality. This campaign, which runs as 48 sheet posters, is based around the tag line: More Positive Thinking from Brains.

5&6. Ginsters try to shed the service station image with this no-frills print

and poster campaign promoting its range of "Real honest food". Agency: Bartle Bogle Hegarty. Creatives: Pete Bradly, Marc Hatfield, Steve Robertson and Justin Moore. Art direction/typography: Chris Chapman.

7&8. The makers of Bavaria beer believe their brew is too tasty to

keep all to themselves, hence a print and TV campaign illustrating how its makers in Brabant intend to conquer Holland and the rest of Europe (sound familiar?) Agency: KesselsKramer. Creatives: Johan Kramer, Erik Kessels. Photographer: Otto Snoek. Print production: Pieter Leendertse

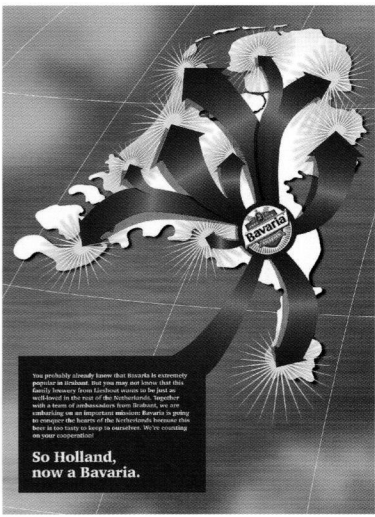

obviously another

obviously another

obviously another

9

10

11

9-11. Photographer Jenny van Sommers shot this Kellogg's Crunchy Nut Cornflakes press campaign from J Walter Thompson, adapting familiar foods to include the cereal. Written by Matt Collier and Wayne Robinson.

12-15: Posh totty Tara Palmer-Tompkinson promotes posh crisps from Walkers. Agency: Abbott Mead Vickers.BBDO. Creative: Rob Oliver. Photographer: Kate Plumb. Dress designer: Tristan Webber. Hat designer: Stephen Jones

Posh Crackers from Walkers
12

Posh Crisps from Walkers
13

Posh Crisps from Walkers
14

Posh Pappadoms from Walkers
15

ANHEUSER
World Select

Ten brewmasters. Four continents. One Beer.

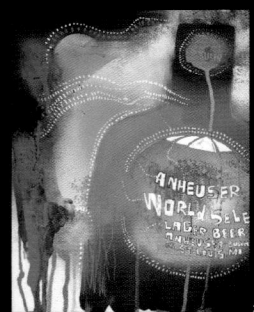

1

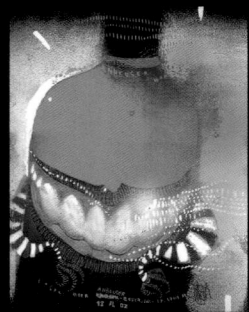

2

3

Boston-based ad agency Hill
Holliday's latest print campaign to
promote Anheuser World Select,
Anheuser-Busch's new pilsner beer,
encompasses a huge billboard in
New York designed by Brazil's Lobo
(finished poster shown, 1). Lobo's
contribution (development artwork
for the campaign shown, 2-4) is one
of many projects created for the
brand by a selection of design teams
from all over the world. Apparently,
the colour green was significant in
the brief as this is the first full-
alcohol beer from Anheuser-Busch
that is bottled in green glass. "The
brand has utilised an organic
approach from Lobo, tying the
bottle's colour to nature," says Hill
Holliday's Jeremy Schwartz. Client:
Anheuser-Busch. Agency: Hill
Holliday. Art director and creative
director: Jeremy Schwartz.
Production Company: Lobo/The
Ebeling Group. Creative director:
Mateus de Paula Santos

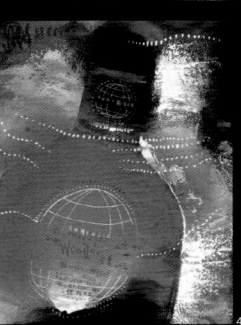

4

1

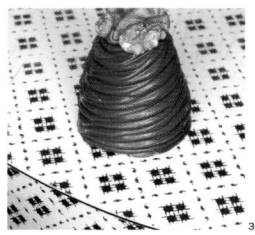

3

4

2

Tim Morris has been shooting for the likes of Vogue and The Observer for the past 25 years. Pictures 1-3 were taken for The Observer Food Monthly magazine, to illustrate a preview of Nigel Slater's biography Toast. "The book's all about the food Nigel ate through his life. As a kid, tomato sauce and foods like that were forbidden," Morris explains. "So I wanted my shots to have a 60s feel... a tin of mandarins would have been a real luxury then, the same with a Walnut Whip." The retro feel of these shots is enhanced by upping the colour contrast. Image 4 is from his personal portfolio. "Most of the work I do is observational still life: with the bottles of sauce here I just walked into a café, took the shot, and walked out... it was that quick." Morris likes to keep things spontaneous, "And I always frame my shot in-camera," he adds, "they're very rarely cropped." www.timmorrisphotographer.com

1

2

3

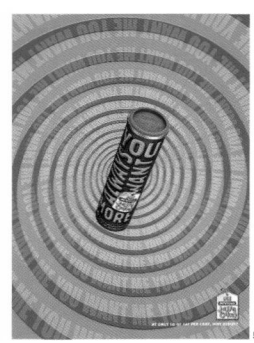

4

1-4. Continuation of the Molson Canadian beer campaign in which male drinkers are encouraged to make themselves seem more attractive to women through various cheeky forms of deception. These include a series of fake business cards from luxury companies for those who want to pretend that they have expensive hobbies and a set of cute photos to keep in your wallet, showing off your sensitive side. Agency: Crispin Porter Bogusky. Creatives: John Parker and Evan Fry (business cards), John Parker, Alex Burnard, Mike del Marmol, Evan Fry and Dave Schiff (photos).

5. Jaffa Cakes press ad from Publicis. Creatives: Ira Joseph and Jackie Steers. Photography and spiral effects: Actis Studios. Typographer: Paul Martin.

6. New York-based design studio Vault49 illustrated, designed and produced a promotional mail-out pack for catering firm Last Supper. The pack consisted of this decorous poster, printed in five colours plus gold foil, which was housed in a foil-blocked wallet and posted in a hand-screenprinted package.

7. Drink menu for Chronicles, a bar and restaurant housed in the former Reading Chronicle newspaper building. Creative director: Barnaby Firth, Cream Design

5

6

7

8-10. Smirnoff 96-sheet poster concept work, commissioned by JWT but never used. Designed by Bless.

11. Lemon Jelly and Dot Com Refugee mugs from Airside. Available from www.airsideshop.com

12. Cute gravy boat gag alluding to the fact that you're not going to have much of the brown stuff left if you plump for Oxo. Agency: Abbott Mead Vickers.BBDO. Creatives: Mary Wear, Andy McKay. Photographer: Sophie Broadbridge.

13. www.jamieoliver.com by Poke taps into the blog craze: the chirpy chef tells us of his hilarious trip to Wimbledon with his mates (Jamie's Diary) and debate rages over the best scone recipe (Forums). Users can also see the world through Jamie's mince pies courtesy of the camera in his mobile (Moblog). Poke's Nik Roope says that Oliver has been keeping an online diary since 2000 so "tapping into the Blogosphere seemed a natural advance for us. He's very technology literate so developing a blog-based environment was a great way to ensure he could add content to the site from his laptop or his phone anytime, anywhere." Photos: Chris Terry, David Loftus.

14. Cover for Jamie Oliver's new book, Jamie's Dinners, from Penguin. Art director: John Hamilton

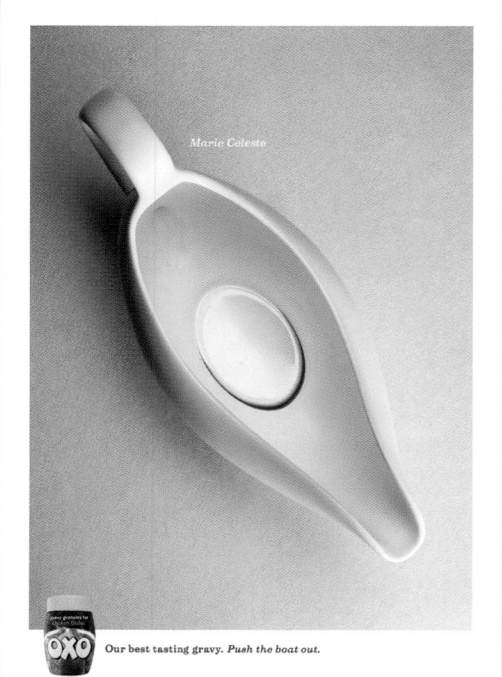

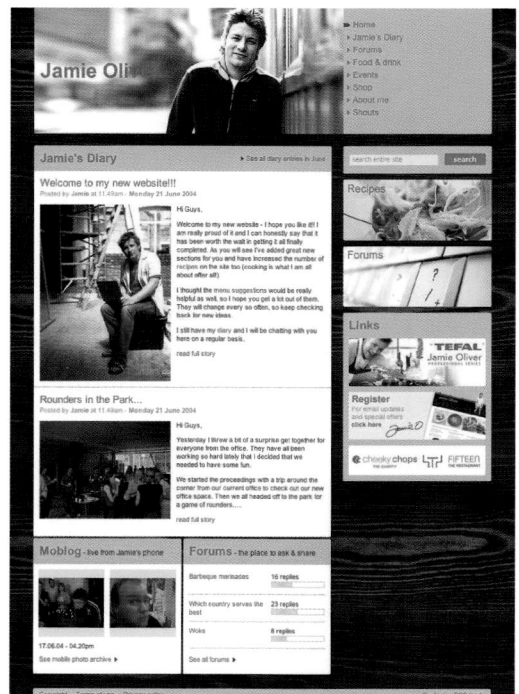

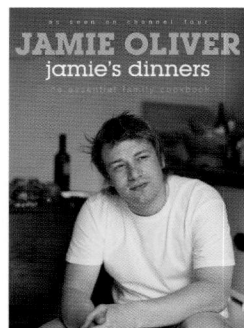

Plastic spud laments arrival of grain-based snack Grainwaves. Creatives: Nick Worthington, Lachlan Macpherson. Agency: Publicis Mojo Auckland. Directors: The Glue Society, @radical.media, Sydney

A car crash in a pub, to show how little booze it takes to impair judgement. Creatives: Paul Jordan, Angus Macadam @ Leo Burnett. Director: Ringan Ledwidge, Small Family Business. Client: DfT

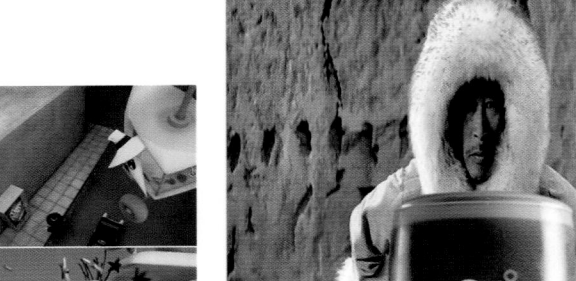

Mountain Dew breathes life into MAD cartoon Spy Vs Spy. Agency: BBDO New York. Creatives: Bill Bruce, Doris Cassar. Directors/production company: Traktor. Special effects: Method Studios

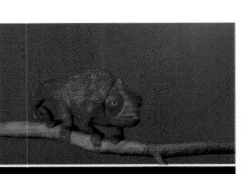

A chameleon stays resolutely red in this spot promoting new flavours (but not colours) of Tizer. Agency: BDH\TBWA. Creatives: Chris Lear, Doug Laird, Danny Brooke-Taylor. Directors: Fizzy Eye, Nexus

Iconic Guinness commercials of yesteryear are re-vamped with an Extra Cold twist in this new campaign for the beverage. An Eskimo, for example, does the famous Guinness dance to track Guaglione by Perez Prez Prado while waiting for his drink to settle. In another re-worked spot, the Guinness surfers only get as far as the foam before backing out of a far too chilly sea. Agency: Abbott Mead Vickers.BBDO. Creative: Mark Fairbanks. Director: JJ Keith @ Exposure Films

How do nasty traffic wardens, baggage handlers and bus drivers sleep at night? Horlicks. Written by Chris Sainsbury and Louise Roberts at Grey. Directed by Rick Lemoine, @radical.media

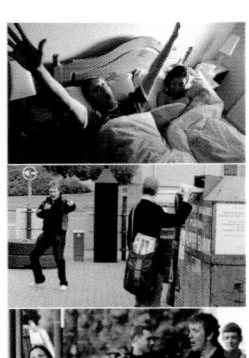

Entertaining McDonald's ads featuring an obsessed football chanter. Best line: "You're going home in a painted narrow boat." Creatives: Ed Morris, Trevor Webb @ Leo Burnett. Director: Theo Delaney @ Hot Spur & Argyle

McVitie's crumbs get everywhere, but none go to waste: "We make the biscuits, you make the crumbs". By Adam Kean and Alex Taylor at Publicis. Director: Christian Loubek, Independent

Goodfellas star Ray Liotta is the tough-talking wise guy in this dregs-saving new spot for Heineken. Agency: Clemmow Hornby Inge. Creative: Tony Barry. Director: Bryan Buckley @ Hungryman

Pilot is the latest epic TV and cinema spot from Lowe for Stella Artois. It features a British WW1 pilot who is shot down over occupied France. A man hides him in his bar but, when a German patrol turns up and tells no one to move, the barman can't bear not being able to turn off the flow of Stella from tap to glass over at the bar. Finally, our barman cracks, pointing to the large trunk by the door which is hiding the pilot. Director: Ivan Zacharias. Creatives: Vince Squibb, Jason Lawes and Sam Cartmell

The aggravating Danny Baker and the excellent Peter Kay team up in this latest installment for John Smith's. The ads show Kay cocking up Baker's attempts to conduct a soap powder doorstep challenge. How? By applying his no-nonsense philosophy to the question of whether he would agree to swap his one packet of biological powder for two big packets of ordinary powder. Course he bloody would. Agency: TBWA\London. Creative: Paul Silburn. Director: Danny Kleinman

Brickyard VFX removed all traces of rigging in lo-tech spots portraying Snapple bottles as superheroes. Agency: Deutsch. Production Company: Bob Industries. Director: Spencer Susser

Trippy combo of live action and animation, in this surreal spot for gourmet restaurant chain Chipotle. Agency: Mother, New York. Director: Anders Hallberg, Believe Media. Animation: Hornet Inc., NY

Another beautiful Waitrose spot, this time showing the origins of its whiskey. Written by Chris O'Shea and Ken Hoggins at Bank Hoggins O'Shea. Directed by Stuart Douglas, @radical.media

Designed by Form, Shelf Life (cover shown, 1) is a collection of unintentionally amusing brands from around the world; the kind that people usually encounter while on holiday. India's Gits poppadams nestle alongside such gems as De Donkere's Basterd sugar from The Netherlands (2) and Sweden's Skum confectionery (3). The book was written and compiled by Rosie Walford with Paul West and Paula Benson at Form. Published by Bloomsbury at £9.99, more details are available at www.shelflife.co.uk.

4. Customised, anodised aluminium tray for the service and display of food at Australian coffee shop, di Manfredi. Creative director: Vince Frost. Designers: Bridget Atkinson and Paula Yu. Design development: Stefan Kahn. Manufacturer: compact desk. Design studio: emeryfrost. Intro have created new brand guidelines for Japanese restaurant chain YO! Sushi! Using the strong colours of the already existing price coding of dishes (shown, 5), and straightforward shots of each dish (6), the information in the new menu, housed in a fetching Muji wallet (7), is as easily digested as a bowl of miso soup. Design: Mat Cook and Ian Eves @ Intro. The Geisha bar opened in Nottingham late last year with an identity and interior graphics by Studio Output.

Prior to the restaurant's launch, a concertina-folded booklet (8) featuring vibrant illustrations was sent out to selected households in the area. The interior of the bar was designed by Macaulay Sinclair while Studio Output were commissioned to create the back-lit glass panel which sets off the main bar (10) and also designed the mural which decorates the entire length of the 16 metre wall opposite (9). Output's involvement is ongoing as the interior panels are rotated every three months

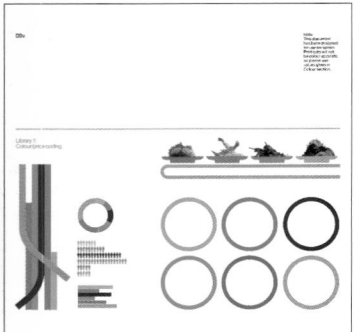

11-14. UK graffiti crew They Made Me Do It were commissioned by agency Cake to decorate a number of American Football helmets. The helmets were mounted in display cabinets in London bar Pop to support a Coors Fine Light Beer-sponsored Super Bowl viewing on 6 February. 15&16. Birds Boutique Café, situated in an old Cape-Dutch building in Cape Town, belongs to Mathilde and Heike Stegmann, mother and sister of designer Frauke Stegmann, who helped develop the interior and signage. Work in progress is the theme: "The inspiration was shacks and townships, the process of appropriating and recycling used products," says Stegmann. Trestle tables add to the informal look, while stools are made from crates with cushions on top bearing a forest-fairytale-fox print. "There are various books on birds which I gathered, each holding a pink menu with a golden embossed bird stapled to it. The coffee cup with the golden birds was specially designed for the working kitchen," adds Stegmann. "All the rest of the crockery: plates, milk jars etc are made by my mother." 17-21. An appropriately-shaped graphic device ties together emeryfrost's identity for Manta, a new Sydney restaurant. Creative director: Vince Frost. Designer: Anthony Donovan

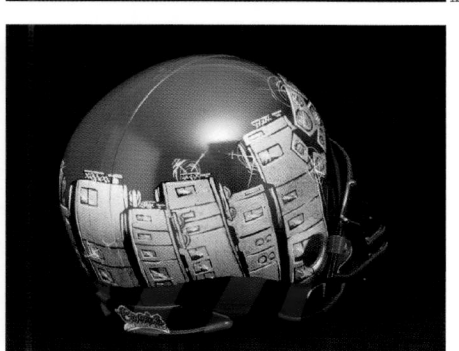

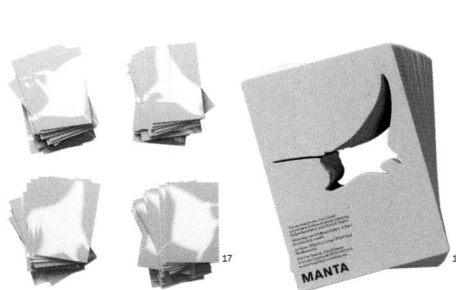

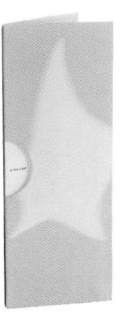

Taking your graphic designer and architect to the cinema must count as one of the strangest briefing meetings ever, but that is how restaurant owner Mark Chan began the development of OQO, a bar/restaurant in north London. Chan arranged to meet architect Jeremy Walker from Hawkins Brown and John Simpson (director of graphic design studio, SEA) at The Screen on the Green in Islington to watch the Japanese animated film, Spirited Away. This was to be part of the inspiration for the project. "We wanted a name which had no meaning and which was short and symmetrical," says Simpson. "Mark was also very keen to have a visual identity which could be used as a template for other bars or restaurants he intends to open in the

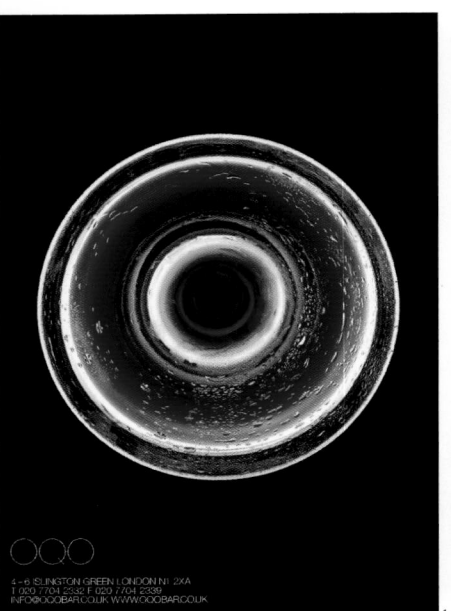

4–6 ISLINGTON GREEN LONDON N1 2XA
T 020 7704 2332 F 020 7704 2339
INFO@OQOBAR.CO.UK WWW.OQOBAR.CO.UK

1

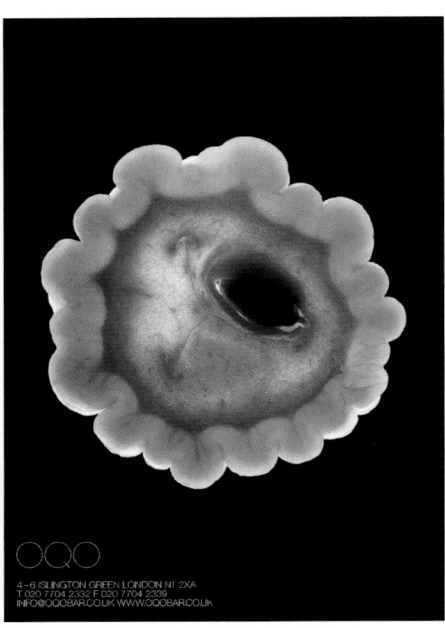

4–6 ISLINGTON GREEN LONDON N1 2XA
T 020 7704 2332 F 020 7704 2339
INFO@OQOBAR.CO.UK WWW.OQOBAR.CO.UK

2

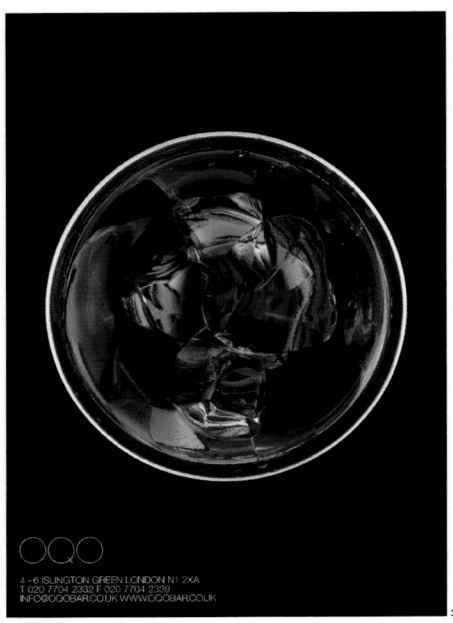

4–6 ISLINGTON GREEN LONDON N1 2XA
T 020 7704 2332 F 020 7704 2339
INFO@OQOBAR.CO.UK WWW.OQOBAR.CO.UK

3

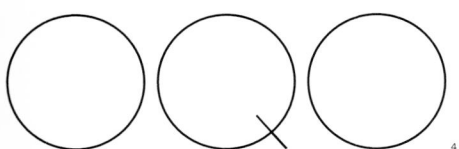

4

5

future." The bar was primarily to serve cocktails and the restaurant Chinese Tapas. "We decided to use selected food items and cocktails shot from above to echo the Identity," Simpson explains. Photographer John Ross back lit the individual items, concentrating on the close-up detail of the objects. "After six hours of shooting cocktails and drinking most of them, we had some stunning results which we used throughout the interiors of the bar and on individual items like menus, matchboxes, posters and coasters. The success of this identity was down to the collaboration between a number of disciplines: architecture, graphics and photography. It seems that designers are no longer pigeon-holed and we are finding that good design can cross over many boundaries," Simpson says.

1-3. Posters featuring Ross's shots of cocktails and food. 4. OQO logo. 5. Menus. 6-12. OQO restaurant and bar interiors and signage. Graphic design by SEA. Architect: Jeremy Walker from Hawkins Brown

7

8

6

9

10

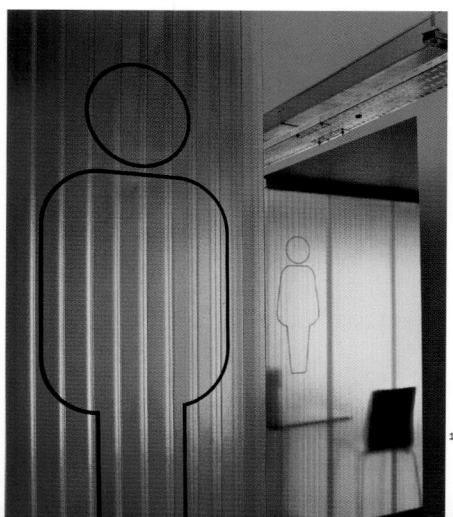

11

12

of Enterprise IG, this redesign of Peroni beer aims to "highlight the Italian heritage and provenance" of the beer which comes in special presentation packaging. 2. Penderyn is the only whisky distilled in Wales.

idea of Welsh gold and recently won Enterprise IG the Best Designer award at the Welsh Language Board's Bilingual Design Awards. 3. The Waitrose Cooks' Ingredients range has over 60 products for food lovers, from oils to

Designed by Lewis Moberly. Design director: Mary Lewis. Designer: Christian Stacey. 4. Glasgow design agency ThirdEyeDesign has created the packaging for newly launched luxury chocolate brand Kshocolat which is stocked by 140 stores in

Nichols and Liberty. 5. Waitrose Espresso beans, designed by Robin Hall at Davies Hall. 6. Thorncroft cordials, also by Robin Hall at Davies Hall. 7. These two Momo wine bottles are the first in what will eventually be a

the biodynamic vineyard, Seresin Estate, based in New Zealand. Biodynamics, in case you're interested, is a method of farming that seeks to actively work with the health-giving forces of nature: it's the oldest non-chemical agricultural

for variety. Designers: Mike Dempsey and Sophie Paynter at CDT Design

1

2

3

4

5

6

7

Penny Cottee was a finalist
in the Still Life Series
section of the 2005 AOP
Assistants' Awards for her
intriguing pictures of food
packaging (1&2)

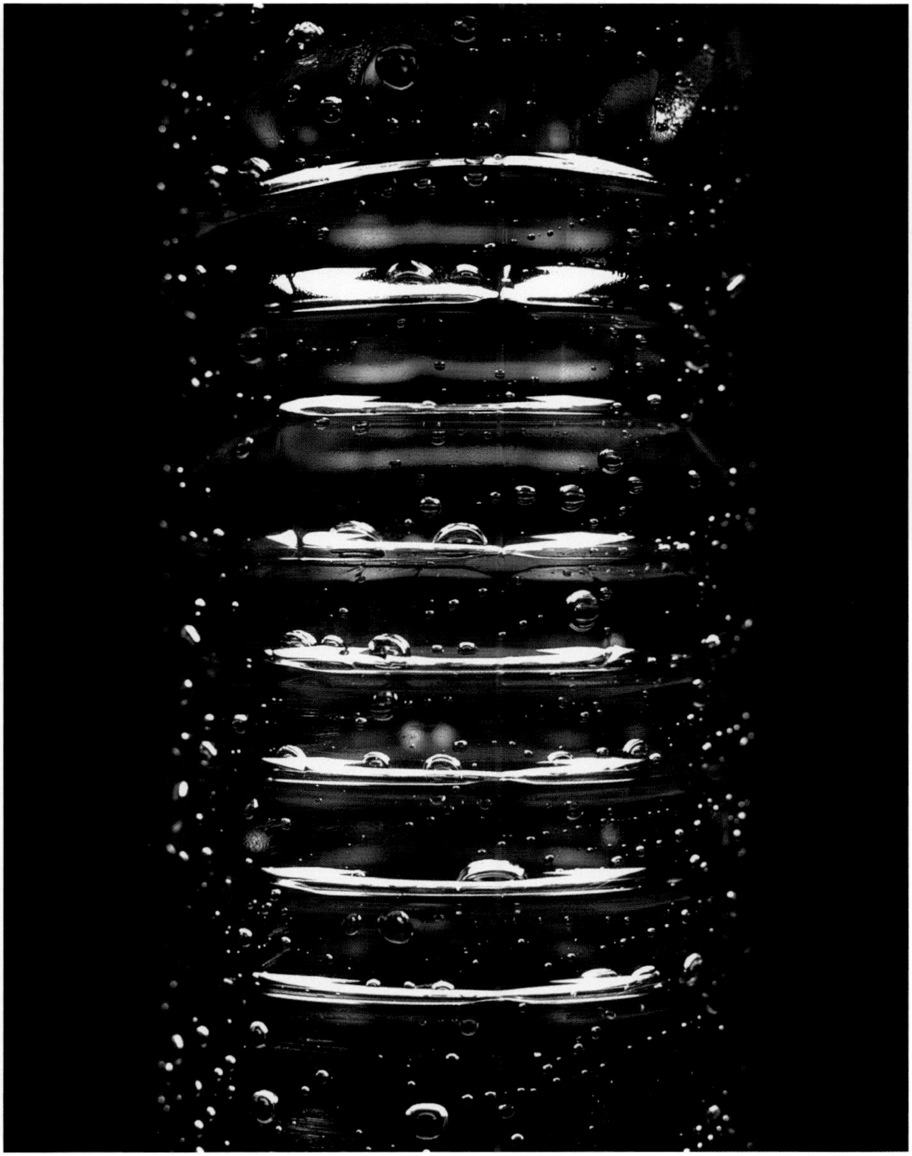

1

2

1-3. Two projects exploring the health-giving properties of breakfast cereal. For the Wheaties print campaign, the food packaging features various sports personalities, which are then placed in surroundings resembling environments typical to their sport. For example, swimmer Michael Phelps is placed on a blue tablecloth, undulations in the fabric resembling ripples in water. In another ad for whole grain cereal Total (3) nutritionally questionable components of your typical full-English breakfast are listed, but minus a few vitamin-oriented vowels. Agency: Saatchi & Saatchi, New York. Creatives: Tony Granger, Paul Kwong, Glen Levy, Craig Love. Photographers: George Petrakes, Dan Mahon (Wheaties), George Petrakes (Total).

4&5. Pure, wholesome goodness is the theme of these 50s-style illustrated posters for organic milk Altogether Better. Agency: Fallon. Creatives: Sam Heath, Frank Ginger, Richard Flintham, Andy McLeod. Illustrators: Harry Wingfield, Jason Holley

3

1

2

4

5

6&7. Skinny Girl is the name of this slightly sinister print campaign for fine chocolate chain Chocolate Gallery. Targeting young, female confectionery lovers, it aims to banish the skinny girl inside who wants to deny herself the pleasure of some chocolatey indulgence. Agency: Leo Burnett Singapore. Creatives Victor Ng, Jon Loke. Illustrator: Ying. 8. Brazilian design studio Lobo created this print campaign for Turning Leaf wine. The campaign, called Touch Of Magic, associates the product with a magical transformation and presents the wine bottle as a larger than life element embedded within a woodland scene. Illustrators: Andrezza Valentin and Mateus Santos. 9. This either-way-up poster for cider Merrydown Vintage was designed by Mark Denton and was the inspiration for CDD's new Merrydown Vintage TV spot Robots which Denton also directed (see overleaf). The robot is merry when his glass is full and down when it's empty. Creatives: Dave Dye and Sean Doyle. 10. This ad from AMV.BBDO for the RSPCA's campaign against the use of battery hen farming plays on the traditional sporting rivalry between England and Germany. In this case, Germany has taken the lead in the fight to ban battery cages, committing to a total ban by 2012; so it's 1-0 to them. "With your support they won't beat us," suggests the copy. Art director: Tony Hardcastle. Copywriter: Mark Tweddell

6

7

8

9

10

1. Headmaster Bob explains what he likes about Snapple. Then his pupils, dinner ladies and colleague list likable things about Bob. Like his hair. Agency: Cliff Freeman & Partners. Creatives: Brad Emmett, Lee Seidenberg. Director: Chris Smith @ Independent

Media, LA. 2. Talking dog tries to get his paws on the kids' Wall's Balls. Agency: McCann Erickson. Creatives: Nicola Hole, Mark Rowbotham. Director: Graham Rose @ Rose Hackney Barber. 3. Gary Lineker becomes Mr Potato Head in latest

Walkers spot. Agency: Abbott Mead Vickers.BBDO. Creatives: Daryl Corps, Ben Kay. Director: Peter Peake @ Aardman Animation. Post: Rushes. 4. Titles for Al Dente TV show on BeTV by Base Design with Pikaboo. 5. Film pastiches such as Vertigo and Jules et Jim

illustrate the true horror of being forced to split the sticks in your Twix. Agency: Grey. Creatives: Adam Chiappe, Matt Saunby. Director: Nick Gordon @ Academy Films. 6. Magnum gets sexy. Agency: McCann Erickson. Creatives: Martyn Smith,

Mark Hurst. Director: Bruce Aveillan @ Quad Films, Paris. 7. Mouthy cockatoo rescues woman from sleazy lounge lizards in Bud Light spot. Agency: DDB Chicago. Creative/ direction: John Immesoete @ Backyard, Venice, CA. 8. Lucozade Sport Hydro Active restores

moisture drop by drop. Agency: M&C Saatchi. Creatives: James Lowther and Bill Gallacher. Directors: Warren du Preez and Nick Thornton Jones, Brave Films. 9. HP Sauce is the Official Sauce of Great Britain. Agency: Mustoes (UK). Creative: Mick

Mahoney, Marco Puig. Director: Rob Sanders @ Amarillo Films. 10. The same CDD team that created the Merrydown Robot poster (shown previous page) produced this new TV spot for the cider. Director: Mark Denton @ Therapy Films

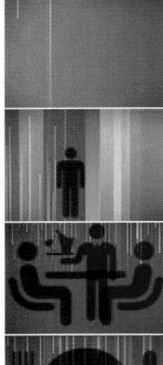

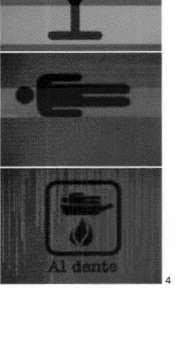

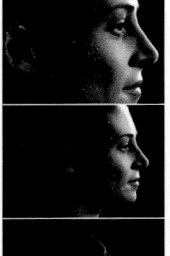

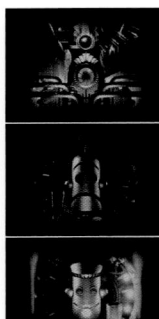

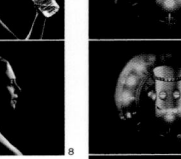

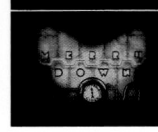

Self-
Promotion

1. Tank have created a lavish, large format promotional magazine for department store Liberty (spread shown). Featuring elegant photography of a selection of goods available from the shop, Give Me Liberty is loose bound so that its pages can be used as wrapping paper. Creative directors: Andreas Laeufer and Masoud Golsorkhi. Designer: Simone Pasztorek

2. Turner Duckworth's Little Red A-Z conveys the company's attitude to clients. One of the studio's guiding design principles is assigned to each letter and illustrated in an appropriate manner. Each book is wrapped in paper printed with found propaganda imagery from the Chairman Mao era in China. A sticker on the first page of each copy bears the recipient's name.

3. Spread from Dutch studio Koeweiden Postma's hardback book, In The End It's All About Love.

6. Promotional stickers, made by Neville Brody's Research Studios, for a party held in Paris.

Employers may complain that interviewees fail to present their work properly but these two mailers, both containing CDs, are extremely well designed. Twenty year-old Luke Prowse (mailer shown 4&5) decided against university, preferring to enter full-time work instead. Contact him at Luke@stereotypography.com. Chris Moorby meanwhile (7&8) is a graphics student at Barnsley College who has already produced work for Airside and Lab Magazine. www.computerlove.net/moorby

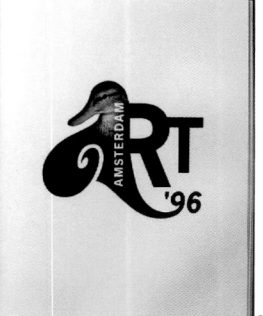

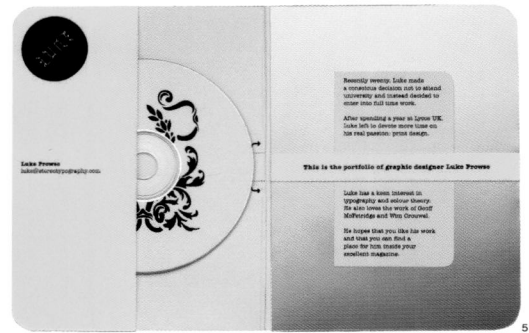

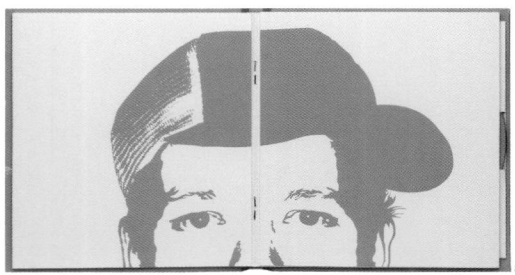

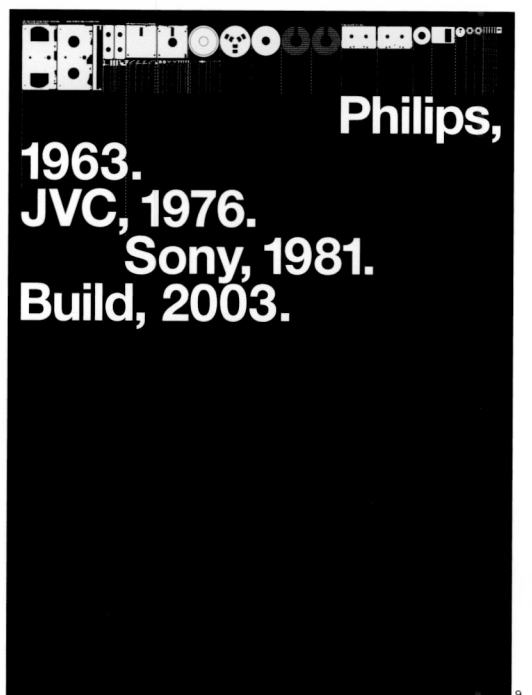

Philips, 1963.
JVC, 1976.
Sony, 1981.
Build, 2003.

10

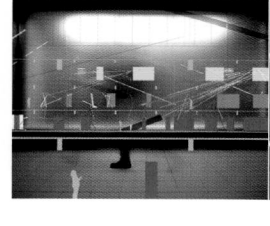

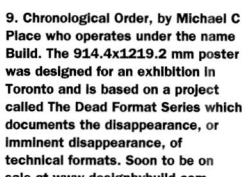

11

9

9. Chronological Order, by Michael C Place who operates under the name Build. The 914.4x1219.2 mm poster was designed for an exhibition in Toronto and is based on a project called The Dead Format Series which documents the disappearance, or imminent disappearance, of technical formats. Soon to be on sale at www.designbybuild.com

10. Park Studio's fun promotional pack comes in a badge-adorned carrier bag containing wrapping paper and a set of Christmas cards, each simply displaying a different anagram of Merry Christmas (such as Mr My Shirt Races). Also includes a brochure displaying past projects.

11. Sydney-based Wishart Design have combined creative forces with

fellow Australians and motion graphics specialists PictureDRIFT to increase their range of client services, from identity creation through to motion graphics. Shown are stills from a slick promo movie highlighting their combined talents.

12. Brochure for 26, the not-for-profit organisation of writers and language specialists that aims to promote the

use of writing in business. Designed by Harry Pearce at Lippa Pearce

13&14. Postcards from designer/artist Anthony Burrill. "I bought the original signs in a shop and just switched them round in a surrealist way," comments Burrill. "I just thought they'd be a nice postcard: people can put them on their door"

12

13

14

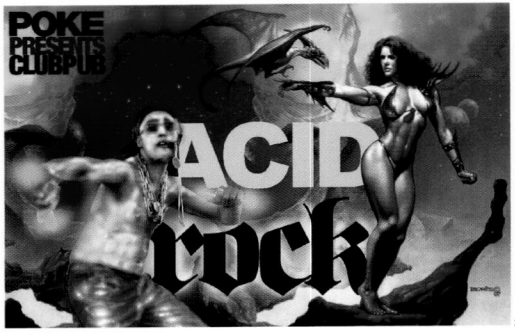

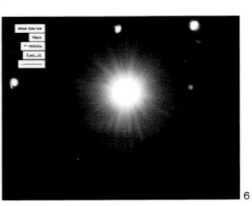

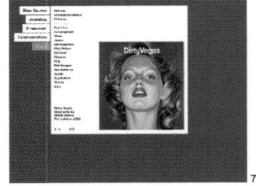

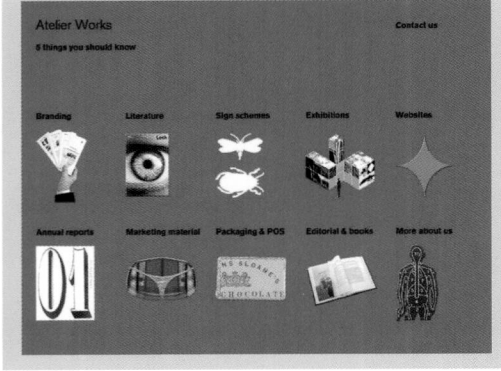

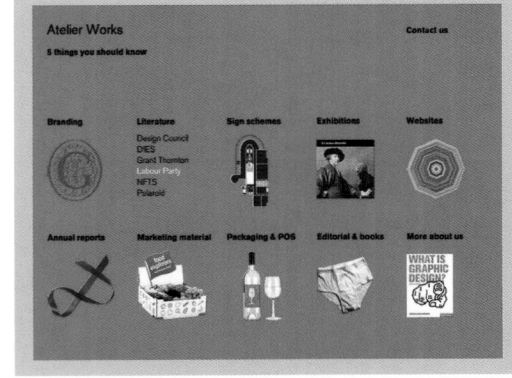

1. Poster advertising the next Club Pub, the club night/get-together for designers organised by new media studio, Poke (pictured 2). All attendees are requested to bring their own 15 minutes of music recorded onto cassette: the tapes are played during the night. The poster features a digitally-enhanced Nic Roope, partner at Poke. For details of the next event, see www.clubpub.org

3-8. Website for design studio Blue Source, www.bluesource.com. "Our ambition was to have a very simple site that did not require a team of experts to maintain it and that functioned as a place where we are able to represent ourselves efficiently through regular updates," says Blue Source's Seb Marling.

Every minute, a new image scrolls over the homepage. A specially drawn bitmapped font is used throughout referencing outmoded computer operating systems. Information is broken down into five main areas: biographical details, agency news, contact information, portfolio, plus a hidden section of the site as signified by a broken line of dashes. Inside the hidden area are hundreds of images including reference materials, work-in-progress and works that never previously saw the light of day.

9&10. Website for Atelier Works. An anagram of the company name appears top left on a pared down homepage which presents the company's work cleanly and simply, www.atelierworks.co.uk

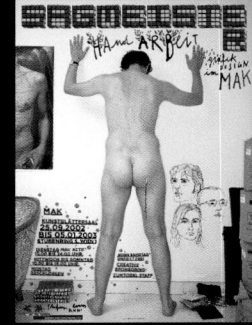

Stefan Sagmeister has always been one to take the concept of self-promotion literally. These three posters publicise exhibitions of his studio's work in Vienna, Zurich and Tokyo. The Zurich version (shown left) features Sagmeister and colleague Mathias Ernstberger in customised suits. "They represent charts showing the number of times pieces have been pictured in design magazines and annuals. Over the years the Lou Reed poster has been shown 101 times, (so it is shown largest) while the Anni Kuan brochure has been pictured only seven times, which makes it the smallest," says Sagmeister. The Tokyo version (below) is a classic before and after situation. The top picture is Sagmeister, weighing in at 178 pounds. The bottom one is taken one week later, after he has consumed all the food items shown and gained another 25 pounds, "Not an enjoyable binge," he comments.
Designers: Stefan Sagmeister, Matthias Ernstberger and Sabine Hug (Vienna version only).
Photography: Tom Schierlitz, Bela Borsodi (Zurich version)

1. These appealing reel boxes from Hornet, a production and design company with offices in New York and Los Angeles are reminiscent of 1950s children's toy packaging. Designed by Susan Hildebrand, who also designed Hornet's identity.

2. California-based production company Motion Theory take pride in how their moving image work is delivered. These reel cases resemble large hardback books and employ the graphic elements and colouring used in the company's stationery.

3-5. Enjoyable A5-sized book, styled like a sketch pad and jam-packed with the illustrations and distinctive handwriting of Marion Deuchars. Developed by HHCL/Red Cell and entitled "There's What Is... And There's What If..." it showcases some radical thoughts from the agency on a number of selected brands including Tetley Tea and Blackpool (shown). One of our favourites is the idea for a cruise liner to offer its services to Club 18-30 "You might need to put in high perspex guard rails, but you'd never

be far from a bedroom," they point out wisely. Quite.

6-9. Selection of self-promotional T-shirt designs by commercials and promo directors Shynola

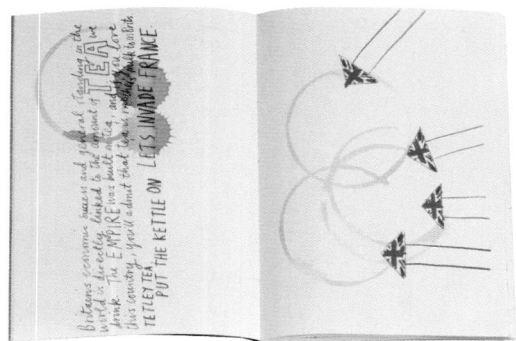

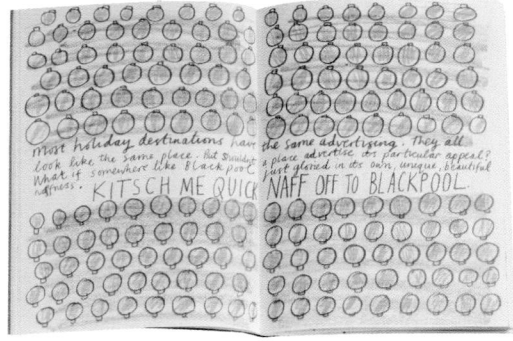

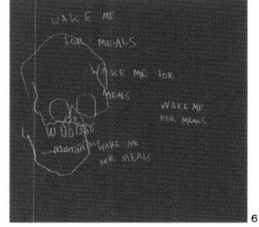

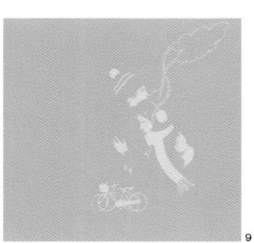

10

11

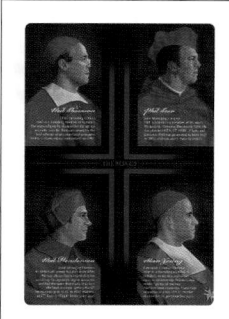

12

13

14

15

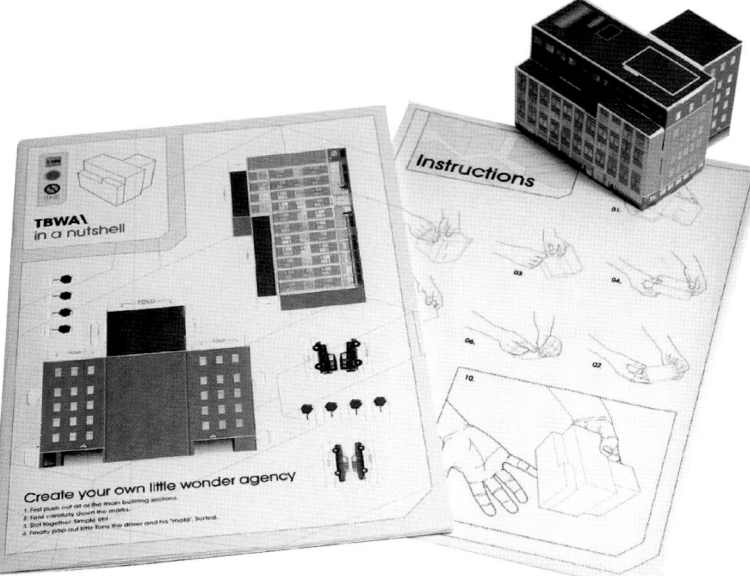

16

10. Gorgeous fleeces, distributed by award-winning production company Gorgeous Enterprises to friends and associates with new babies. This particular one is modelled by the delightful George Elvis Wood, son of Barnsley at The Mill.

11-13. Advertising agency St Luke's produced this corporate credentials brochure which takes a tongue-in-cheek look at the agency's proposition, that belief in the audience builds belief in the brand. Religious iconography brings the concept to life. Creative director Al Young and his partner Jules Vizard developed the leather-bound brochure. Portraits: Liam Kennedy. Colour photography: Lee Powers. Cardinal portraits: Jon Rogers.

14&15. KID UK, a book celebrating the tenth birthday of children's TV channel, Nickelodeon. The book aims to cement Nickelodeon's reputation for understanding what kids are all about. It's based on interviews conducted with children (we're talking normal kids here, no stage school types allowed) about their general interests. Produced in-house at Nickelodeon. Design/art

direction/interviews: Paul Ayre, Rohat Cellali-Sik. Photography: Simon Rawles.

16. TBWA\in a nutshell is the name of this brochure, which includes a self-assembly miniature version of the agency building, plus content about their disruptive activities for clients. Designed in-house. Art director: Bryn Jones. Illustrator/ typographer: Alex Fairman. Cardboard engineer: Tim Riding

Ross Holden has an interesting take on the standard black leather portfolio case. To carry his latest illustration work round to clients, he made this suitcase (bottom left and right) which holds a selection of recent projects and sketchbooks. The illustration on the front of the case uses a technique that Holden has developed in much of his new work – drilling or punching holes to draw elaborate images and fonts. Linking in with the design of the case, his books are also painted with the name of his working identity, Unglue My Limb (top right). Holden also created a mailer (top left) that includes different examples of his work, Polaroids and a poster and arrives in a take-away bag. www.ungluemylimb.com is set to continue the identity online, and provide a less cumbersome version of his mighty wooden portfolio

1. Self-promotional campaign for New York-based illustration studio Quickhoney. The stickers were plastered around the city.

2-6. Illustrators Vault49 produced this self-promotional volume. It comes in a custom-made box (2&3) which Vault49 screenprinted by hand in their studio. Inside the box, three copies of the same book displaying samples of their illustration work are wrapped in translucent paper (4). The book itself (spread shown, 5, cover shown, 6) is printed using five colours plus a varnish

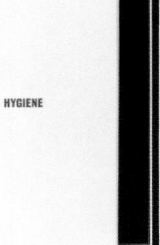

1&2. The latest of the Pentagram Papers series of bi-annual booklets exploring the curious and the stimulating. This one, by Fernando Gutiérrez, showcases the ingenious objects created by Cubans suffering under the US trade embargo.

3&4. 250 Projects and 25 years in New York celebrates Pentagram's anniversary in the city. The cover

maps the location of its clients in Manhattan. Art Director: Paula Scher. Designer: Sean Carmody. Editor: Kurt Koepfle.

5&6. CDT was commissioned to design a limited-edition book and direct marketing campaign for Robert Horne to challenge the misconceptions of designers about printing on uncoated paper. Nineteen

Old Wives' Tales were illustrated and related to classic myths and facts about printing on uncoated paper. Art direction: Christian Altmann. Designer: Sophie Paynter.

7. Fold-out mailer from Duffy, London. On one side of a large sheet of light paper are reviews of their work from the media. On the reverse is one large image. The whole thing

comes in a brown card envelope with text screen-printed in white.

8. ESOUND 10, from the EMI esounds series of sampler CDs. Each CD contains a compilation of new releases from the label's acts and comes with a fold-out illustrated poster. Illustration: Adam Pointer. Art direction and design by Traffic. Compiled by EMI Trade Marketing

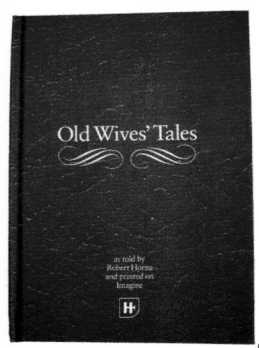

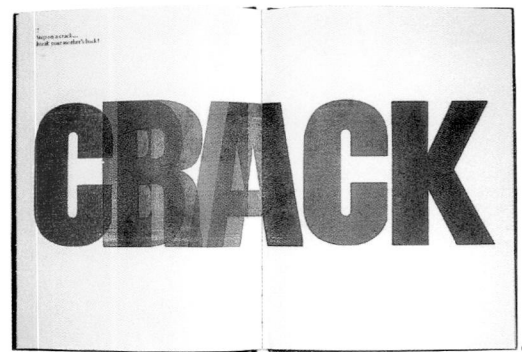

*Wish you a Merry Christmas?
Why should we. Why do we have to do anything
for Christmas. It's only one day! Just because
of something that's supposed to have happened a
million years ago or whatever. Jesus Christ.
Can't we all just get on with life like normal?
Why does everyone have to be so bloody happy at
Christmas. Anyway, if you need us, we're in our
studio. And can you knock before you come in.
Some privacy would be nice, if that's not too much
to ask. And we're not tidying it up.*

TO ALL OUR FRIENDS, A VERY MERRY CHRISTMAS
OUR LAST ONE AS A TEENAGER

THE 20TH ANNIVERSARY OF LEWIS MOBERLY

10

11

12

HEART
FAILED (IN
THE BACK OF
A TAXI)

13

14

15

CALENDAR
2004

16

17

9. Poster by Lewis Moberly to celebrate its twentieth anniversary. Art director Mary Lewis says, "The poster is for friends and colleagues who will recognise Lewis Moberly's love of copy, pleasure in typography and desire to surprise and delight". Designer and copywriter: Christian Stacey. Printed foil block in red onto textured Whipped Cream Curious Soft Touch paper.

10. Wrapping paper from Foundation 33. Utilitarian variations include a version listing all the days of the year (you just circle the appropriate one) and a repeat pattern made up from gift tags, which celebrate everything from Mothers' Day to Christmas (the user fills in the "to" and "from" details in the pertinent version). The wrapping shown (56) is ironically smothered in the price

stickers that you'd usually try to remember to pick off.

11 UNA designers desk diary. Each week is numbered in a different language using the Fregio Mecano typeface on a full page. When the week has passed, that page can be torn out and stored in the flap at the back of the clear plastic cover. A new cover is then revealed bearing the number of the next week. A short story by Meghan Ferrill runs through the book.

12. Self-promotional mailer by Baron & Baron featuring the studio's work as a set of stamps. Perforations run around the edge of each image.

13. A tight budget led to this low-tech self-promotional project from art director Marc Atlan. Printed on

newspaper bearing enigmatic slogans and oversized images, it aims to reflect the range of emotions that the designer goes through. This spread, as with the rest of the work, was based on a photograph taken by Atlan. "I took this picture in a cab in Florence on assignment for Comme des Garçons," he says, "It's about speed, movement and focus."

14&15. Airside have reworked their Lemon Jelly, Lost Horizons sleeve for a Christmas card. Now though, the familiar landscape is covered in snow. The cards come in packs of ten: five daytime versions and five nighttime. For their 2004 calendar (16&17), Airside opted for a 12-inch, wall-mounted format. It comes with a sheet of 40 stickers to help flag up important dates

A selection of seasonal greetings from the many cards, posters and crazy paraphernalia that flooded the Creative Review office this Christmas. Highlights among the greetings cards (1) include (clockwise from top left) "The Adoration of the Magi" beautifully rendered entirely in meat and veg by Nikki Crumpton, partner/head of planning at agency Fallon. NB:Studio sent a combined card for every occasion including Valentine's and Mother's Day. Third Eye's black and white scrawled effort was created by the production and marketing managers. Julian Morey's simple, reflective card wished everyone a mirror Christmas, while Moving Brands opted for graphic representations of tape spools in silver, gold and white printed on clear acetate. North reminded us of a decade's work in design by taking us through ten years of client logos. Agency Abbott Mead Vickers joined up with the Central Illustration Agency to produce an innovative Christmas greeting: a set of playing cards where each card was designed by one of 52 illustrators from the CIA stable. Contributors included Ian Bielby, Brian Grimwood, Simon Spilsbury, Ray Smith and David Holmes. Louisa Allgren at AMV created the concept and Steve Davies, also at AMV, designed the graphic on the back of each card and box. Several cards used Arjo Wiggins' Curious Touch textured paper (used by CR on the slipcase for our April 03 issue), the best being this by Big Active featuring a blind embossed illustration by Jasper

Goodall. The Chase's concertina effort put together seasonally apt street names while another design group, BOB, opted for an edible card, gamely baking their company name and sending the wares out with season's greetings. Finally Johnson Banks sent up that annual irritant, the round robin, this time updating friends on "family" news at the design studio. Adorning their card: fetching sketches of the team.

Everyone loves a good collective noun, as Pentagram well know, which is why their Christmas "card" (2&3) was packed full of them (along with some apposite photos). Best nouns: a "knot" of toads and a "romp" of otters.

Mother have something of a reputation when it comes to self-promotion, which is enhanced by these latest efforts. 4. Instead of sending out Christmas cards this year, they repackaged some of the gifts sent to them by other companies and sent them out instead: your very own Mother Re-Gift. 5-7. Mother's Explorers [sic] Map of the Antarctic is a lovingly put together facsimile of an atlas, including a key to symbols indicating such unlikely features as a Robbie Williams look alike and cycle paths. Inside are 104 pages of carefully grid-referenced white space. The inside back page features more from the series such as The Explorers Map of Dense Fog and The Explorers guide to Heaven. Presumably, all the apostrophes must have got lost in the snowy wastes

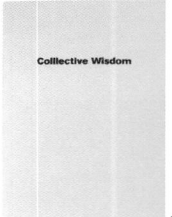

Collective Wisdom

A   of dragons

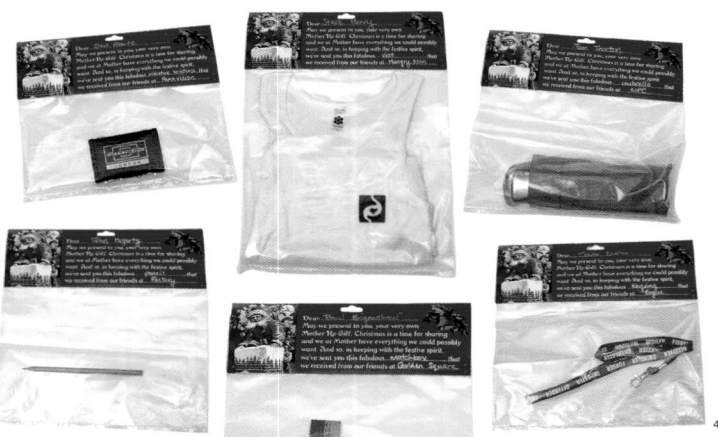

EXPLORERS
MAP
of the
ANTARCTIC

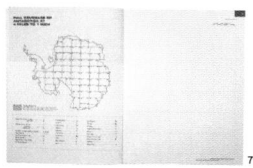

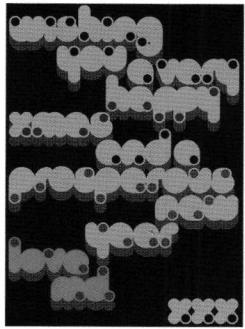

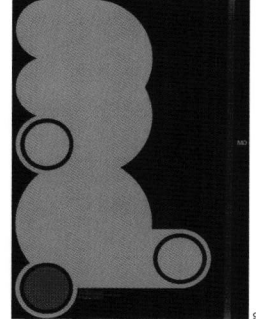

8&9. This double-sided, seasonal poster, by London-based Malone Design, was screenprinted on a claret coloured stock. The yet-to-be-named typeface was created specially for the poster – a full character set is being developed.

10. Bibliothèque's festive poster pictured a piece of iron pyrites, better known as Fool's Gold.

11. From ad agency Maison Zimbler

comes the MZ 2005 Portable Notebook. Packaged to look like a laptop, it's actually an Etch-A-Sketch, complete with "twist and shake technology interface".

12. The Gorgeous Christmas album was production company Gorgeous Enterprises' seasonal offering. The record includes home-spun versions of Rudolph the Red-nosed Reindeer and White Christmas, as miaowed by various musical cats. And it was

recorded in Portland Mews.

13&14. My Christmas is Gone, a book of photographs of discarded Christmas trees was produced by 4creative. Art directed by Jim Chambers, who also photographed the rather sad looking fir trees.

15&16. Manchester-based design studio Love's Christmas offering came in the form of a book of corporate guidelines to the office

Christmas party. Inside were suggested typefaces such as Flirt Ultra and Pished Light, a guide to acceptable behaviour and a Skirt Length to Pay Rise Ratio diagram

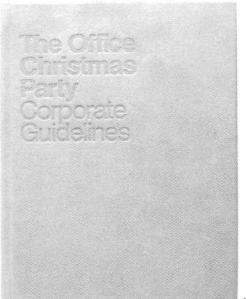

In A Still Night, Studio AKA's animated Christmas card, a cute character trudges through the snow singing a very crackly, German version of Silent Night. See it at www.studioaka.co.uk

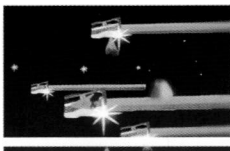
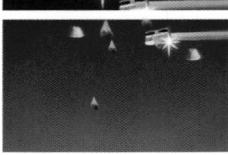

Up The Resolution created D&AD's seasonal e-card. Unsurprisingly, it features yellow pencils which streak across a wintry sky until they are sharpened... Shavings fall to earth to form Xmas trees

A message of good will from Duffy & Partners, New York, who also celebrate their 20th birthday this year. A collage image builds but is eventually blotted out by the simple message: "Peace"

To promote his newly-launched collectable figures, Minipips, designer Griff created a series of promotional animations through his company Up The Resolution to be distributed on DVD and virally

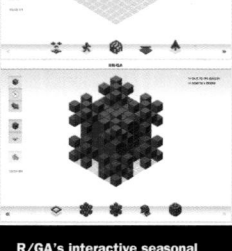

R/GA's interactive seasonal greeting invited visitors to an online gallery, where they could build their own virtual sculptures. The shapes build gradually and satisfyingly on screen from small red cubes

These three virals accompany some dubious-looking perfume sent out by HarrimanSteel and are, they explain, a "blatant piss-take of esoteric/vacuous perfume commercials that hit our screens every December"

Animated greetings from the heart of Studio Soi, a German-based animation studio. The film features Soi characters waving from woodlands, fields and urban landscapes. Really simple and really beautiful too

St Nick squares up to St Luke in the boxing ring and promptly punches his lights out in this nicely filmed online greeting from advertising agency St Luke's. Santa's elves bawling from the ropes are very good

The D&AD's Interactive TV category (sponsored by BSkyB) was announced in this commercial which features famous jingles badly sung by visitors to a Japanese karaoke bar. Agency: HHCL/Red Cell. Creatives: Jonathan Burley, Ian Williamson. Director: Russ Lamoureux @ Hungry Man

BOOK SMARTS #3
WORDS OF FINITE WISDOM

BOOK SMARTS #1
THE TRUTH ABOUT NOTHING

BOOK SMARTS #2
SEMI-SURVIVAL GUIDE TO THE FUTURE

1

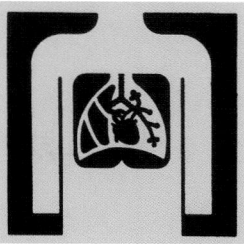

WHOEVER SAID BEAUTY COMES FROM WITHIN NEVER TOOK A BIOLOGY CLASS.

2

SOMEONE WILL PULL THE PLUG.

3

HUMANS ARE ANATOMICALLY CORRECT.

4

SAUCE
SHOWREEL

5

1-4. Book Smarts is a series of three pamphlets from US ad agency 86 The Onions satirising the kind of self-help books or small collections of quotes to be found by the cash registers of most book shops. "No-one will learn anything from reading them," promises writer Chad Rea. Illustrated by Anthony Burrill.

5. Radio director, Neil Harrington sees radio direction as "something you add on top [of an idea] to bring it to life". So, naturally, he called himself Sauce. Paul Pateman, of AMV, worked with Harrington to design this mailer: an oversized sauce packet that both looks and feels authentic. The sauce (a gel pack) gives the correct feel whilst also protecting the rectangular CD which contains examples of Harrington's work.

KesselsKramer's latest tome is called, fittingly, Made in a Church and features case studies and communications work from the agency (cover and spread shown, 6). It's been designed as a hymn book to relate to the ecclesiastical office environment of the company. A forthcoming book of all their work, entitled 2 Kilos of KesselsKramer, is supported by a print campaign (7&8) and will be published by Pie Books, Japan in April.

9. Poster promoting the exhibition, Ideas Shop, which was held in the Academy Hills entrance area of the Roppongi Hills tower. The project was developed by Tokyo-based creative agency, dreamdesign

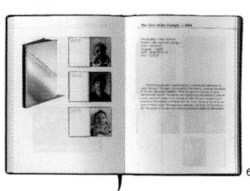

6

www.piebooks.com

coming soon:
2 kilo
of kesselskramer

7

www.piebooks.com

coming soon:
2 kilo
of kesselskramer

8

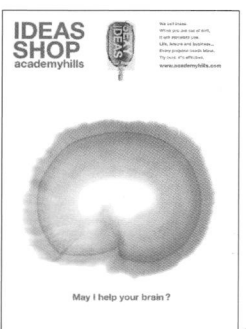

IDEAS SHOP
academyhills

IDEAS

www.academyhills.com

May I help your brain ?

9

1-3. Invitation to an oriental-themed party at design studio Intro. The dual-language, double-sided poster (3) was folded down to sit in a stitched envelope (1).

4-6. Marmalade magazine turned the streets of London into one big gallery (albeit a noisy, smelly one) with Not On Sale Now, a series of fly posters carrying positive messages about the experience of city living. Contemporary artists and designers responding to the brief included James Taylor, Vault 49, Neil McFarland and Dan Witz.

7. This mailer from illustrator Mick Clarke is cleverly personalised with the recipient's name. It tells the story of the mailer's journey through the post to the recipient's desk, their subsequent visit to his website and call to commission him for work. See www.mick-clarke.co.uk

8. Poster/mailer featuring the original names of some notable bands: did you know that REM were once called Can Of Piss? Designed by Wayne Daly

9. A series of experimental images by photographer Jenny van Sommers playing with light and form.

10&11. New York-based designer Gelman and UK illustrator Paul Davis produced this large format, promotional print piece. After meeting at a D&AD judging, the pair decided to collaborate. Gelman sent Davis a box of his print work: "He asked me whether, maybe, I could rearrange his work – draw on it – make it different," Davis says. "I started thinking about where design is supposed to function: placement, media buying and all that. What struck me after taking a couple of rolls of film of his work was how very funny it looked in the wrong place. That was it – I took about 1000 (maybe more) shots of exactly that. Wherever I was, in 2004, I had his work in my possession and would grab it out of my bag and shoot it whenever it seemed a potentially humourous, wrong situation. The design is simple, the type is simple and the idea is simple. We are simple! Personally I want a great big juicy overpaid advertising commission because of it."

12. From Alphabet City: Out on the Streets, a children's alphabet book by Michael De Feo. Each letter is illustrated with an original painting by De Feo, wheat-pasted onto the streets of Manhattan and photographed. Published by Gingko Press. www.alphabetcitybook.com

13-15. Desk Dummy looks at first sight like a typical printers' blank – the bound samples of paper sent out by paper companies. But it has one important difference – it is covered with the jottings and musings of designer Nick Eagleton at The Partners. "I had a pile of left-over blank dummies and it came to me that I could use them as a scrapbook on the trials and tribulations of being a designer," he says. Eagleton then persuaded PaperCo to publish a book of his work as a promotion for Tullis Russell's Advocate paper.

16-18. Airside's 2005 calendar comes with a page of stickers (17) to mark special occasions. Each week of the year is set on its own page containing an image of an Airside creation

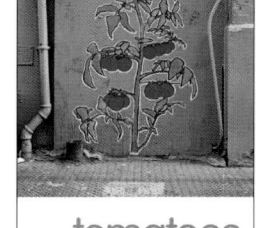

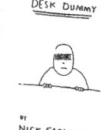

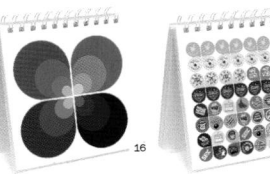

Cabanon Press is run by illustrators Tom Gauld and Simone Lia who formed the small imprint in 2001 whilst at the Royal College of Art. Since then they have self-published several books including parts one and two of Fluffy, by Lia, Gauld's Guardians of the Kingdom and the first volume of his Three Very Small Comics. His second volume of miniature comic books is available now and contains two handmade stories and one poster, packaged in a neat brown envelope (5). Invasion (extract shown, 1-4) is a 14-page adventure story that returns to one of Gauld's obsessions: the comings and goings of characters within a stark medieval world. In this comic, the story concerns two men who meet on a barren isle. The other existentially tragic tale is The Robots Broke Out of the Factory and Fled as Far as Their Batteries Would Allow (extract shown, 7-10) where the demise of six robots is delicately portrayed in Gauld's scratchy ink drawings. And as if that title weren't long enough, the enclosed poster, Our Hero Battles Twenty-Six Alphabeticised Terrors (6) charts the 26 foes that a sword-wielding character has to face, one after the other; from the humble Axeman, to a gang of Zombies. The poster was originally created for Pentagram's Ballpoint exhibition (CR June 04): it was inspired by the books of Edward Gorey and B-movie monsters. The set is available from selected bookshops at £4 and also from www.cabanonpress.com where more of Gauld and Lia's work can be seen

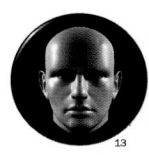

11

12

13

14

15

16

17

18

New York's hip downtown boutique mEmes hosted an event for graphic designer Gelman at the end of last year (12). For the duration of the event, all regular merchandise was taken down from the shelves and replaced by a special GLMN/GELMAN collection of T-shirts (14-18), skateboards (11), hats, buttons bearing a 3D image of Gelman (13) and stickers. Gelman also provided

20 blank, fluorescent, orange mesh trucker caps together with 20 thick black markers so that party-goers could decorate them. Completing the self-promotional overload, a topless female bartender served drinks with a gold GELMAN logo painted on her chest.

19-21. Design consultancy Navyblue's self-published book

Waiting For is, says design director Clare Lundy, "to prompt people into thinking about what it is they are really waiting for in life". In it, two Navyblue staffers reveal and illustrate what they are waiting for. Included in the book are a series of age-progressed portraits of the designers going through from 23 to 33, 43, 53 and, finally, 63 years old. Lee Mawdsley's original shots were

aged by the National Missing Persons Helpline using techniques developed to help locate missing persons. The book will be used as a promotional piece by Navyblue and their partners on the project, Fulmar and PaperCo.

22. Stockport College's 2005 prospectus for its BA(hons) Design and Visual Arts course is lovingly art

directed by course tutor and graduate of the course, James Corazzo. The illustration on this spread is by Liam Healy, another graduate of the course

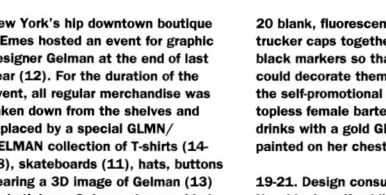

19

20

21

22

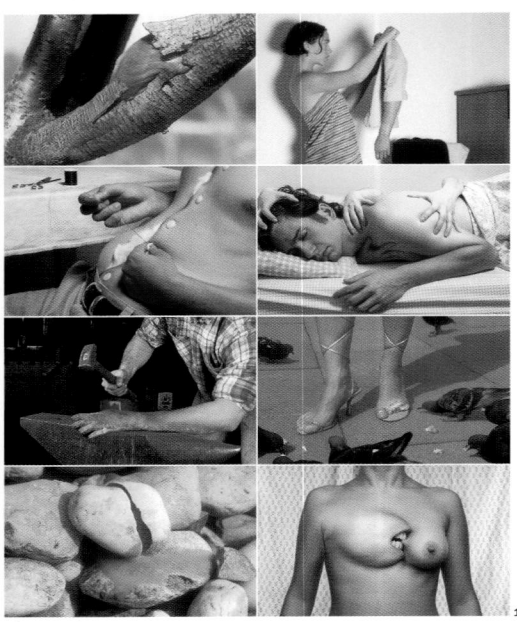

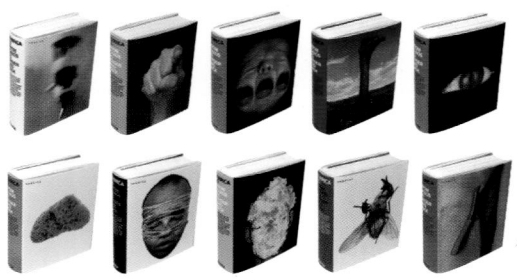

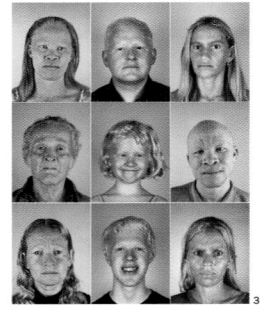

1-4. Fabrica 10 book: a weighty celebration of the first ten years of Benetton's research centre, includes a decade of experiments, projects, attendees, visitors and ideas ranging across all media from photography to advertising, illustration, graphic design and new media. The original idea for Fabrica, developed with the infamous Oliviero Toscani, was to establish "a bridge between the visionary dream – a workshop in which to design communication of the future – and concrete experiments in the field, somewhere between utopia and the reality of a world that is in a state of chaotic change". That vision certainly shines through in this volume, which documents the creative process, alongside coverage of self-initiated projects such as these portraits of albinism by Pieter Hugo (3), Margot Quan Knight's surreal photographs (1) and famous Benetton campaigns including Toscani's controversial death row series, while offering a nice insight into the goings on at the centre. Containing over 2000 illustrations, a DVD and a range of ten different dust jackets (4), this hardback translated into English, Italian and French, is in bookstores now.

5&6. Lowe creatives Adrian Lim and Steve Williams are supporting Watford art deco, art house cinema The Rex with a series of film posters produced as a personal project. Shown are posters for screenings of Giant and It's A Wonderful Life. Printer: Geoff Saisi at Admagic.

7&8. Booklet accompanying Circus Performance II, an exhibition of work from RCA MA students selected by strategic consultancy Circus. The design of the book plays on our assumptions about the way information is presented. Text on the back cover is printed upside down and reads: "This is not the title of this booklet. Your susceptibility to traditional methods of reading means that, despite reading this title, you will still open this booklet on what is essentially the back of the book. And what's more, it is upside down"

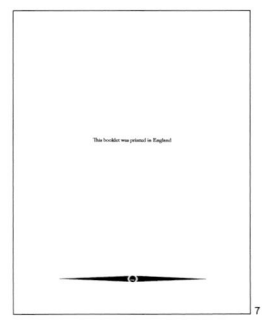

Arts &
Culture

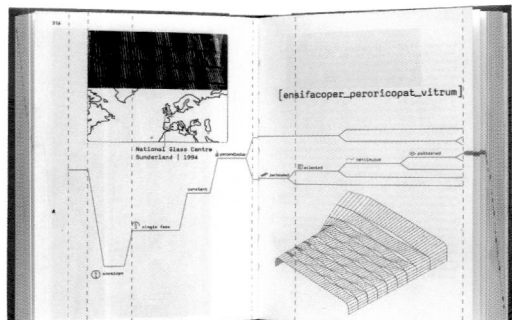

1&2. Breeding Architecture, a book to tie in with the ICA's current Foreign Office Architects exhibition. Concept: Ramon Prat. Design: Rosa Lladò, Estella Robles.

3. Sculpture and local artefacts act as waymarkers for the Plymouth Waterfront Walkway, a ten-mile segment of the South West Coast Path. Sculptor Gordon Young (CR Aug 02) led the project, an initiative of Plymouth City Council. This tiny book offers some background about the objects one encounters on the walk. It was designed by Josh Young (Gordon Young's son) and Monica Pirovano. Photography by Pirovano, Mark Molley and Rocco Redondo.

4. Liberty window commission for the V&A Gothic exhibition by Warren du Preez and Nick Thornton Jones.

5. Poster for Northern Broadsides' production of The Merchant of Venice, by Elmwood. The company specialises in raw, stripped down versions of Shakespeare, often performed close up to the audience, hence this treatment. Art directors: Richard Scholey and Alan Ainsley. Designers: Alan Ainsley, Stephen Shaw and Ben Greengrass.

6. Quality Britain is a magazine produced by the British Embassy in Tokyo, distributed across Japan since the beginning of this year. Designed by Johnson Banks.

7. Artist David Batchelor's light-box installation in Selfridges' window is part of FEAST, curated by ArtReview

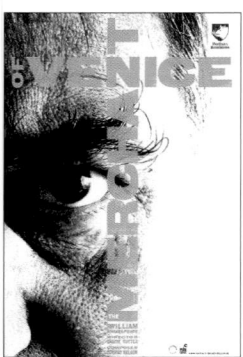

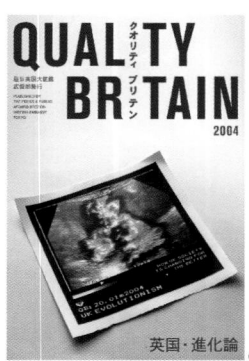

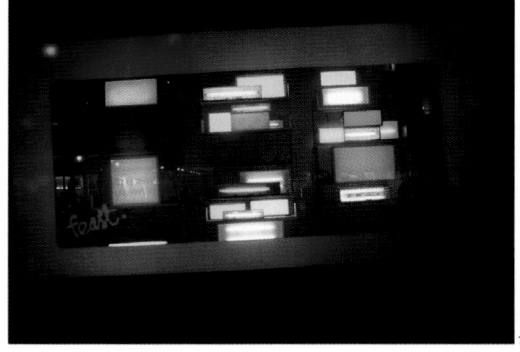

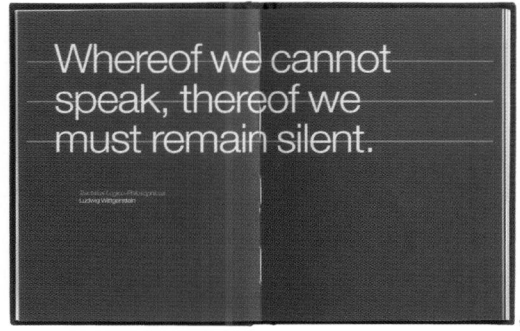

8&9. Accompanying catalogue to touring exhibition on communication in contemporary art. Produced by SEA the A6 book, printed on a selection of stocks is case-bound and blockfoiled.

10. Cover for The Druid King, A Novel, by Norman Spinrad. "The aim

was to distinguish this book in the historical fantasy section of the bookstore... [which] is full of gallant horsemen astride their white stallions," comment designers Doyle Partners, New York. Type is made up from twigs in a similar treatment to David Byrne's Lead Us Not Into Temptation sleeve (CR Nov 03).

11. Markus Moström designed this poster for an exhibition for recent scholarship winner to the Royal Swedish Academy of Arts, glass and ceramics designer Ingegerd Råman.

12. French design duo Jacob & Jannelle have developed a typographical signature style for the

Contemporary Art Centre of La Ferme du Buisson. This poster utilises an image by exhibiting artist Pierre Giner.

13. Fourteen of London's leading art galleries commissioned Cunningham Design to produce this brochure to encourage students to visit galleries

Selection of recent work for arts and cultural clients by Pentagram's London and New York studios.

1-3. Environmental graphics installation for the National Design Triennial: Inside Design Now show at the Cooper-Hewitt, National Design Museum by Paula Scher. Ellen Lupton, one of the curators of the Triennial, selected Scher for the show but wanted to focus on her recent architectural work. Scher had the idea to marry her painting with directional signage and do an installation. She created graphics for directional rugs and the inside and outside of the lift running between the two levels of the show. Photos: Peter Mauss/Esto.

4&5. Two posters for the Yale School of Architecture by Michael Bierut. Shown (4) is a poster for the Spring 2004 series of lectures, exhibitions and symposia at the School. Architecture and Psychoanalysis (5) was a symposium held at the School.

6. Poster for the American Institute of Architects (AIA) New York Chapter 2003 Heritage Ball, this year held at Chelsea Piers on the Hudson River. By Michael Gericke.

7. Poster for The Story, a play about journalistic ethics, at The Public Theater, NY. Designed by Paula Scher and Joe Marianek.

8. Identity for the Virginia Museum of Fine Arts by Woody Pirtle and Timea Dancs. The identity coincides with the development of a new extension by architect Rick Mather.

9. Book design by Abbott Miller and Johnschen Kudos for At First Sight: Photography and the Smithsonian, a retrospective of the Smithsonian's relationship with the medium of photography. The book is to accompany a major exhibition at the Smithsonian next year, also designed by Abbott Miller.

10&11. London's Globe Theatre commissioned this book in order to document the first five seasons at the re-built venue. Play features photographs of each production along with notes about its staging and quotes from the plays themselves. Pentagram partner Angus Hyland and designer Charlie Hanson chose typeface Minion for the cover and headings as it suggests the type found on printed materials contemporary to the original theatre

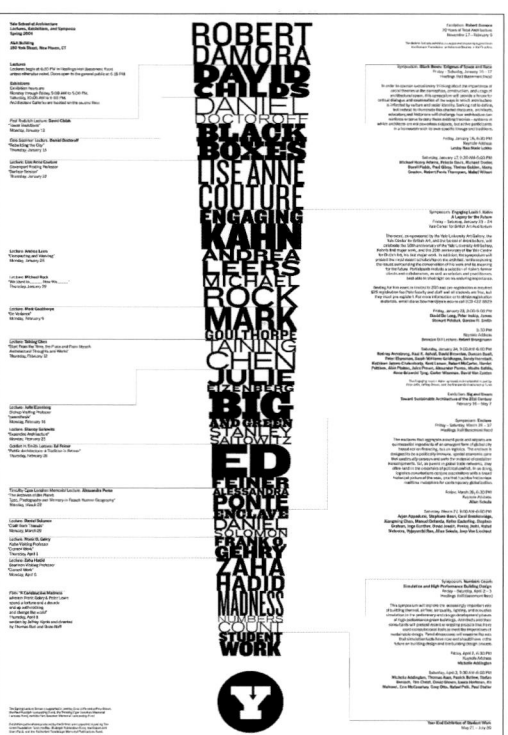

4

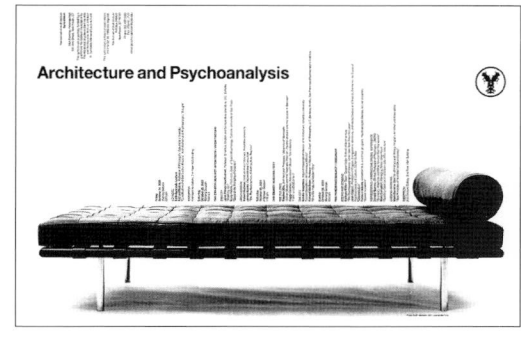

5

6

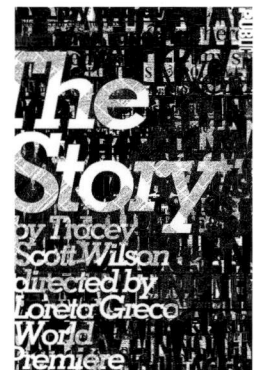

7

VMFA

8

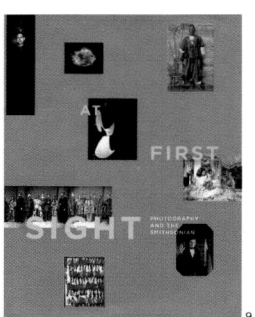

9

10

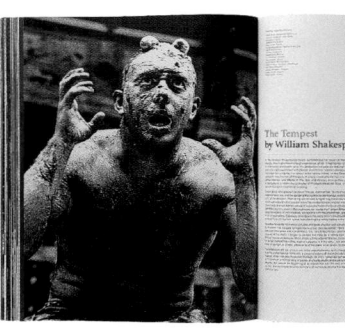

11

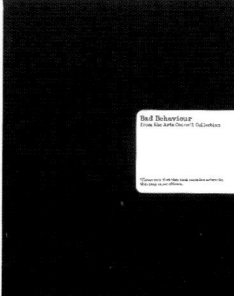

1

2

3

1. This catalogue from A2-GRAPHICS/SW/HK supports Arts Council touring exhibition, Bad Behaviour. It brings together work by subversive artists from the 1980s to the present day. Commissioned by the Hayward Gallery, this elegant design features a foil-blocked, embossed cover, with an adhesive label that wraps around the fore-edge of the book.

London-based designers Non-Format recently held a workshop with graphics students at the Oslo School of Art. Jon Forss and Kjell Ekhorn got the students to produce work exploring the use of luminous ink. Here's one of the resultant posters, shown as it appears in daylight (2) and as it appears in the dark (3).

Kilimanjaro magazine is a new large format independent publication. It's the brainchild of art director Loran Stosskopf and creative director Michael Odukoya. Issue two (cover and spread shown, 5 and 6 respectively) explores the idea of recycling and contains various features, photographs and illustrations relating to the theme. A smaller colour supplement (cover shown, 4) contains more of the same on different stocks. For stockists and more info, visit www.kilimag.com

4

5

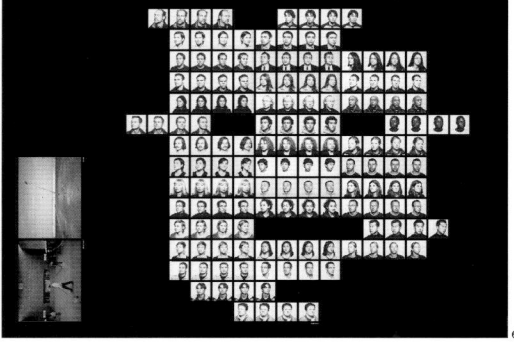

6

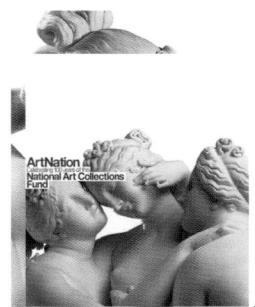

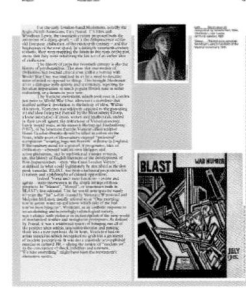

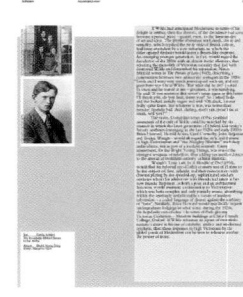

7

8

9

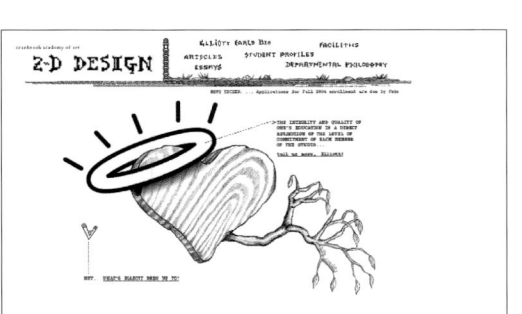
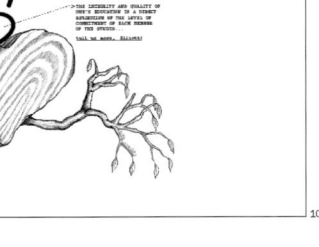

10

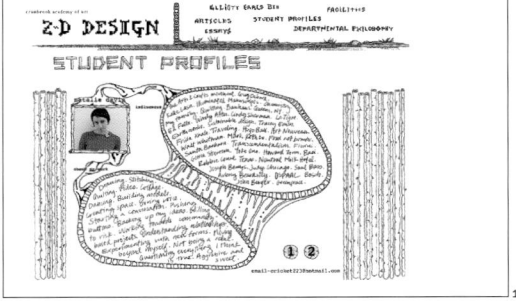

11

7. Cover of Berklee College of Music prospectus, designed by Chris Allen at Siegel & Gale, New York.

8&9. ArtNation magazine was published in association with the Independent on Sunday to celebrate the centenary of the National Art Collections Fund. The magazine highlights the works that the fund has helped to acquire for the nation.

Designers MadeThought were brought in to add a contemporary edge to the content, allowing it to appeal to a younger audience.

10&11. The website for Cranbrook Academy of Art's 2-D Design course reflects strongly the influence of its head of department, Elliott Earls. Concept, design and implementation by Ned Snider. Flash design and

implementation: Katya Moorman

12. Website for the Whitechapel Gallery by Bureau for Visual Affairs. In order to make content easily accessible, every area of the site is visible in one view. Each section follows the same seven column grid.

13. Website for the Smithsonian Center for Education and Museum

Studies by AKQA. The site serves as a gateway to the Smithsonian's extensive educational resources. The navigation breaks users into three distinct audiences: educators, students and families.

14. GR/DD have created a CD-Rom prospectus for Central Saint Martins College in which the idea of a touch-screen interface is cleverly mirrored

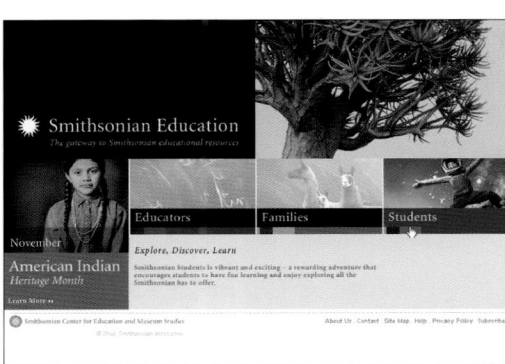

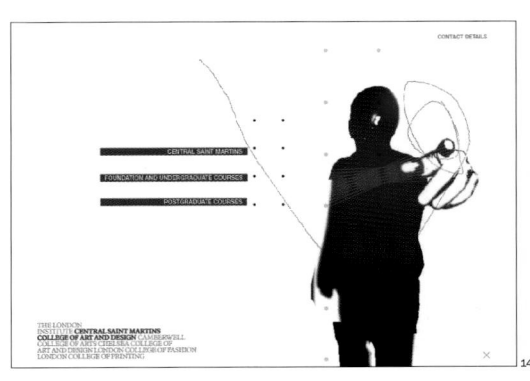

12

13

14

| multina-tional coffee conglom-erate dictates disem-bodiment from church spires no eye but for sheen of collagen | lips swoosh of com-position purple paint coated hand-prints evidence invisible while supplies last laugh | scratch varnish trellis hood orna-ment gleam want ads and human sign obe-sity and anime | dead presi-dent mis-match erap intent hayop mathe-matic bonus buy breakfast cereal for | screen monitor pixilation of extreme magnifi-cation brush stroke hint of angel trick of the eye wanting to read | ceramic tile veranda remote control hand mother mary invent dignify |

Spreads from the forthcoming book Graphic Poetry, developed by Sheffield-based design partnership Wig-01. The book features writing from contemporary poets around the world. Each poem selected for the book has been visually interpreted by a designer, illustrator or image-maker. Spreads shown from the book include Julian House of Intro's interpretation of Barbara Jane Reyes' poetry (1), WIG-01's take on the words of Brian Burch (2), plus Marc Boutavant's illustration of Kaethe Fine's work (3) and some delightful typography from Alan Kitching based on a poem by Maureen McManus (4). Book concept/design: Andrew Townsend

MORI ARTS CENTER

MORI ART MUSEUM
MORI ARTS CENTER

TOKYO SKY DECK
MORI ARTS CENTER

ROPPONGI ACADEMY HILLS
MORI ARTS CENTER

TOKYO CITY VIEW
MORI ARTS CENTER

ROPPONGI HILLS CLUB
MORI ARTS CENTER

A B C D E F G H I J K L **MORI ARTS CENTER** S T U V X Y W Z 5

6

7

8

9

10

11

Barnbrook Design had the massive job of developing all the visual communication for the Mori Arts Centre, a state-of-the-art luxury development situated at the top of the statuesque Roppongi Hills Tower, in Tokyo. The complex incorporates a mixture of living, shopping and gallery spaces. It includes the Mori Art Museum, Tokyo Sky Deck and City View, as well as the Roppongi Academy and Roppongi Hills Club. These different facilities are brought together in one identity: a spectrum of coloured lines or lightwaves, which can be separated out where necessary to denote the identity of each specific centre (5), with a bespoke font used throughout. Red is the prescribed colour of the Mori Arts Museum which is situated on the fifty-second floor of the towerblock. Work for the MAM includes these icons which were developed for use in museum publications (6-9), plus the book for inaugural exhibition Happiness: A survival guide for art and life (cover shown, 10). Barnbrook also designed this poster (11) promoting the exhibition

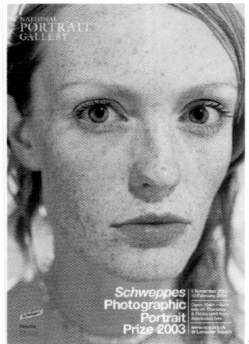

1

Landscape? 2
new major contemporary
art for the Towner collection

7 February –
28 March 2004

Tuesday – Saturday
12-4pm
Sunday 2-5pm

Towner Art Gallery
High Street Old Town
Eastbourne BN20 8BB

Telephone
01323 417 961

Admission Free

2

DESIGN HISTORY AT 21

3

NB: Studio designed these posters for the Schweppes Photographic Portrait Prize 2003 at the National Portrait Gallery (1) and Landscape? 2 (2), the forthcoming show at the Towner Art Gallery, Eastbourne. The latter show includes artwork by Julian Opie, whose painting Missing You was used on the poster.

3. This poster was designed by apracticeforeverydaylife for an exhibition celebrating 21 years of the History of Design MA jointly run by the Royal College of Art and the V&A Museum. Kirsty and Emma of apracticeforeverydaylife also designed the exhibition itself which took place in the RCA.

4. Amsterdam-based designer Alvin Chan has designed this graphic identity for Australian photographer Earl Carter, overprinting yellow ink on silver ink on white stock. "The typographic treatment is default and basic," says Chan. "For me this down-to-earth approach fits the image of Earl."

5&6. Blame Everyone Else, a collection of the work of illustrator Paul Davis designed and published by Browns. The book includes 14 different paper stocks and has three different dust jackets. Editing and creative direction: Jonathan Ellery. Designers: Lisa Smith and Jonathan Ellery. www.orders.artdata.co.uk

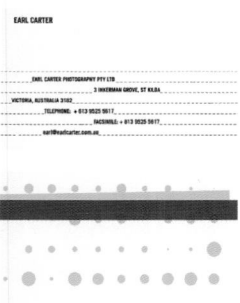

4

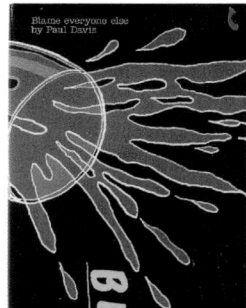

5

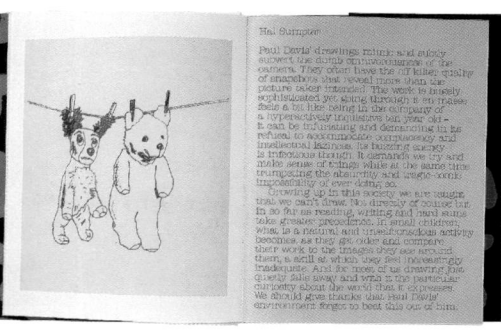

6

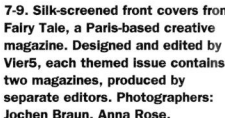

7

8

9

10

7-9. Silk-screened front covers from Fairy Tale, a Paris-based creative magazine. Designed and edited by Vier5, each themed issue contains two magazines, produced by separate editors. Photographers: Jochen Braun, Anna Rose.

10. Poster by Agenda Design for an exhibition of weave designer Ann Sutton's work at the Crafts Council.

11. Toronto's 763 Gallery commissioned Park Studio in London to create posters for its Respond exhibition. The posters are made up of strips of pattern and colour which are perforated to encourage interaction and the easy tearing off of each strip.

12. Poster-sized invitation to a one-day David Bailey exhibition held at London advertising agency Lowe and sponsored by Olympus. Copywriter: Adrian Lim. Art director: Steve Williams.

13&14. Peter Blake, Commercial Art, a seven-inch booklet which accompanied an exhibition of Blake's work for commercial clients at the London Institute Gallery. The show was curated by Brian Webb and the catalogue designed by Brian Webb and Chris Gloster of Webb & Webb Design

11

The great thing about holding a one-day exhibition is that you don't need to invite the critics or any of those other useless buggers from pretentious arty-farty magazines who normally only come to slurp your wine, pinch all the canapés and spout bollocks about your photos. No point, since the great unwashed aren't going to be gawping at your pictures afterwards, there's no need to even publicise the event. What you end up with instead is a nice little private view – far more exclusive and infinitely more civilized. Which is precisely what I'm doing between 6.30pm and 9.00pm on 11th December 2003 at Lowe, Bowater House (that ugly 60s office block opposite Harvey Nicks in Knightsbridge). There'll be a whole load of stuff there which ranges from the 70s through to the present day, in my really rather brilliant exhibition called Bailey's Old Shit and New Shit. Oh, and it's sponsored by Olympus. I apologise in advance that it's being held at an advertising agency, because that means that you'll inevitably bump into the odd wanker, but don't let that put you off. If you're coming, the polite thing to do is RSVP to bailey@heraldcommunications.com

12

Peter Blake Sculpture

13

14

1. Interleaved programme designed by Moving Brands for the Grand Hotel fundraising gala at the Donmar Warehouse. Art Deco graphics echo the styling of the play, Grand Hotel, and the form of the booklet suggests a series of doors, each opening to reveal another layer. Black, leather-textured paper and gold ink convey a feeling of faded luxury and ensured all advertising was consistent with the look.

2. Cover to Moscow Style, a book documenting the graphic design, art, architecture and fashion scene in the Russian capital to be published this month by Booth-Clibborn Editions. Designed by Conny Freyer and Eva Rucki at Troika.

3. Fluke Magazine from Studio Lobster. Explains its creator Richard Short: "The magazine is North-East based and pushes the boundaries for culture and the local arts. It showcases the region's bright young things alongside reviews and interviews with international DJs."

4&5. Invitation and catalogue cover for Depth of Field: the place of relief in the time of Donatello, an exhibition at the Henry Moore Institute in collaboration with the V&A. Text is set in Bembo as it originates from fifteenth century Venice. Images in the catalogue are introduced on loose, irregularly sized slips, tucked into the spine as if collated by the essayist. Design: William Hall.

6&7. Programme covers for the London Chamber Orchestra. Designers: Mike Dempsey and Sophie Paynter, CDT. Illustrations: Sophie Paynter.

8&9. Great Magazine cover and contents spread. This monthly publication is designed by Spin for The Photographers' Gallery, London

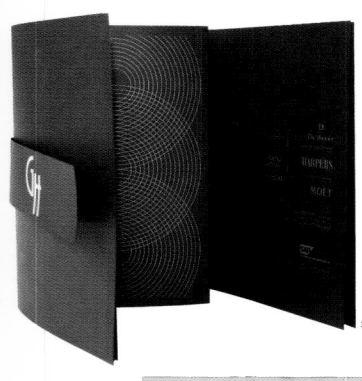

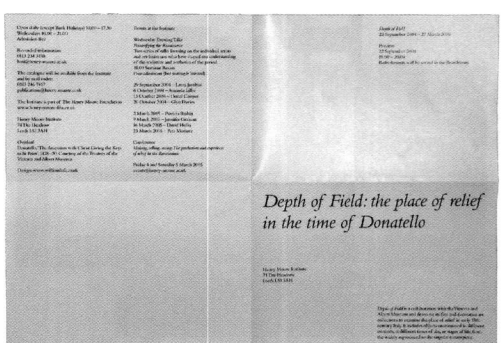

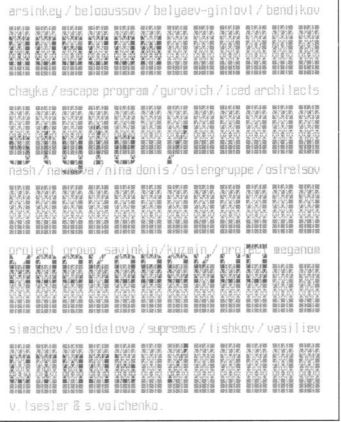

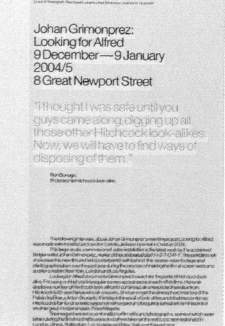

10. Andrew Cross – An English Journey, a book published to accompany a screen-based exhibition at John Hansard Gallery. The work was an investigation of the changing English landscape, and attitudes towards it, via views from a freight truck's journey from Southampton to Manchester. It is the latest in a series of books designed by Richard Bonner-Morgan for the Film and Video Umbrella.

11. Expérimenter le Réel, a magazine-style catalogue for the Cimaise et Portique contemporary arts centre in Albi, France. The show was split into two parts so designers Base BCN took the same approach for the catalogue: readers can start either at the front or back and work their way to a text section in the middle.

12&13. D.design's Derek Samuel created this booklet to accompany a travelling exhibition of images of famous race, stud and polo horses by photographer Michael Penn. The show, titled Beauty and the Beast, is currently in Dubai but moves to New York later this year.

14&15. Front and back of the Tate Report 2002-2004 designed by Fernando Gutiérrez at Pentagram. The Report includes details of acquisitions and progress reports on each of the four Tate galleries. Design assistant: Chris Duggan. Pentagram partner Angus Hyland has also designed Phaidon's new series of photography monographs. The first in the series focus on Weegee (cover shown, 16) and Erwin Blumenfeld (17). Hyland worked on the project with Sharon Hwang

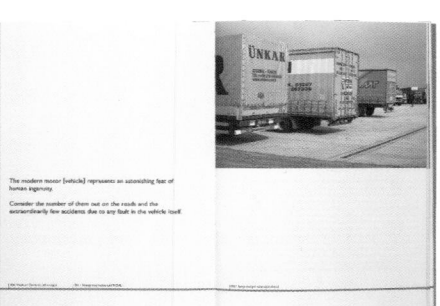

10

expérime le réel

la vie devant soi

11

12

IMAGES OF THE WORLD'S MOST FAMOUS AND BEAUTIFUL HORSES

13

14

TATE

TATE REPORT 2002–2004

15

PHAIDON

16

PHAIDON

17

1-6. From New York-based Sagmeister Inc, double page spreads commissioned by Austrian magazine .copy. Every month, the magazine asks a different studio/artist to create a series of dividers, each opening a new section in the magazine.

Cumulatively, the images read "Money does not make me happy"

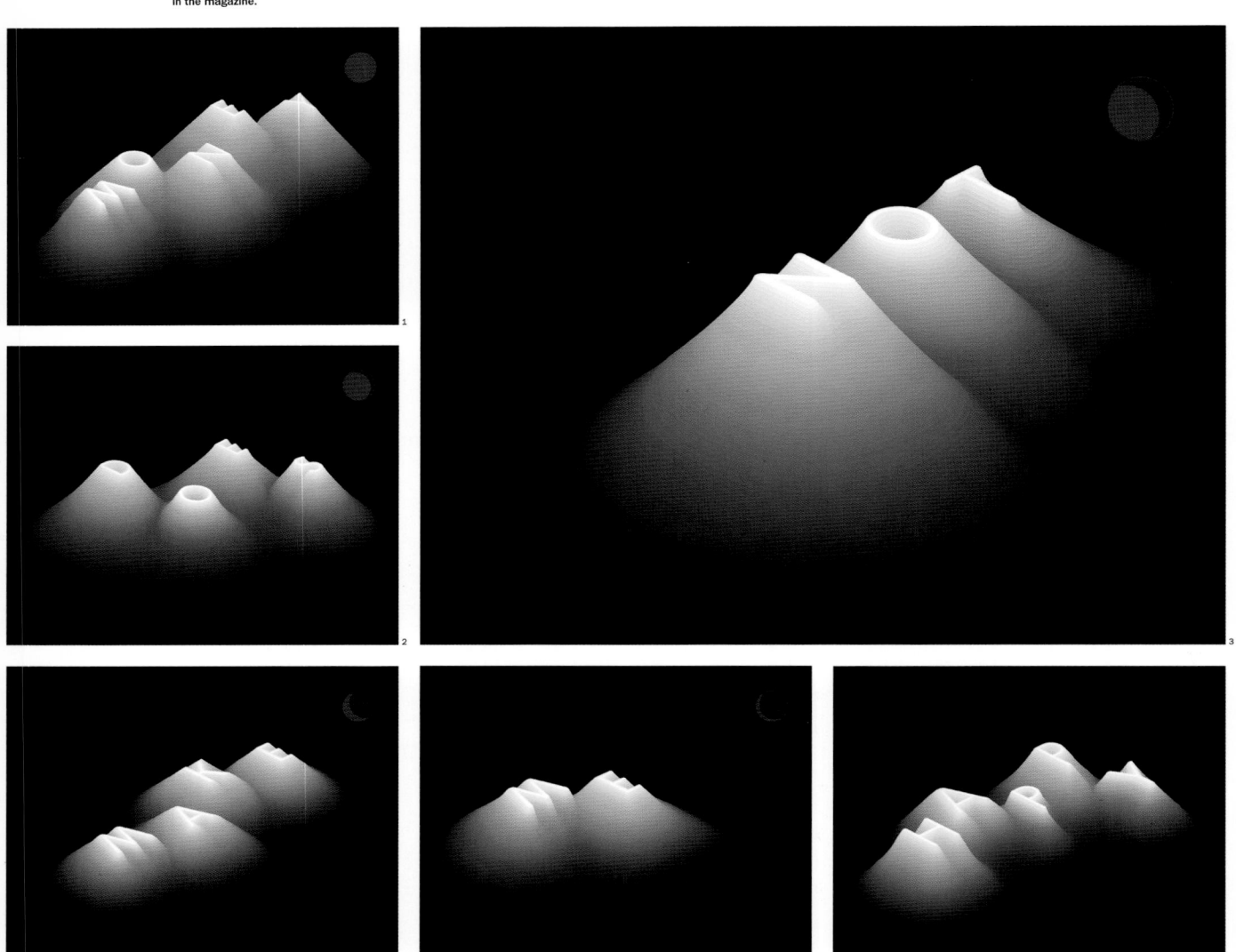

Much has, rightly, been made of the stunning architecture of New York's revamped Museum of Modern Art, but graphic design also plays a part in the Museum's new aesthetic. Moma's Departments of Graphic Design and Digital Media worked with various consultants to create a design programme that complements Yoshio Taniguchi's building. Matthew Carter has restored Moris Fuller Benton's Franklin Gothic typeface of 1912 to create a new face, MoMA Gothic, which forms the MoMA acronym and is used in signage and printed material. Kevin Dresser of Dresser Johnson was commissioned to create custom iconography (including for the outer windows, 8, and restrooms, 9. Photos: James Kuo). The graphics and wayfinding system (7, photo by James Kuo) was developed by Bruce Mau Design, beginning with a 40-feet-high, one-inch-thick glass banner at the entrance (10. Photo: Timothy Hursley). As visitors enter the lobby, they are greeted by a nine-panel display screen created by Imaginary Forces. It employs a constantly shifting "kinetic barcode" created from animated slivers of the 20,000-plus works of art in the MoMA database, over which is superimposed information about the Museum (11& 12). Creative director: Mikon van Gastel. Programming: Oliver Delano and Alessandro Sabatelli of slinc.realtime with Kurt Ralske). There is also a new proprietary colour for the Museum, MoMA LC Red, developed with Pantone. It features in this artist party invite (13) designed by Ed Pusz, production by Claire Cory, photo by James Kuo. A magazine ad campaign (14&15) announces the new look, declaring that Manhattan is Modern Again: design by Elan Cole

7

8

9

10

11

12

13

14

15

1. Poster design by Philippe Apeloig who won a competition to design the logo, identity and all promotional material for Brésils Brésils, a series of cultural events taking place in France throughout 2005 celebrating Brazilian culture. 2&3. Design group Spin have numerous clients in the arts and culture sector. Recent projects include this poster promoting theatre Rose of Kingston's production of As You Like It and another for the current Dan Flavin exhibition at the Haunch of Venison gallery in London. 4. London-based Rose design produced a series of posters for The Tate's Great British Art series. These three posters represent Tracy Emin, Francis Bacon and Paula Rego. Photography: Jason Wilde. 5. Poster for Grand, dance by Graeme Murphy with piano in mind, by the Sydney Dance Company. Costume: Akira Isogawa. Art Direction: Vince Frost. Design: Tim Murphy. Photography: Stephen Wardby. Design studio: emeryfrost. 6. APFEL|AB (A Practice For Everyday Life and Anthony Burrill) devised the name and design of this call for submissions and promotional material for a show at the Salone del Mobile in Milan which will exhibit work by British students. 7 (opposite page). Poster for an exhibition of Sagmeister Inc's work in Chaumont, France. "It features all the people who had a significant influence on our work. They were all hand-painted by tourist illustrators found in New York's Central Park," explains Stefan Sagmeister. Art Direction: Stefan Sagmeister. Design: Matthias Ernstberger. 3D illustration: Aaron Hockett. Illustration: Gao Ming, Mao. Client: Chaumont, France

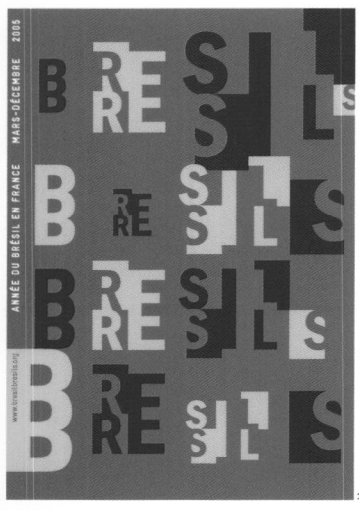

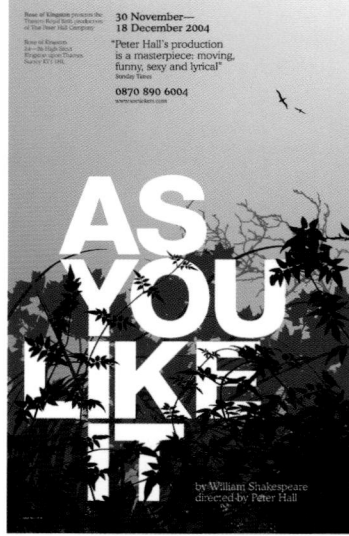

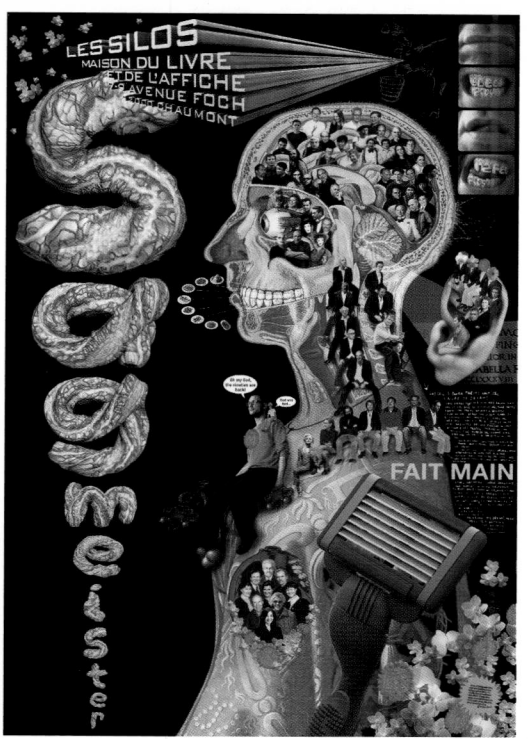

7

The work of old masters including Da Vinci's Lady With An Ermine (8), and Rembrandt's Return of the Prodigal Son (9) are put to lewd use in this saucy campaign for New York's Museum of Sex. One visit, we're told, and "you'll never look at art in other museums the same way again". Creatives: Andrew Whitehouse, Justin Gomes, Gary Goldsmith, Dean Hacohen, Earl Cavanah, Lisa Rettig-Falcone. Agency: Lowe New York.
10&11. The Barbican Film identity carries on North's work for the arts centre. The logo takes its inspiration from the fact that the Barbican Cinemas still project from film.
12. Poster by Airside for the Crafts Council exhibition, Knit2Together. The typographic identity for the show uses the knitted stitch to create a font which is carried across print work.
13. To raise money for Cancer Research UK, Brighton-based bespoke tailor Gresham Blake has collaborated with various artists providing custom made white suits to be used as canvases. Poster by Red Design

8

9

10

11

12

13

Paula Scher and her team at Pentagram have created environmental graphics for the new expansion of the Children's Museum of Pittsburgh. Since 1991 the museum has been housed in the landmark Old Post Office Building in Pittsburgh's Allegheny Square section. In 2000 the museum commissioned an expansion that would link the Post Office with the neighbouring, vacant Buhl Planetarium. The new expansion, by Koning Eizenberg Architecture, bridges the two buildings with a three-story structure that provides a new entrance and additional exhibit space. Combined, the buildings now comprise 80,000 square feet of exhibit space, with new exhibition areas installed throughout. The architects crowned their expansion with a polycarbonate screen that visually links the two existing buildings and, in a collaboration with the environmental artist Ned Kahn, doubles as a shimmering wind sculpture composed of plastic tiles that move in the breeze. Scher's signage takes its cues from the expansion architecture. Lobby signage and the donor wall (11-13) are composed of colourful fluorescent Plexiglas panels. The color sensibility is inspired by the lighting (by lighting designer Anne Militello, who previously worked with Scher on the New 42nd Studios building in New York) and by the floor, for which much of the buildings' original terrazzo was retained. The letters of the marquee signage on the museum entrance (1-4) extrude from the building and are lit by neon from within a wire mesh, creating three-dimensional letterforms that look possibly like something out of superhero comics

2

3

4

5

6

7

In the galleries, identification signage appears as a playful treatments of words: "Garage" has been set in rubber tread (9); "Theater" appears in forward on one side and reverse on the other, as though projected (7); "Studio" was created by kids painting over a stencil on the floor (6). Throughout, the signage is inspired by the activity of the museum, and employs inexpensive materials and fixtures that are easily repaired or replaced.

The signage typography (set in Futura) has become so linked with the museum that its in-house graphics department has begun using the font as a de facto insititutional identity.

Art Director: Paula Scher. Designers: Paula Scher, Rion Byrd, Drew Freeman, Joseph Marianek, Adriana Deleo. Firm: Pentagram

Design, New York. Project Photography (Signage): Peter Mauss/Esto. Project Architects: Koning Eizenberg Architecture

8

9

10

11

12

13

1. Identity for The Noguchi Museum in New York using typeface FF Balance. Art director: Abbott Miller. Designers: Abbott Miller, Jeremy Hoffman, Pentagram Design, NY. 2&3. Letterhead and identity for the Rokeby gallery in London by Bureau for Visual Affairs. The identity "integrates the current show title in both website [also by BfVA] and letterhead whilst presenting a clean and contemporary appearance – establishing a close link between the gallery and its shows and artists," BfVA say.

4-7. With the launch of its new multimedia centre, ArtStart, The National Gallery is leading the way in the marriage of art and technology in the gallery environment. Touch-screen monitors now provide visitors with access to 2300 paintings, all of which have been digitally scanned at an extremely high resolution. The touch screens provide access to the collection via four categories and, on examining a particular work, the user can zoom in on the surface of the painting. The small white box in the right-hand navigation window (4) can be dragged over any work, revealing the tiniest of details and textural variations. Visitors can also create their own tours of the gallery and print out their individual routes. The interactive system (which was three years in the making) was developed in conjunction with digital agency NYKRIS. It has just recently been shortlisted for the design category in the BAFTA Interactive Awards. 8-11. Invite and catalogue for ShowCASe – Contemporary art for the UK, developed by Barnbrook Design. The exhibition showcases new works acquired for museum collections by the Contemporary Art Society, an organisation promoting and developing collections of contemporary work

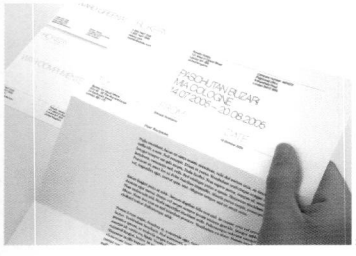

ROKEBY

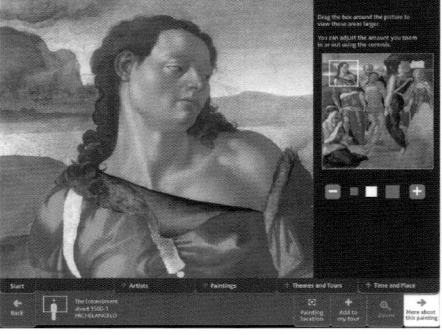

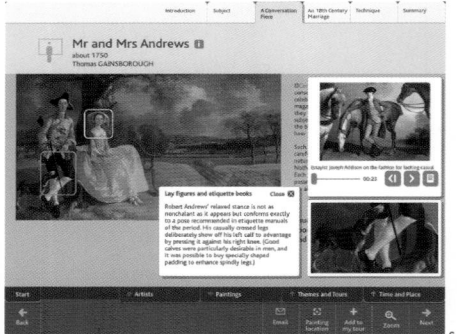

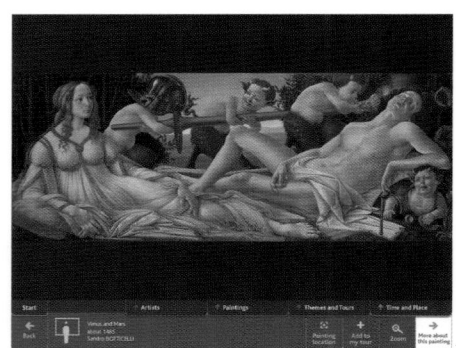

Fashion

1. Nekoman is a new Manga character created by Japanese art collective Tashahisha. The large-pawed one, plus another character Super Nekoman are sold in 55DSL shops in Tokyo, Milan and London, as well as select toy shops in Japan.

2&3. The phrase "fashion victim" takes on a whole new meaning in this cruel campaign for Dochnal & Zien Haute Couture. Creatives: Maciej Nowicki, Sylvia Rekawek and Justnya Nakielska of agency JWT Parintex, Warsaw. Photographer: Lukasz Murgrabia.

4&5. Stylishly sparse Spring/Summer 04 catalogue from Aboud Sodano for designer Paul Smith. Photography: Sandro Sodano.

6&7. Youth label Fullcircle are advertising their Spring/Summer 04 collections against backdrops by Japanese artist Hiroshi Kan. The clothing brand have also commissioned 30 new paintings from Kan for an exhibition which will take place at London's Blink gallery from 25 March through to 8 April. Shown 6 is one of Kan's original paintings while 7 shows the finished Fullcircle press ad

●FULLCIRCLE

8&9. A new Levi's Europe website, www.eu.levi.com, has been designed by London-based digital communications agency, Lateral. Creative director: Simon Crabtree. Designers: Sam Collett, Ted Hunt, Laura Jordan, Mark Hanlon. Animation: Rob Gibson.

10&11. The new Diesel catalogue advises us ominously, to "love nature while it lasts". Thus these shots of smartly-clad beauties, hugging trees and communing with the soil. The catalogue is part of a broader campaign shot in Los Angeles by Henrik Halvarsson, the result of a cooperation between Diesel Creative Team and Dutch partners KesselsKramer.

12. Cashmere and Pearls: a suitably opulent packaging idea from BOB Design for client Pringle of Scotland. The soluble "pearls" actually contain a gentle detergent for hand-washing your cashmere twin-set.

13&14. Photographers Toby McFarlan Pond and Guido Mocafico shot these fantastic images of monsters by Christian Lacroix for Le Book. They've since been turned into a fiendishly good calendar. McFarlan Pond took the actual dolls and then drew them using lights – no retouching was necessary. Art direction by Michel Mallard.

15. Accessory story for Japanese Vogue, shot by Coppi Barbieri

Crystal

The gem of twice. Photographed by Richard Burt

1

New Bags
and Baubles
Accessories to carry you high and wide
Photographed by Barbara Donnelly

2

VOGUE

MARCH
£3.30

THE NEW FEMININITY

**PRINT DRESSES
CHIFFON
CRYSTAL
FIFTIES
HOLLYWOOD LUXE
& THE PRETTIEST PINK**

Chocolate:
an obsession

KARMA COSTS
12 women
reveal how
much they
spend to
feel good

**THE WOMEN
WHO INSPIRE
FASHION'S
LEADING MEN**

THE HITS FROM THE
INTERNATIONAL
COLLECTIONS

3

VOGUE
Contents March 2004

310

4

beauty
Health, hair, make-up, skincare, spas, scent

Totally
tropical

5

Living

Plastic fantastic

6

VOGUE SHOPS

fifties
How to wear this season's retro look with flair

7

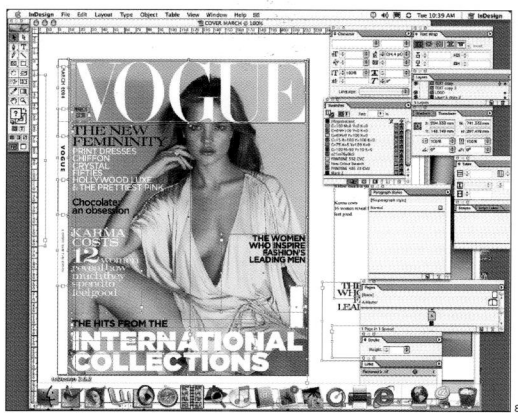

The March issue of Vogue will see a major redesign inspired by the magazine's classic past. "My favourite Vogue year has always been 1959, specifically American Vogue," says the magazine's creative director, Robin Derrick. "I've always loved those magazines because they were so beautiful."

Derrick has looked to the classic elegance of layouts by legendary Vogue art director Alexander Liberman and those by Marvin Israel, who was at Harper's Bazaar in the same period. "It's very understated, just trying to use positioning and space," he explains of his chosen look for Vogue's new fashion spreads. "But the challenge was to make the more commercial front of book. [The 1959] magazines don't work as hard as modern magazines need to do at the front. I've always tried to get Vogue to be busy and clean – either the pages work very hard or they are just beautiful."

In particular, says Derrick, he was attracted by Liberman and Israel's use of serif type, typically combining several different but similar faces in the same issue. "Serif fonts feel modern again. It's weird – when I was working on Arena with Neville Brody, the only font you could use was Helvetica because nothing else seemed modern," he says. "The last time I redesigned Vogue I did it all in American Typewriter to try and make it accessible and fun but, although it worked well in the front of the book, it never seemed classy enough in the centre of the magazine."

In order to source the fonts used in 1959, Derrick called in designer and typographer Julian Morey. "The first thing I did was to go off to the St Bride's type library and find the original fonts," Morey explains. "But the New York foundry that they came from has gone bust and they aren't available digitally. There wasn't time to cut new fonts so I

tried to find things that came close and we got it down to four or five different faces."

For headlines, standfirsts and cover lines Vogue will use the serif fonts De Vinne, Craw and Promoter. Gotham, a Jonathan Hoefler sans serif face, will also be used. The body copy has changed from Times to Century Schoolbook. "It's a total break from where they were," says Morey. Derrick however, is not completely happy with the cut of some of the faces: it is likely that, over the next few months, several of the fonts will be re-drawn to form a bespoke set for the magazine.

Another major change is that the new issue will be the first to be produced by Vogue using Adobe's InDesign layout programme. "We switched because it's a very precise tool," says Derrick. "Also it's Photoshop compatible and we are using more and more digital imagery: it seemed to offer the chance to

handle digital pictures better than Quark. What they don't tell you on the box, though, is that it's slower than Quark so we needed some serious machine upgrades to make it work. It's a bit jam tomorrow – everything is promised to be better in the next version – but I do think InDesign is a very good design programme, it's undoubtedly finer than Quark and it's nice to be able to work with that level of precision."

Shown here are (1&2) fashion spreads from the March 04 issue, inspired by American Vogue of 1959 (11 and 12). The cover (3) also links back to those of 1959 (one shown 10) in its use of multiple typefaces. The new contents page (4) features Vogue written in the Promoter typeface. Pages in the front of the book carry through the use of serif type (5-7). The March issue was the first to be laid out using InDesign: work in progress shown 8 and 9

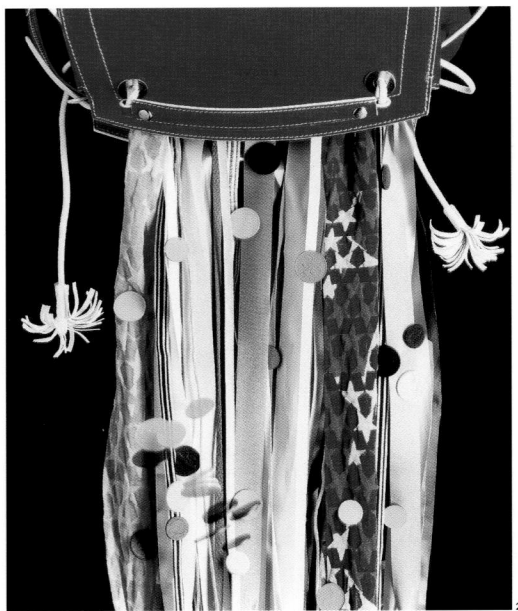

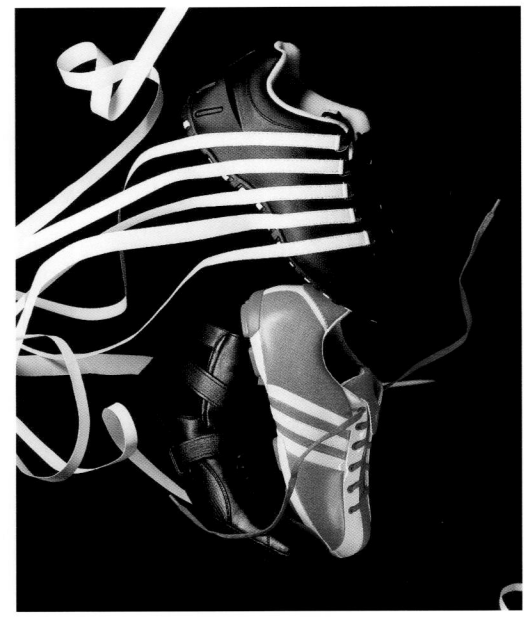

1. New York's Design Machine recently completed the identity for Estella, a children's fashion boutique in downtown Manhattan. The simple serif logotype is screenprinted onto brown paper carrier bags.

2&3. Photographers Barbara Metz and Eve Racine produced a series of images for a fashion story in Dazed and Confused's December 2003 issue. "We wanted to create images that weren't just mere descriptions of fashion items," explains Racine. "Rather, we built and photographed sophisticated scenes, where each item is introduced within its own surreal landscape." Photography: Barbara Metz and Eve Racine. Art direction and set design: Ben Sansbury. Styling: Sarah Cobb

4. Non-Format and photographer Jake Walters produced this series of images for fashion magazine, Tank. Digital photographs were transformed into individually coloured letters so that the blocks of text form the image. The words were taken from songs on the theme of suicide (including, left, This Is The End by The Doors). The images formed an eight-page fashion story in Tank's January issue

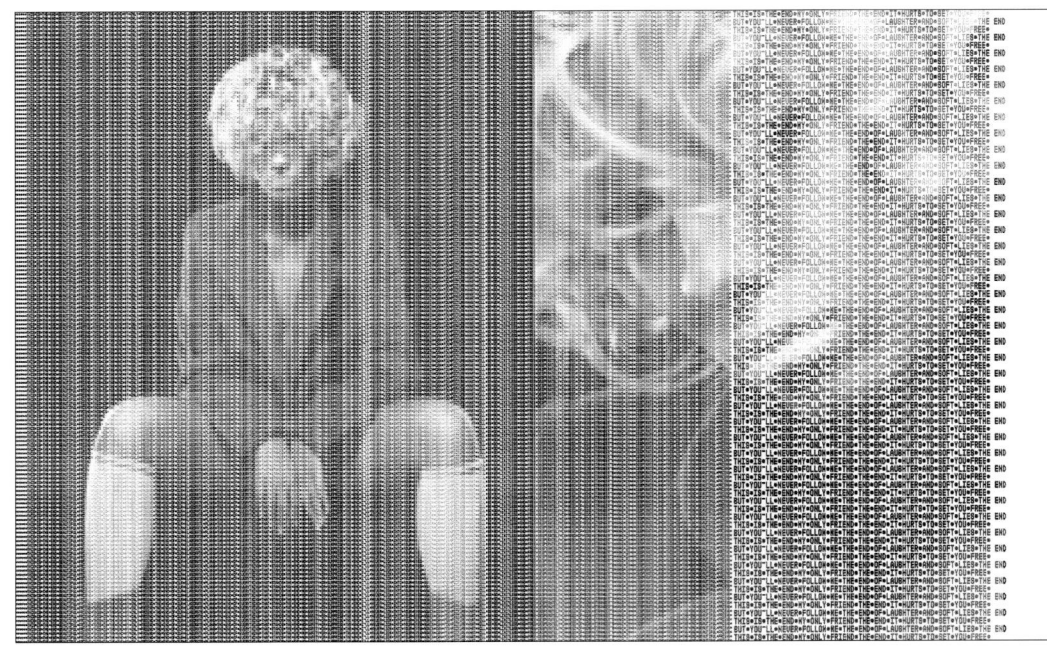

5&6. Pentagram partner Fernando Gutiérrez designed this promotional book for Luc Berjen shoes. Printed on glossy 3mm thick card, with an embossed Luc Bergen logo on the cover, the book uses a simple and elegant visual language throughout. Clean white spreads and a light sans serif type are complemented by a series of beautiful line illustrations by Kam Tang. Design assistant: Susan Jamieson.

7&8. Silas II, the clothing label's new website, works as a companion piece to the original version (Silas I). Like its quirky predecessor, there is no flat colour, the interface being composed, instead, of photographs of a sculpture by the site's art director Ben Sansbury. Click on a specific section and the sculpture slides left or right across the screen (making a pleasing swishing noises in the process) before allowing the user to zoom into different sections. "Perhaps the model represents a monolithic space station leaving planet Silas," comments Sansbury. See www.silasandmaria.com. Design/build: Ben Sansbury and Arron Bleasdale (wedostuff).

9. New York graphics collective Faile silkscreened this range of hoodies by hand. They feature both classic and new Faile images and are available exclusively from www.hanon-shop.com

OUR
DESIGNERS

5

OUR
NEED

6

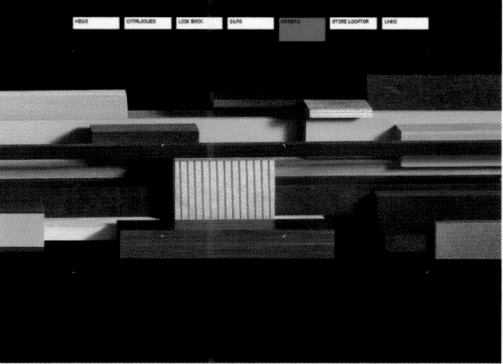

7

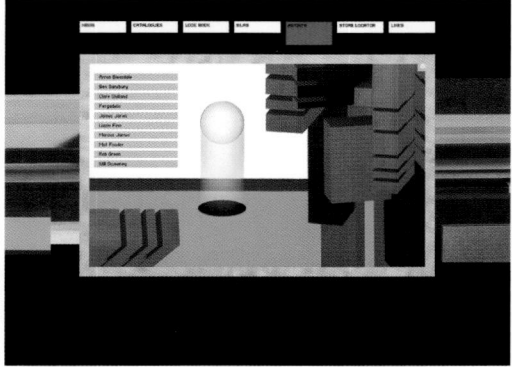

8

9

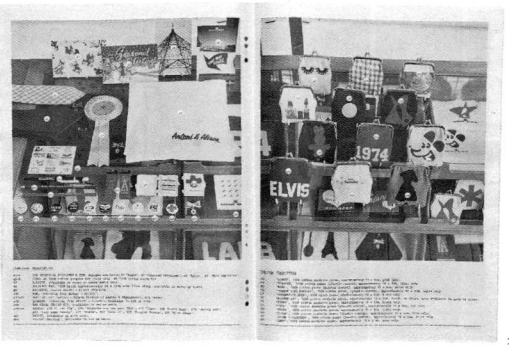

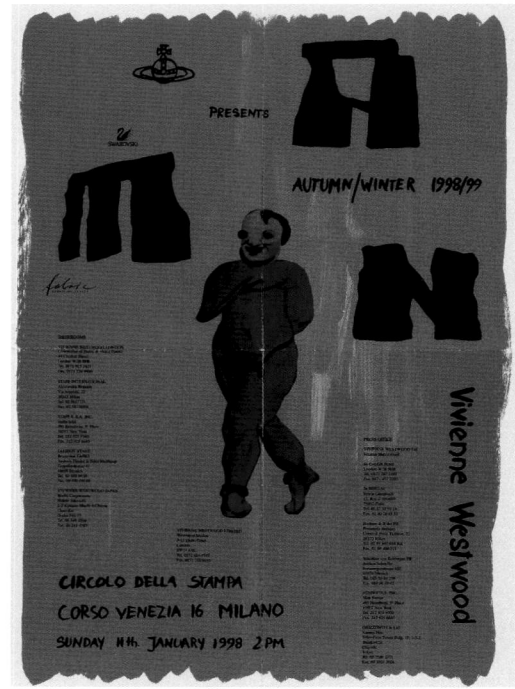

Fashion & Graphics comprises case studies of communications material produced for 23 different fashion designers. Each designer and their collaborators are interviewed revealing the working relationship between fashion and graphics. Work featured includes Antoni & Alison's 1998 mail-order catalogue – a newspaper printed on presses used by local papers and designed with Graphic Thought Facility (1); Comme des Garçons' spring 2002 advertisement by Ronnie Cooke Newhouse and Steven Wolstenholme with photography by David A Bontrager (2); Fraser Moss and Jimmy Collins' work for You Must Create (including foil used for packaging clothes, 3) and the invitation to Vivienne Westwood's Man collection show, autumn/winter 1998/99, designed in-house (4). Fashion & Graphics, by Tamsin Blanchard, designed by Frost Design, is published by Laurence King, priced £28

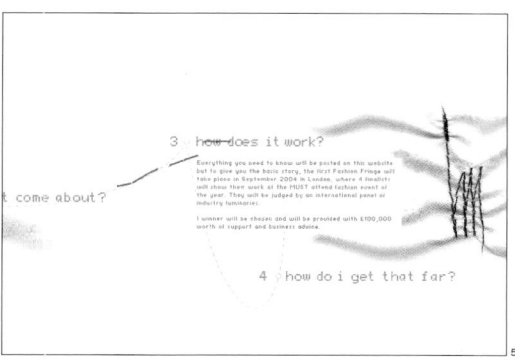

5

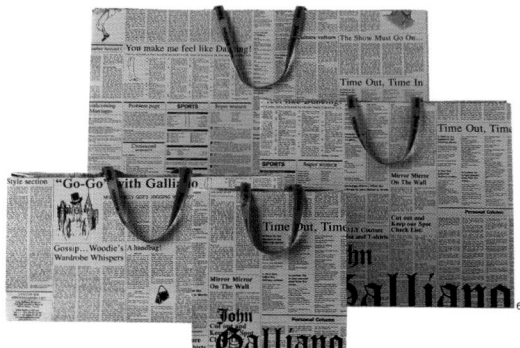

6

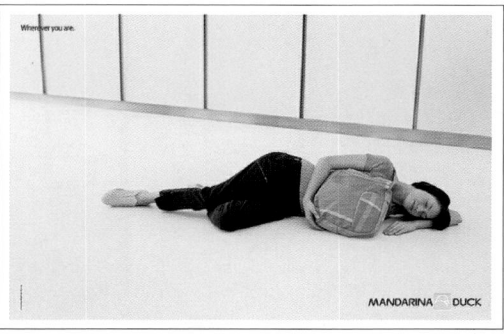

7

5. Less Rain designed this website for Fashion Fringe, a new UK fashion design competition. Open to anyone, the competition gives people the chance to put on their own catwalk show (one winner wins £100,000 of career support). The navigation system allows you to stitch your way through the online information. "All the content is laid out in a tree structure, with dotted lines connecting all chapters, helping you stitch to the right direction, as if they're chalk marks on a garment," explains Less Rain's Vassilios Alexiou. www.fashionfringe.co.uk

6. The current visual identity for John Galliano from Michael.Nash Associates was launched late last year. The brief covered all forms of branding from packaging and stationery to garment labels.

7. Happiness is... a bag by Mandarina Duck, or so this ad campaign implies. Photographs from Jason Evans show models curled up contentedly with their luggage. Design/art direction: Tom Hingston and Simon Gofton @ Tom Hingston Studio. Styling: Simon Foxton.

8&9. Linn Olofsdotter created a series of 23 illustrations for the catalogue for Flor, a new women's clothing brand from Brazil. Agency: Fnazca (Saatchi & Saatchi), São Paulo. Art Director: Fábio Simões.

10. A hand-written logotype by Suburbia lends a sense of history and heritage to new luxury goods label, Corto Moltedo. "We decided to skip the sans serif modernist approach and do something that goes back to the days when you'd use the signature of the company's owner for the logo," comments Lee Swillingham, creative director on the job alongside partner Stuart Spalding. Work is currently underway on packaging, point-of-sale and other elements for the brand

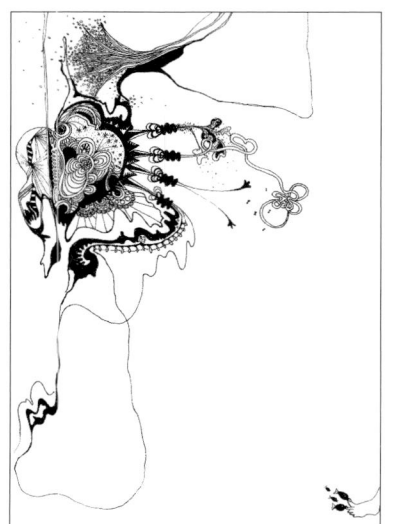

8

9

Corto Moltedo

10

beauty

womenswear

Victorian decoupage meets Hieronymus Bosch is how DDB creative director Mark Reddy describes the agency's new press campaign for Harvey Nichols. The four ads are each made up of over 100 separate shots comped together to create rich, bizarre tableaux symbolising the different departments of the store (beauty spread shown, 1).

"The original brief was 'fashion playground'," says DDB art director Grant Parker who created the campaign with partner Patrick McClelland. "We felt it should be about the experience of shopping at Harvey Nichols and the sensory overload that you get there." The team developed the theme of Heaven On Earth which was then changed to HN on Earth after it was discovered that both the Heaven

nightclub and Gap have the name Heaven trademarked.

Illustrator David Bray was briefed to create initial visuals (6-9): "Bosch and The Garden of Delights was the main reference," says Parker, "plus we gave him pointers on the hedonistic feel we wanted: we didn't want it to be twee."

Bray's drawings were then given to Tim Bret-Day to interpret photographically. "I'd been wanting to use Tim for a long time, he's incredibly sensual and he has been using a lot of digital photography with very complex arrangements of a huge number of parts. We couldn't think of anybody else who would take it on," says Reddy who believes that the project would have been impossible before digital photography due to its complexity – each image is made up of over 100

individual shots (two shown, 4&5). "A lot of fashion imagery is very stand off-ish, this is the opposite of that," Reddy says "It's definitely more is more rather than less is more. We didn't want people to be able to see everything in one go, we wanted them to find 20 other things that they hadn't noticed before, that would keep you looking and would involve you."

DDB designer, Mary Lam created a family of 12 logos (two shown, 2&3) to reflect the different areas of the store and special events. The logos will appear on the ads and be carried through to windows, in-store graphics and packaging.

Photographer's assistant: Mark Townsend. Retoucher: Lee Stuart at Ceta. Prop/set designer: Charlotte Lawson. Additional illustrations by Steve Dell

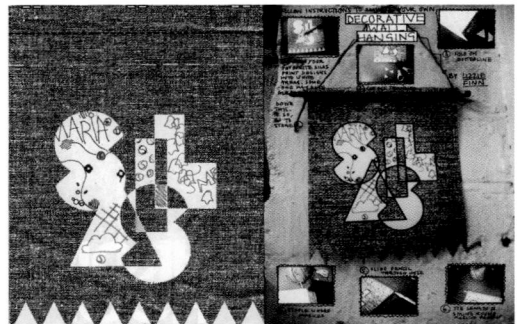

1&2. DIY is the theme of Silaszine No.2. Designed by Ben Sansbury, it features clothes from the streetwear label plus handy hints from the Silas team about everything from how to make your own designer toy – using toilet roll, some double-sided sticky tape and a couple of buttons – to assembling your own decorative wall hanging (above, as explained by the excellent Lizzie Finn). The best bit: Rachel's facts.

3. Dark Tales, Only to Read at Home is the latest catalogue from 55DSL

to be created by KesselsKramer. Produced to support the clothing brand's Arctic/Sports-inspired collection, the book features the inhabitants of Helton Hollow – an eerie town where strange things happen to strange people – who are brought to life through the distinctive illustrations of comic book artist Ashley Wood. Creative director: Dave Bell. Art director: Nils-Peter Lövgren. Copywriter: Tyler Whisnand. Strategy: Chris Barrett.

4. Ad for Dunhill Stingray skin wallet, shot by Jenny van Sommers for Yellow Door.

5&6. Boxfresh continues its "we are you" theme in this Spring 05 look-book. Gareth McConnell's street-cast shots drip council estate chic while menswear designer Peter Hoppins' cover illustration references the finest Chav influences. Art direction: Jamie Speck (Boxfresh graphics and marketing manager). Stylist: Cynthia Lawrence John. Printed by Dayfold

7&8. maharishi has long championed camouflage and takes a large slice of responsibility for the rise and rise of camouflage in fashion over the last decade. Creative director and founder of the label, Hardy Blechman, spent six years researching camo, from its roots in nature through to its use in the military and current popularity and use in modern civilian culture. The result of all this labour is a book, DPM Disruptive Pattern Material. The encyclopaedic manual, split into two volumes totalling 944 pages, is nothing if not exhaustive – it contains over 5000 images, many of which are previously unpublished, of various camouflage patterns used in a wide range of scenarios, with the aim of being the most authoritative camouflage manual available. Published by DPM Publishing, £100. To find out more and order a copy, visit www.dpmpublishing.com/dpm

Tying in with the publication of DPM, maharishi are opening dpmhi, a new store in London with a gallery space and website that will represent mhi (an abbreviation of maharishi), DPM, toys books and sneakers... The five storey building at 2-3 Great Pultney Street, Soho, has been redesigned by French architect François Scali. It will boast a maharishi camouflage floor rendered in mosaic. Products on sale will include Krylon's Camouflage range of spray paint – available in typical camo colours, brown, green, sand, black, grey and white (example shown, 9) and toys such as this Michael Lau CC19 Junkie, mhi variant toy (10). See www.dpmhi.com for more info.

11. Window graphic for the Carhartt shop in Neal Street, Covent Garden. The texture is made up from Carhartt "C" logos and cut from frosted vinyl for a rain-like effect. Design by Nathan Gale/Intercity.

12. Martha Cooper documents the street styles of early hip hop in Hip Hop Files, Photographs 1979-1984, published by Turnaround, £30

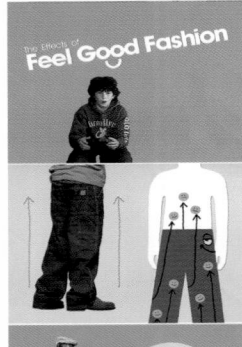

The feel-good response triggered by Old Navy denim molecules reacting with low-price particles in the brain is playfully brought to life by graphic artist Geoff McFetridge and the compositing and finshing talents of Brickyard VFX's similarly-named Geoff McAuliffe. This spot, entitled Yard Work, shows a youngster seemingly enjoying The Effects of Feel Good Fashion by jumping at a chance to mow the lawn. If only it were that simple in real life. Ad agency: Deutsch LA. Directors: Dayton/Faris

In Levi's new TV spot, a guy on a BMX rolls up alongside a girl roller-skating gently along and suggests she hitches a ride by grabbing on to his low-slung jeans. The way the girl and boy interact and are dressed doesn't feel rehearsed or over-styled: Instead, she seems shy and he nearly falls off his BMX. As the pair roll off into the sunny distance, laughing, there is a sense of teenage romance in the air. Creatives: Jim Hilson, Toby Allen. Agency: BBH. Directed by Nick Gordon at Academy

tut tut

Sexy girls, trendy boys, motorbikes, sun-drenched landscapes... all the usual marketing cliches, but one thing is missing: there's no "great big offensive logo". Why? French Connection's FCUK is so renowned we no longer need to see the words, a typeface is enough. Free thinkers unite or a brand getting too big for its boots? You decide. No doubt it'll shout loud and clear to its target audience. Creative team/directors: Trevor Beattie, Bil Bungay. Agency: TBWA\London. Production company: RSA

Frustrating scenes where stuff doesn't fit – from a too-small parking space to a needle that refuses to thread – are used to illustrate the sheer luxury of a bespoke Timothy Everest suit. Entitled Perfectly Fitted, this spot uses clever sound design: a frenetic Aphex Twin number followed by a smooth, mellow soundtrack, to accentuate the idea of going from that which jars, to that which fits precisely. Director: Laurence Thrush. Production company: Growth Films. Creative: Shelly Townsend

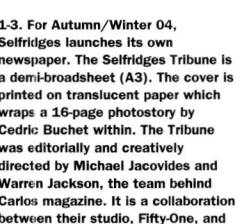

1-3. For Autumn/Winter 04, Selfridges launches its own newspaper. The Selfridges Tribune is a demi-broadsheet (A3). The cover is printed on translucent paper which wraps a 16-page photostory by Cedric Buchet within. The Tribune was editorially and creatively directed by Michael Jacovides and Warren Jackson, the team behind Carlos magazine. It is a collaboration between their studio, Fifty-One, and John Brown Citrus Publishing and

replaces JBCP's previous Selfridges magazine, Show.

4. Fashion story by Coppi Barbieri for Arena featuring mannequins instead of models. Styling: Georgina Hodson. Hair by Duffy @ Premier.

5&6. Charming pencil-drawn invite to a preview of an Anni Kuan collection, designed by Sagmeister Inc. The booklet was sewn shut horizontally: to open it, recipients

literally had to tear it in half. Illustrator: Julia Fuchs.

7&8. New work for Benetton from photographer David Sims. As part of the Autumn/Winter 2004-05 United Colors of Benetton campaign, it is the first installment under the creative command of art director Joel Berg.

9&10. Catalogue for Paul Smith Collection AW04 (Japan) by Aboud

Sodano. Art director: Alan Aboud. Photographer: Robert Wyatt. Designer: Chris Bedson

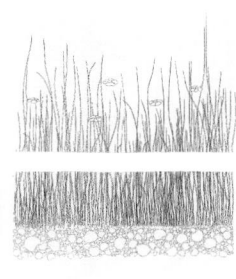

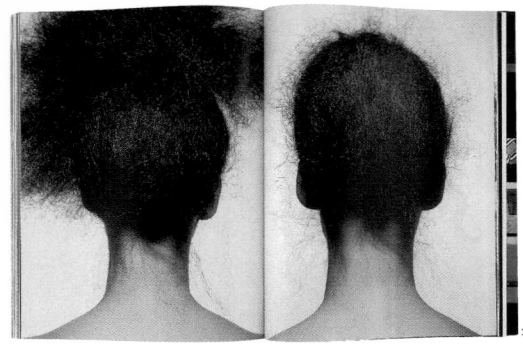

1

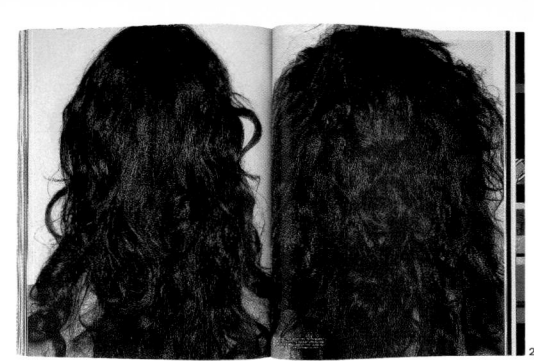

2

3

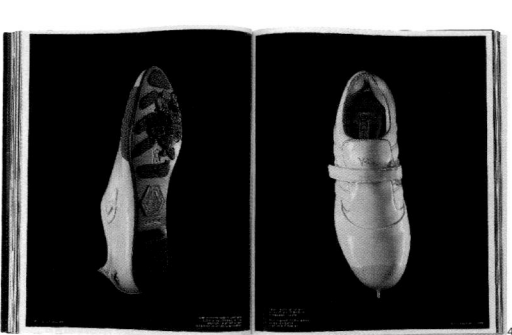

4

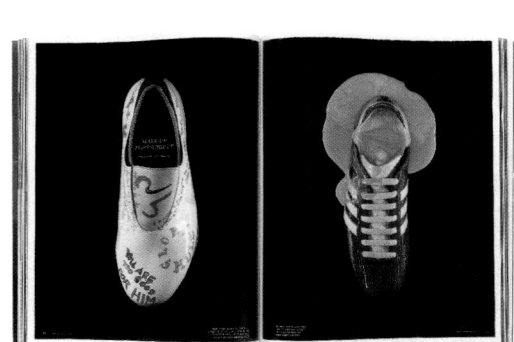

5

6

7

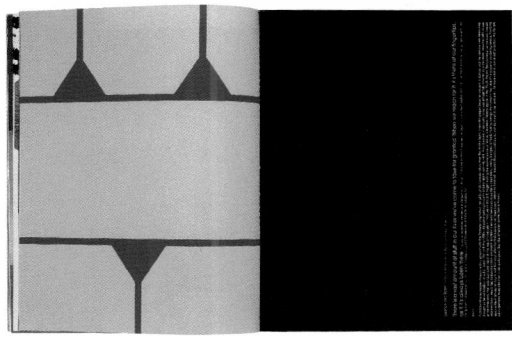

We trawled through the newsstands to find the weird and the wonderful among current fashion and style magazine photo stories:

1&2: The Great New Hair from Self Service, spring/summer 04. Photography by Guido Mocafico.

3. Dragonfly from i-D, September 04. Photographed by Richard Burbridge.

4&5. Make-Up Fortschritt from Qvest, May-June 04. Photography by Attila Hartwig.

From This Is A Magazine, Compendium #3, the printed collection of work from www.thisisamagazine.com.
6. Glass Ball #3 by Azisaka Koji.
7. Left-hand page: Disney Fuck by Vejde Gustafsson. Right-hand page: Anthem by Joel Lardner. Strip at bottom: Lights Out by Clay Weiner.

8&9. Bikini and Necktie by Gelman. From an article on the origins of ordinary objects in Clear, Volume IV, issue 2.

10&11. Wild Things from Surface, September 04 issue. Photography by Kenji Toma.

12. A Slow Drive With Mats Gustafson from Carl's Cars, issue 8, in which the famed illustrator takes a trip with his aged neighbour.

13. Madame Butterfly from Squint, 04/Floral issue. Photo and illustration by Tina Tahir

1

2

3

CYTLING KAHIN RODE ILLUSTRATIONS 4

High street shoe store Shellys gets a makeover courtesy of London-based design and brand consultants Love Branding. The work included redesigning the rather outdated logo (1) giving it a more contemporary feel (2) as well as developing packaging and in-store designs.

3. Mailer for the summer 05 collection of women's shirt designer, Blanc Kelly. Silkscreened white on black paper. Created by Base.

4. Iron Maiden fans will doubtless love Ice Crusaders, a bizarre print campaign telling the tale of two adventurous Diesel-clad heroes, who clash with aliens and other malevolent forces in a mythical landscape made of ice. This campaign was created by the Diesel in-house team in collaboration with Max Bertolini, the man behind such classics as Nathan Never and Silver Surfer. He's seriously worth a look, see www.maxbertolini.com

5. Website for Shoot photography production company by Bureau for

Visual Affairs. A modular system was chosen so that the site would be eassy to update while showing off the work for maximum impact.

6. Fizzy drink Mountain Dew becomes the latest brand to diversify into a clothing line courtesy of US agency Gyro. Hot rod-inspired graphics adorn T-shirts etc.

7. Spin is a marketing and communications agency based in Sydney and Melbourne. This site was created for Lee Jeans, aping the

style of porn sites (apparently) and features a host of dreaded pop-ups. See www.leejeans.com.au

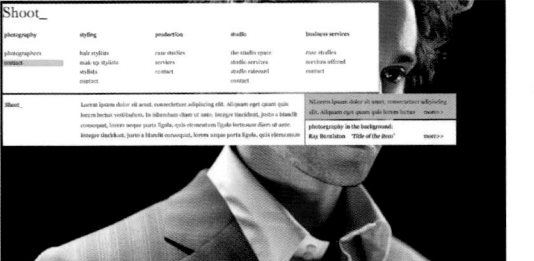

5

6

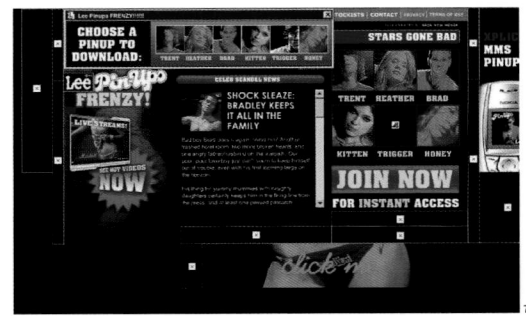

7

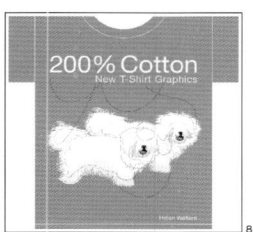

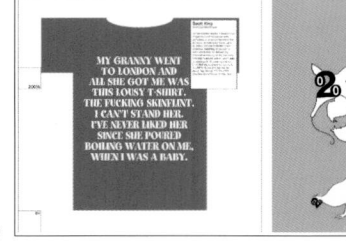

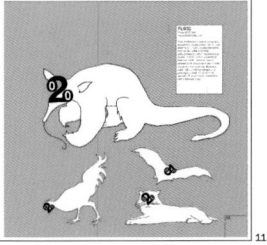

8-11. 200% Cotton boasts 1000 colour examples, in the form of illustrations and photographs, of the humble T-shirt as a vehicle for artistic expression (cover shown, 8). Designed by FL@33, the book is written and compiled by Helen Walters, following on from her precursor, 100% Cotton. Split into five chapters, Walters looks at designs created for brands and clients; T-shirts that have now become part of a design company's sideline project; shots of T-shirt-wearing strangers from cities around the world; a look at the world of the obsessive T-shirt collector; and a selection of unique T-shirt designs created especially for the book based on the brief, "200%" (Scott King and FL@33's efforts shown, 11). Other work shown here includes designs from Danger and 10.Deep (9) and a selection of people's T-shirts caught on camera (10). 200% Cotton is published by Laurence King, priced £19.95.

12-14. Aspesi Spring/Summer campaign from Dirk Van Dooren at tomato. "The idea was to create something that is of a different scale to the norm: something simple, surprising and humorous," comments Van Dooren. "Women's magazines tend to be filled with faces of a certain type so this suggested to me the idea of a face, but with the nose always represented by the clothing."

15. French designer Laurent Fétis created this logo for Thomas Engel Hart, a young US fashion designer based in Paris

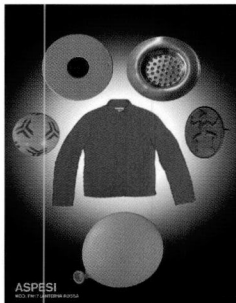

BALENCIAGA

As ever, Fabien Baron's Baron & Baron studio leads the way with high end fashion advertising campaigns. Here is a selection of its Fall 04 output. Creative direction for all by Baron & Baron.

1. Using celebrities, particularly actors, has been one of the main trends in fashion advertising this year. Here, Maggie Gyllenhaal stars for Miu Miu. Photographed by Terry Richardson.

2. Balenciaga. Photographed by David Sims.

3. Hugo Boss Orange Label. Photographed by Fabien Baron.

4. Michael Kors. From a filmic campaign set at a glamorous airport and photographed by Mario Testino.

5. Another actor-based campaign: Keira Knightley stars for Asprey. Photographed by Craig McDean.

6&7. High class campaign for Burberry. Photographed, with not a check in sight, by Mario Testino

BOSS

MICHAEL KORS

ASPREY
LONDON

BURBERRY

BURBERRY

8

9

10

Fashion designer Alexander McQueen has acted as a kind of brand ambassador/collaborator with American Express for a number of years. In order to mark five years of the American Express Centurion Card in the UK (the exclusive black one) McQueen and the card company put on an exclusive event. Michael Nash Associates designed the invitation and logo (8). McQueen

also recently unveiled new site, www.alexandermcqueen.com, courtesy of London-based Poke (9&10). It's a dark, brooding and beautifully crafted piece of work that showcases the latest collections as well as featuring an archive of McQueen's work.

11-13. Stand Off is a magazine developed by the people behind

fashion trade event To Be Confirmed. "It features lots of independent brands, so there's an interesting community of people who are into not just fashion, but music, art, film… they wanted a magazine that captured that spirit," says Tom Hingston whose studio developed the magazine and the identity/promotional items (examples shown, 14&15) for the bi-annual show. "One

of the attractions for us, was that Stand Off wasn't meant for the newsstand so you don't have to fulfil all the criteria you would for a normal magazine," he adds. The signpost-style logo was developed to be both adaptable and playful: "As the show evolves we'll be able to do lots of things with that: from signage at the show, to sweatshirts or T-shirts the staff can wear"

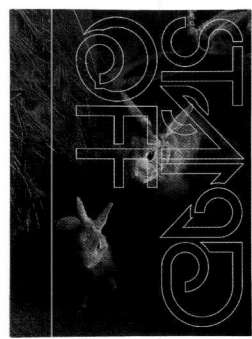

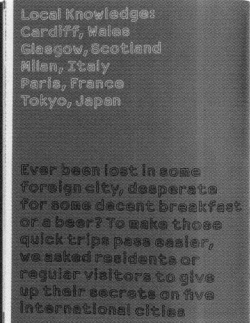

11

12

13

14

15

1&2. StudioThomson designed this swing-tag, invitation and brochure for label Preen. The swing-tag features the company's original handwritten logo, debossed on brown card. The inspiration for the Autumn Winter 2005/06 invite came, explains Mark Thomson, from elements within Preen's new collection, which included garments with childlike proportions, such as large buttons and collars." The typography was inspired by spelling books and a newsprint-style stock lends it a "school playtime" feel.

3. Fashion PR agency Modus announced its recent bi-annual open day with this invitation, printed on A2 bible paper and bearing the uninhibited scribbles of This is Real Art designer and artist Kim Hiorthøy. Client: Modus Publicity. Designer: Kim Hiorthøy/This is Real Art. Typography: Sam Renwick.

4&5. Moon UK created this invite to Robert Cary-Williams' recent London show. An old photocopier helped create the look of the invite – cleverly mirroring the designer's use of distressed fabrics.

6. Aquascutum goodie bag from the Autumn Winter 2005/06 collection – also from StudioThomson. Simple manilla bags were hand-stamped with show information and individually numbered. Within was a hand-made velvet bag, giving the recipient a tactile experience when they reached inside. **7.** Pop-up invitation to the opening of a new H&M store in London's Knightsbridge. The pop-up is of the store itself set among the surrounding streets. The hand-drawn illustrative style was also used for in-store graphics.

Commissioned by Naked on behalf of Chloe Bowers at H&M. Designed and produced by Hannah Measures and Nick Stickland at ODD. Paper engineer: Sarah Wilson. Illustration: David Bray @ PVUK.com. Designer: Mark Butler

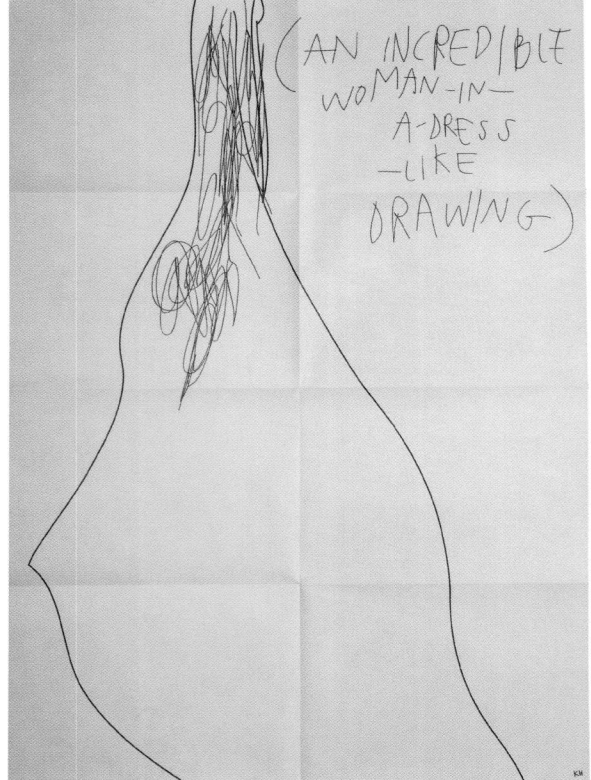

PREEN
by
thornton
bregazzi
autumn
winter
2005/6

tuesday
15th
february
3.30pm

stamford
bridge
football
stadium

chelsea
village

fulham
road

sw6
lhs

fulham
broadway
tube

london
fashion
week
return
bus
service
available
from
front
of
bfc
tent

name

block

row

RSVP
relativepr
@aol.com

telephone
020
7704
8866

facsimile
020
7704
8877

TOPSHOP

PREEN
by
thornton
bregazzi
autumn
winter
2005/6
vacuum

(AN INCREDIBLE WOMAN-IN-A-DRESS-LIKE DRAWING)

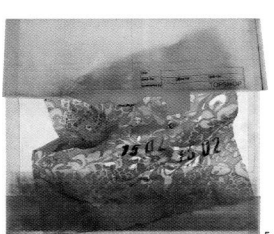

8&9. The exhibition Made in Britain at the Foam Photography Museum Amsterdam, featured the work of 12 contemporary British photographers, among them, fashion designers Antoni + Alison. As its title suggests, the aim of the exhibition was to explore the spirit, characteristics and idiosyncracies of the UK. Antoni + Alison's humorous photo collages include emblematic items such as kitsch pottery and the humble British brick.
10. Lewis Moberly created this brand identity for Girls Girls Girls, a new retail outlet targeting pre-teen girls and their mums. The identity uses a butterfly (symbol of transformation and beauty) in shocking pink with a single letter "g". Design director: Mary Lewis. Design/typography: Poppy Stedman.

11-14. Conquer the world with this cut 'n' play board game and catalogue from Silas/Babette. The aim of the game? To expand your multi-national business empire by acquiring less developed countries. Belarus is going for a steal at $80,000,000, although if Amnesty accuses you of human rights violations it'll cost you $5m to get your fellow players to turn a blind eye. Concept/art direction: Silas/Rob Green. Design/illustration: Rob Green. 15-18. Melted toy soldiers were used to make the swathes of colour in this fashion campaign for Pianurastudio. Explain its creators Andy Simionato and Karen Donnachie (known as a to the k): "We experimented by wetting ink-jet printouts of Karen's photos, eventually we combined the day's shots with the melted blobs. We wanted a dream-world inhabited by Dali-like transformations of the everyday." 19. Vexed Generation collaborated with Puma and Biomega on this folding bike designed specifically for city-dwellers. The Puma Bike is available in Puma stores worldwide

8

9

10

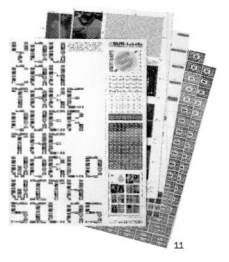
11

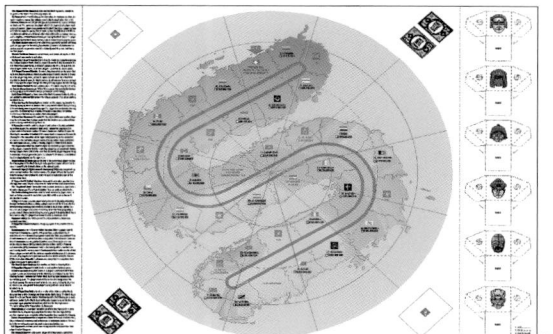
12

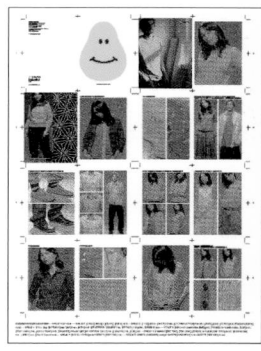
13

14

15

16

17

18

19

1. From Poke comes this website for Swedish designer, J Lindeberg, noted for his stylish golf wear. The menu on the left enlarges as users scroll over it, providing an elegant yet modern feel which is in tune with the clothes. www.jlindeberg.com

2. From a video installation produced by PAM for the Swatch Alternative Fashion Week in March 05. PAM are Paul Plowman, Anthony Burrill and Malcolm Goldie. 3&4. Go to the Silas website and root around until you spy the Arcade section. There you will find fine distractions from office tedium. In Fergus Purcell's Space Rock Overlord (4) you are the protector of the musical cosmos, your job: to save the universe from the "mind-melting android forces of the evil megapopconglomerates", with only a few Flying Vs for protection. Alternatively, vent your rage on Evil Martin, The Bearded Prophet and other James Jarvis characters in his Cosmic Potato Shooter game (3). Turn the sound up. www.silasandmaria.com

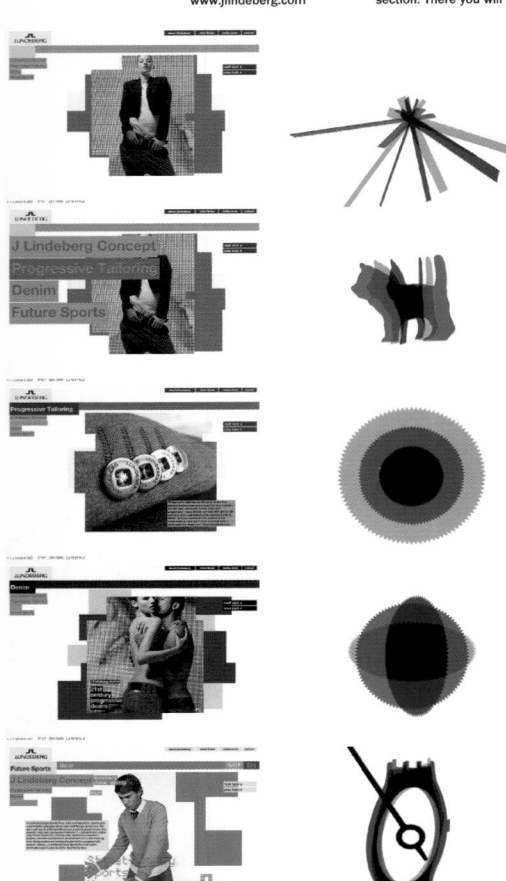

1

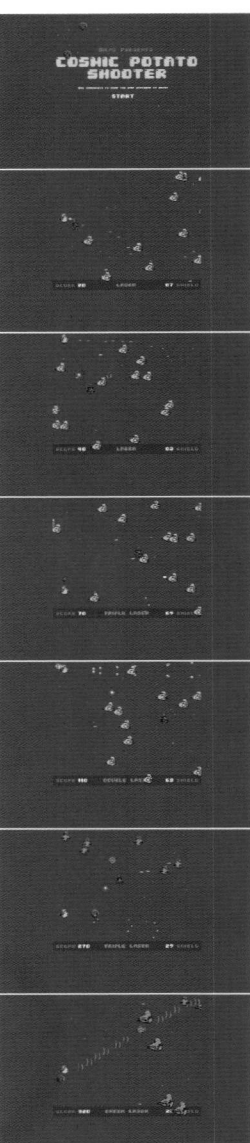

2

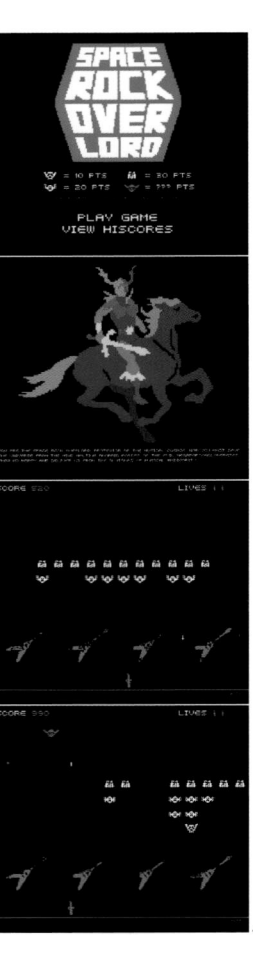

3

4

Central Illustration Agency illustrator Andrew Foster got the chance to add his personal touch to Liberty's latest window displays. In a unique project for the London store, Foster was permitted to paint directly onto the outside of the windows to illustrate the following enticing words: "Grant me, if you will, a few moments of your time. I would like to show you our collection of collections to tempt and delight you." The first section of the text (up to the full stop) runs on the Great Marlborough Street side of the store, with the second creeping round to Regent Street ("I would like to show you our collection" shown, 5-7). Foster (8), a St Martin's lecturer, is used to working on this scale but said that creating such a large piece in public was a new, and daunting, task. The text-based piece involved using paints, paper and pens and took a week to complete. Passers-by, on inspecting the work close up, along with the unstable April weather, are likely to interact and alter the look of the work even further. From the other side of Regent Street pedestrians can see the second sentence in its entirety (three windows shown, 10). Visual coordinator: Katie Baron. Head of visual merchandising: Faye McLeod. 11-14. Over in Knightsbridge, Harvey Nichols also sports a new window display on its Sloane Street side with graphics from London based studio, Zip. The psychedelic work supports the store's new menswear collection. Creatives: Peter Chadwick, Caroline Moorhouse and Daniel Koch

1-3. To mark the one hundred and seventy fifth birthday of leather goods label, Delvaux, Base asked 175 photographers, stylists, designers and painters to participate in a commemorative book project entitled 175:D. The studio selected 175 objects from Delvaux's history, and asked each participant to create a page for the book based on one of the items.

4. Intersection magazine links fashion with cars in this spread from its March-April issue. Various trainers line up as if on a Formula 1 starting grid. Creative director: Yorgo Tloupas. Photography: Holger Pooten. Coordination: Amanda McDonald.

Publisher and photographer Shoichi Aoki established Fruits, the Japanese street fashion fanzine, in 1994. Since then, Aoki's 'zine has documented the fashion scenes that have exploded in the suburbs of Tokyo. Bringing together the best examples from the fashion bible in the book, Fruits, in 2001 his new collection, Fresh Fruits (cover shown, 8) was published by Phaidon in June. There are more examples of Tokyo teens mixing high fashion with the homemade and the book features the cool, the chic and the downright crazy (selection shown, 5-7). Fresh Fruits is priced at £19.95 and more details are at www.phaidon.com. All photographs © Shoichi Aoki, Tokyo 1994-2002.

9–11. Cover and spreads from Beyond Desire, a book about the influences of Africa on Western style (and vice versa), designed by Paul Boudens for the Antwerp Fashion Museum

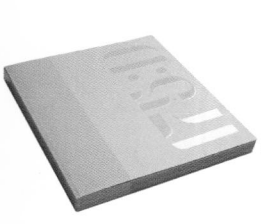

INHOUD

17-19:
00.BEYOND DESIRE:
INLEIDING
Kaat Debo

41-43:
01.HOW DO YOU
LIKE ME NOW?
Philippe Pirotte

81:
02.DE DRANG NAAR
HET EXOTISCHE
Zoe Whitley

83-85:
03.LET'S
GET IT ON:
ZWART
HAAR
Carol Tulloch

105-107:
04.MODE IN
DE AFRIKAANSE
GROOTSTAD
Filip De Boeck & Césarine Bolya

134:
FOTOCREDITS

135-136:
COLOFON TENTOONSTELLING
& CATALOGUS

CONTENT

21-23:
00.BEYOND DESIRE:
INTRODUCTION
Kaat Debo

45-47:
01.HOW DO YOU
LIKE ME NOW?
Philippe Pirotte

82:
02.CRAVING
THE EXOTIC
Zoe Whitley

86-88:
03.LET'S
GET IT ON:
BLACK
HAIR
Carol Tulloch

109-112:
04.FASHION IN
THE AFRICAN
METROPOLIS
Filip De Boeck & Césarine Bolya

134:
PHOTO CREDITS

135-136:
EXHIBITION & CATALOGUE
COLOPHON

NUIT
DE
NOËL
(Club-Happy)
1963
Foto | Photos Malick Sidibé

SAMPLE presents 100 of the most exciting fashion and accessory designers working today (spread of work by New York designer Bruce shown, 13). The book itself comes with a pleated cover (12) and hand-cut pages sliced at different angles. The designers were selected by figures from the fashion world including Ulrich Lehmann and Alexander McQueen. Published by Phaidon in June, £45. Manchester's Eg.G designed the two seasonal 2005 look books for Asics brand Onitsuka Tiger (end-paper shown, 14). The design employed Japanese ornamentation, all hand-drawn in a variety of media by Eg.G's Jo Cartwright. 15. Cover of the Spring 05 issue of 10+ Men (photo: Andreas Larsson), the menswear spin-off from fashion magazine, 10 (whose own Spring 05 cover, with photo by Jenny Gage and Tom Betterton, is shown, 16. Spread, with photograph by Serge Leblon, shown 17). Art director: Daren Ellis. 18&19. This newsprint invitation promotes a preview of designer Anni Kuan's Autumn/Winter 2005 collection. As the invitation wisely spells out, "material luxuries are best enjoyed in small doses", hence the tiny square of 18 carat gold leaf on the cover. Design: Sagmeister Inc, New York. Art direction: Stefan Sagmeister. Illustration/photography/design: Ariane Spanier. Additional design: Matthias Ernstberger. The aim of John Lewis' current in-store promotion, Objects of Desire, is to highlight "12 of the best" products across their 30 product categories. A scarlet fascinator (hair band) features on in-store banners, window displays and also on the front cover of an accompanying brochure (cover, 20. Spread, 21). Art director and designer: Patrice Gueroult at John Lewis Graphic Design Studio. Photo: John Bennett. Stylist: Arabella McNie.

12

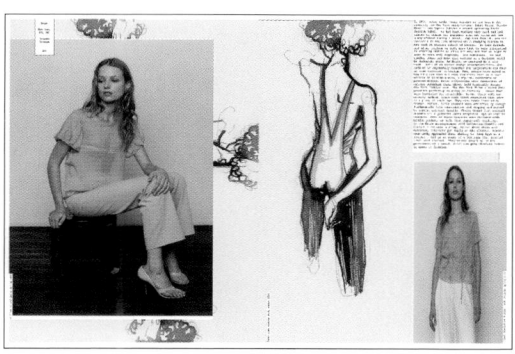

13

14

15

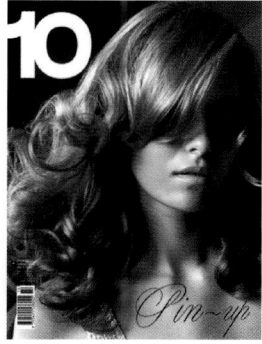

16

17

18

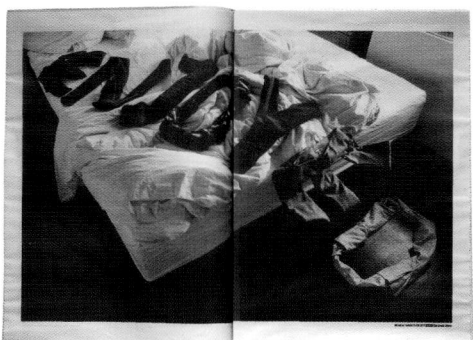

19

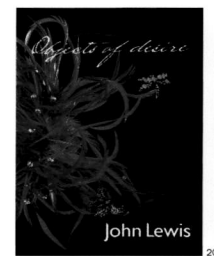

20

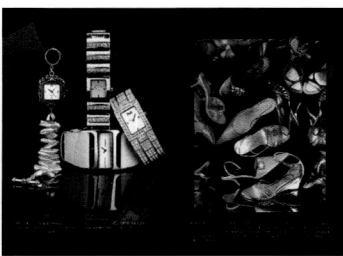

21

Elegant photography and delicate type feature in these two look-books for designer Johanna Ho's Autumn/Winter (1-5) and Spring/Summer (6-10) collections. Says Fabio Ongarato, whose Melbourne-based studio developed the books: "With strong Moroccan influences, hints of vintage and a cheeky innocence, Johanna's summer 04/05 collection was inspired by the 60s photographer Sam Haskins, famous for his Cowboy Kate book." Haskins, now 78, lives in the Blue Mountains in New South Wales, but the designers tracked him down and commissioned him to shoot the campaign. Adds Ongarato: "The next season, we continued to work with Sam – this time picking up on the flamboyant style of various tribal communities from the 70s and 80s. This inspiration was extended right through to the use of interwoven optical patterns and dot screens which appear throughout, referring back also to Johanna's weaving techniques"

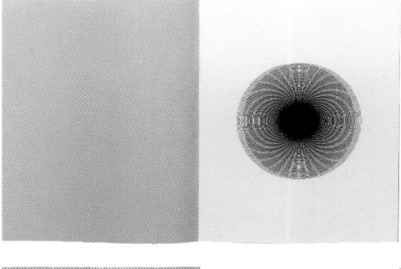

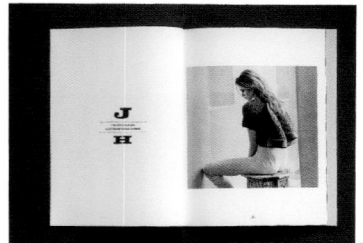

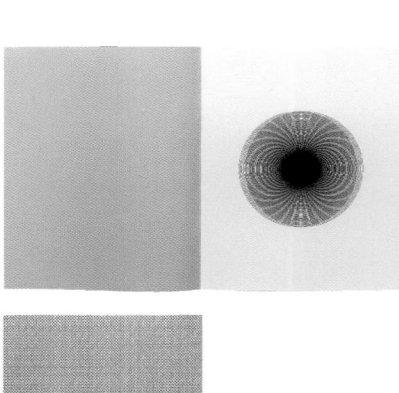

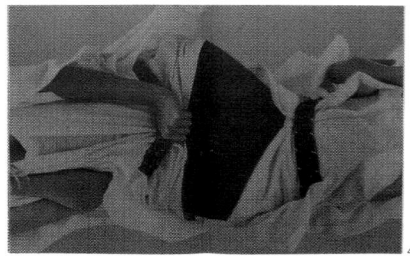

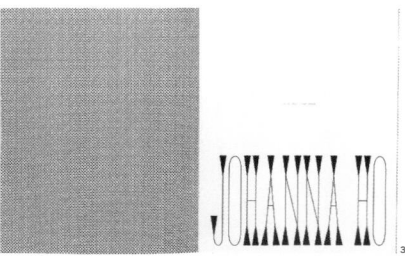

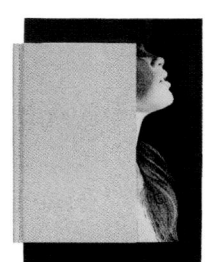

This is issue one of K&K, a biannual, independent newspaper featuring an eclectic collection of art, fashion photography and popular culture. K&K's look will change from season to season – only the grid and baseline grid will stay the same. Published jointly by New York designers, Studio Von Birken and Starstyling Berlin, 500 issues per season will be printed. K&K is available via mail-order or at colette Paris, Isa & Nom de Guerre in New York, pro qm in Berlin and on www.youworkforthem.com. Art direction: Studio Von Birken. Contributors for this issue include: Alex Antitch (photographer on spread shown 16), Bernd Schifferdecker (illustration shown 13), Ryotatsu Tanaka (illustration shown 17), and Peter Farago (photographer for cover, shown 11 and spreads shown 14&15). All photographs of magazine spreads: Ben Pogue. For further information about K&K, see www.studiovon birken.com

11

12

13

14

15

16

17

Clothing label 55DSL has apparently harnessed the power of robots to create garments sporting the most authentic examples of wear and tear. Its latest collection was designed with a number of signature "wears and tears", such as oil stains, grass stains, specific rips and tears: each created by a particular robot made by 55DSL's very own technicians. From a secret factory facility, the 55DSL technicians and robot experts, Robocross, spent six months building and testing robots that rip, tear, burn and stain the clothes. Communications agency KesselsKramer then used the robotic creations as the basis of a campaign for the new collection. Norwegian photographer, Simen Johan, was given carte blanche to record the testing process at the facility – the results included a series of photographs that ran in magazines (1-3) and a unique catalogue for the clothing company (5&6). To find out more about the testing process, and to see it in action, video footage (4) can be seen online at www.55dsl.com.

Creative director: Dave Bell. Art director: Ewoudt Boonstra. Copywriter: Job van Dijk. Strategy: Chris Barrett. Photography: Simen Johan. Robotics: Frank Barnes and Bastiaan Maris (Robocross). Medical Assistance: Charlie Burns. Producer: Julia Llamas

1

2

3

4

5

6

Finance

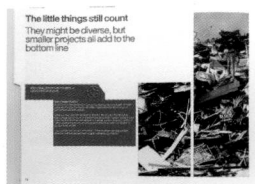

Everything you need to know...

The basics

Our strategy

Our results in 2003

We may be a ports company – but we're not just focused on ports

We're focused on customers...

1&2. Who's Next? asks this poster campaign for the Washington Lottery from Publicis Seattle. Each one portrays the messy aftermath of suddenly discovering that you are a big winner. Creative directors: Kevin Kehoe, Bob Moore. Group creative director: Rob Rich. Art director: Greg Wyatt. Copywriter: Joe Gerlitz. Photographer: Giblin & James.

3-5. Annual report for Associated British Ports by Navy Blue in collaboration with Merchant.

6. Pearlfisher designed this annual report for CEC (Creative Education Corporation). CEC is the holding company for London-based nursery school group, Primary Steps. Pearlfisher creative partner, Jonathan Ford, explains: "We designed the report as a school exercise book, incorporating graph paper, children's drawings and other easily recognisable, visual cues associated with school. The 'book' provides all the accounts and company detail usually provided in

an annual report but the information is presented in a creative and educationally linked way."

7&8. Cover and spread from annual report for Clarks shoes by Frost Design London. The cover references a calendar and the rolling forward of a company's financial figures which occurs at this time, claim Frost. Inside, the main sections of the report are signposted by bold numbers echoing the cover alongside photographs taken at the

Clarks headquarters in Somerset. Photography by Lee Funnell at Graphic Photo

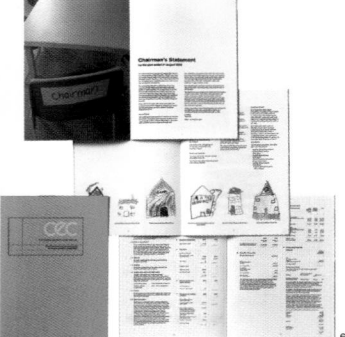

Mother's current campaign for Egg asks "If you don't look after your money, who will?" Each documentary-style spot features a different dodgy business out to con the unwary, from an autograph forger (top), to a pyramid scheme organiser (fourth down), to a canny Scottish farmer flogging bits of "genuine Wembley turf" to the gullible English (bottom). Directed by Brett Morgen through production company, Anonymous.

Investment advisors:
It's a new day.

A storm floods New York in Biblical style, in a dramatic spot for Barclay's Global Investors/iShares. The spot, entitled Clean Slate, features a group of financial professionals trapped in a boardroom until the storm subsides and a sunny, new era of investment arrives. Agency: Venables, Bell and Partners. Creatives: Kevin Frank, Ray Andrade. Director: Andrew Douglas @ Anonymous Content. Post-production: A52

HSBC's local knowledge would prevent faux pas such as making the OK sign in Brazil, where it's very rude. Written by Vince Squibb at Lowe, London. Director: Chris Palmer, Gorgeous Enterprises

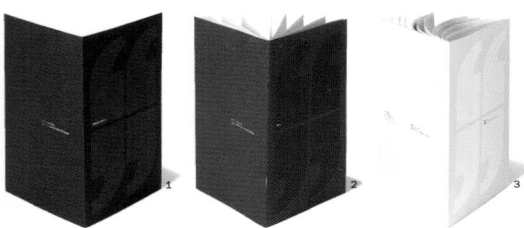

" " Swiss Re
, , Centre for Global Dialogue ₁₃

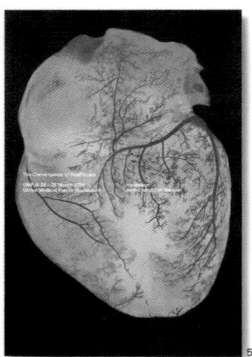

Frost Design London have created the corporate identity and design for the Centre for Global Dialogue in Switzerland. The centre, founded by international reinsurer Swiss Re, has been set up as a forum for events, programmes and conferences dealing with global risk issues. Frost's design solution covers all aspects of related literature and branding. The new identity (shown 13) is centred around a distinctive logotype which consists of red speechmarks arranged to be indicative of the Swiss flag's white cross on a red ground whilst cleverly expressing an invitation for dialogue. Frost's solution also includes the use of a limited but bold colour palette of red, black, white and grey,

while the use of recyclable or biodegradable materials wherever possible reflects the centre's commitment to the environment. Elements of the design project include a restaurant menu (1), a wine menu (2), an A4 writing pad (3) and newsletters (example shown 4). 5&6 The Global Medical Forum Foundation's Report features an image of a heart whose arteries resemble branches of trees, highlighting environmental concerns. 7. Business cards. 8-10 The marketing brochure for the centre

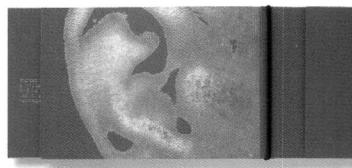

11

Contrary to suggestions that Barclays wanted to "soften" its image or be more "touchy-feely" the bank actually gave London-based design consultancy Williams Murray Hamm the brief of evolving its identity to confirm its position as "financial experts". "Virtually every financial services brand on the high street is pursing values like warmth and friendliness," says WMH director Richard Murray. "Barclays offers traditional values of professionalism and integrity. Banks are inevitably criticised when they change so we

decided to retain the current word marque." The eagle device, which had previously been "played down", has been reintroduced as a symbol of the bank's history, the colour palette has been reduced to just three shades of blue, and there is now just one typeface family. A selection of literature featuring the new look is shown, 11. Creative director: Garrick Hamm.

12-14. Greater Bay Bancorp 2003 from those masters of annual report design Cahan Associates. The report

shows how Greater Bay Bancorp, a diversified financial services organisation, develops its business through superior client relationships and strong community roots. The report pinpoints specific entrepreneurs and links them to Greater Bay Bancorp employees who have helped them find financial solutions to suit their needs. The coloured lines on the front of the report are taken from a diagram within plotting the interconnecting relationships between Greater Bay Bancorp and its clients

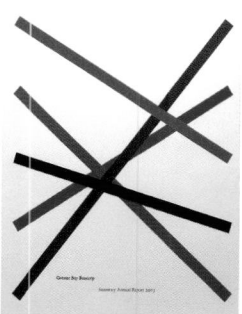

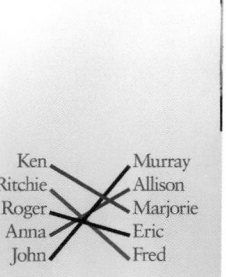

12

13

14

HET
REALISME
VAN
REAAL

REAAL Verzekeringen

1

HET
REALISTEN
SPEL

HOE GROOT IS DE
KANS DAT MENSEN
WEER VAKER
SPELLETJES GAAN
SPELEN?

A   15%
B   31%
C   41%
D   56%

2

MACQUARIE INFRASTRUCTURE GROUP
INTERIM REPORT FOR PERIOD ENDED 31 DECEMBER 2003

MACQUARIE

Chairman's letter
Financial highlights
Half year in review
SR125 South/USA
M6 Toll opening/UK
M7/Aust update
Revenue statistics
Investment profile
Community/Tree profile
Corporate directory

MIG/
INTERIM
REPORT/

4

MILJOENENSCHILDERIJ.

3

1-3. Risk calculation is central to the activities of insurance company REAAL. Agency KesselsKramer's promotional work for the brand is all about calculating probabilities. For example, the probability that you will find an old masterpiece lying around the house is pretty low, so it's prudent to get some good pension insurance with REAAL. A multi-faceted campaign includes this brand book (1) with photography by Jacqueline Hassink. Her images also feature in a deck of Top Trumps-style playing cards (2). Art director: Krista Rozema. Copywriter: Patrick van der Gronde. A TV campaign (3) continues this theme of unlikely probabilities (such as your child making a fortune for you, by inventing flippers). Creative team as above. Directors: James Brown, Johan Kramer. Production companies: Kikkers, KesselsKramer.

4. Australia's Macquarie Infrastructure Group (MIG) holds a number of large international and national infrastructure investments, particularly toll roads. emeryfrost has developed a strong visual language for them, based on graphic road imagery. The corporate colour palette is a metallic silver, grey and orange. Typography references toll road signage. The look is applied across all MIG publications, including the annual Interim Report (cover shown), as well as video and web. Design: emeryfrost, Sydney. Designer: Ray Parslow. Cover photography: Karl Schwerdtfeger.

5&6. Annual report for the Scottish Ambulance Service by Elmwood. Illustrations give basic first aid advice as well as step-by-step information in case of a 999 emergency. Graphics were inspired by ambulance livery and the document uses simple, bold typography to highlight key statistical information. Designers: Paul Sudron, Graham Sturzaker. Creative director: Richard Scholey

LIFE SUPPORT

SCOTTISH AMBULANCE SERVICE
ANNUAL REPORT FOR 2002/2003

NHS
SCOTLAND

5

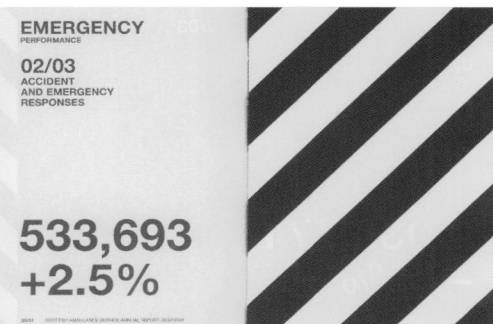

EMERGENCY

PERFORMANCE

02/03
ACCIDENT
AND EMERGENCY
RESPONSES

533,693
+2.5%

SCOTTISH AMBULANCE SERVICE ANNUAL REPORT 2002/2003

6

7

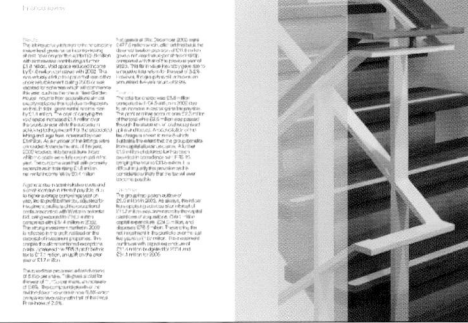

8

Exchanging information.

9

Dont be one.

10

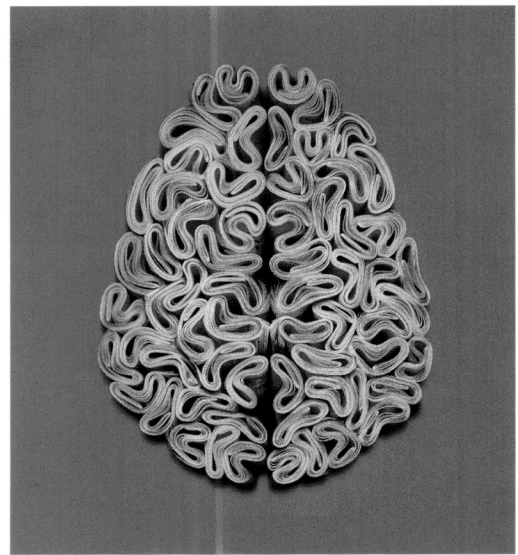

11

7&8. Annual report for property investors, Derwent Valley Holdings, by Cartlidge Levene. The report features images of a recent development by architects Lifschutz Davidson. Vertical bands overlayed onto the architectural images relate to the lines of the building.

9. MetaDesign, San Francisco's annual report for Adobe builds on its work last year for the software giant's packaging. "The art and technology of communication" is the theme. "Because Adobe 'helps people and businesses communicate better', we developed three main chapters that turn that positioning statement into something tangible for each customer," explains creative director, Brett Wickens. "For enterprise customers it is about 'exchanging information', for creatives, 'communicating ideas' and, for consumers, 'sharing memories'. Illustrated customer testimonials demonstrate the benefits of these solutions." Senior designer: Julian Bittiner. Writer: Jay O'Rear. Photography: Todd Hido. Case study images: Peter Saville,

Deutsch Inc., Martin Evening, Dimension Films, Karen Nichols.

10&11. Ambient and press ads for The Economist from Ogilvy & Mather Redcard Singapore. Specially made doormats were placed at the entrances of important banks, financial institutions and selected bars in the city's business district. Creative directors: Craig Smith, Andy Greenaway. Art directors: Richard Johnson, Kelly Dickinson, Naoki Ga. Copywriters: Steve Hough, Simon Jenkins (Brain)

Last year, Browns produced a memorable annual review for Channel 4 using the illustrative skills of Paul Davis. This time, the studio has again gone for the illustrative approach but uses four emerging talents: Elliot Thoburn, Gwyn Vaughan Roberts, Luke Best and Lorna Miller. As last year, there are four different covers, each reflecting the diversity of taste and interest of the typical C4 viewer as they relax at home in front of the channel's programmes. Lorna Miller's group of young flatsharers (8) are, apparently, laughing along with BoSelecta; Elliot Thoburn's young bloke has a beer in front of The Hajj (4); Gwyn Vaughan Roberts' odd couple are watching The Deal (5) while Luke Best's family are engrossed in Wifeswap (1). Other images include a portrait of new chairman Luke Johnson (3) plus feature-style illustrations of articles about individual programmes (The Deal shown 2, Wifeswap, 7)

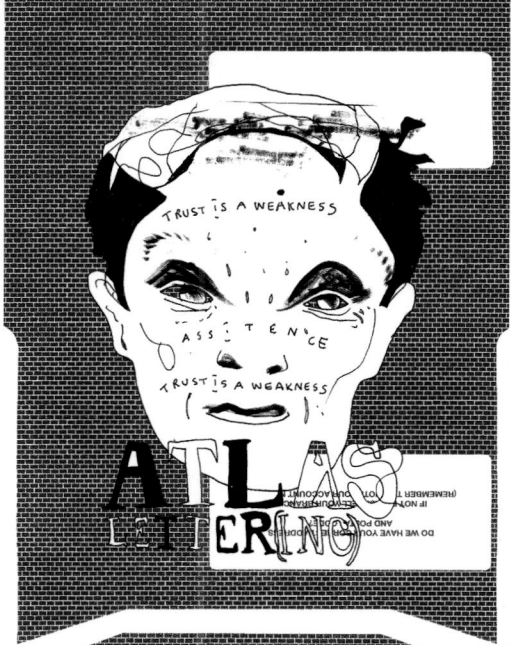

TRUST IS A WEAKNESS

ASS I T E N CE

TRUST IS A WEAKNESS

ATLAS LETTERING

THE ONLY THING I WANT TO BE IS RICH AND OUT OF HERE.

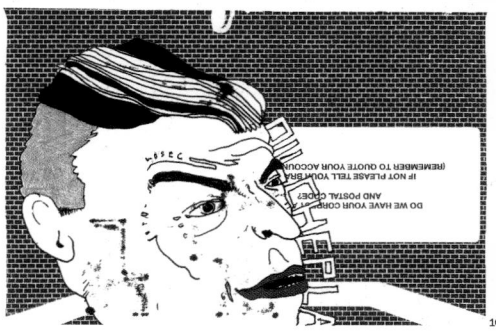

HELLO

9-11. The backgrounds for these images, by London-based illustrator Ross Holden, come from the insides of the envelopes used by his bank to send him letters. "The images are the starting point for a small collection of work based around the massive amount of debt ordinary people find themselves in," explains Holden, "and the increase in debt-suicides from finding yourself stuck in a financial cul-de-sac. I was looking at the patterns inside my bank envelopes, some feature bricks, some feature gold bars – the bricks being the castle, the gold bars being the bounty. Basically, the idea was to use these patterns on everyday items from milk cartons to maybe curtains, bed sheets, work ties, carpets, everyday household shit – a reminder that when you're in debt nothing really belongs to you and there's no escaping it." The work is a personal project that will form part of a series of exhibitions set to appear on Holden's website www.ungluemylimb.com

Charming spot for bank Dexia, that shows how one's money can be brought to life. Agency: Duval Guillaume, Brussels. Creatives: Philippe De Ceuster, Joost Berends. Director: Andy Morahan, Wanda/Bikini

"Every time I pick up Orlandos trousers, I find his underpants inside."

In this spot for Dutch insurers Centraal Beheer Achmea, two cleaners are horrified to find their posh workplace in complete disarray. Cursing the "devil children" of the house for partying, they proceed to clean up the mess until one opens the front door, sees police outside and realises that the house is actually a crime scene. Creatives: Dennis Baars and Erik Falke, DDB Amsterdam. Director: Nicholas Barker @ Rogue

The spring in this confident chap's step is due to having Mastercard, not cash, in his pocket. Agency: McCann Erickson NY. Creatives: Sharon Ehrlich and Daniel Rodriguez. Director: Stylewar @ Smuggler

Devoted, under-appreciated puppeteer works hard for his money in this heart-rending spot for Intelligent Finance (see p24). Creatives: Tom Ewart, Dave Sullivan, CDD. Director: Ed Gill @ Academy

Transport

1&2. Fallon's campaign for the Skoda Octavia again dares car buyers to ignore what everyone else thinks. "Beware. Sheep on road," says one. "The office canteen isn't the best place to test drive a new car," says the other. Creatives: Dave Masterman and Ed Edwards. Photographer: Todd Hido.

3. You can now take the Eurostar all the way to the ski slopes, as this poster by Neil Dawson and Clive Pickering of TBWA\London illustrates. Typographer: Dan Beckett. Retouching: FEP.

4. Press and poster ad from BBH for Audi playing on the notion of DNA, the gist being that the new A3 is a perfectly engineered match for you. Creatives: Ben Hartman, Neil Durber. Artwork: Al @ Mission Impossible.

5&6. Transport for London poster campaign from M&C Saatchi. Each poster shows an imaginary pop star who can't perform due to their untimely teenage road-accident death. Creatives: Tom Spicer, Kit Dayaram. Typography: Rob Wilson. Photography: Jason Joyce

7. VW Touareg ad from DDB New Zealand. Creatives: Darran Wong Kam, Hywel James. Photographer: Alan McFetridge.

8. The latest from Leo Burnett's Fiat Vans campaign which, in an appropriate tie-in, runs with The Sun's football supplement. Fiat Vans are customised with wittily appropriate accessories for a particular team. Creatives: Andy Bunday and Jon Lilley. Illustrated by Andy Bunday originally and by Metin Salih going forward

An American TV presenter misinterprets British culture in these hilarious US spots for British Airways by M&C Saatchi, New York. Creative: Paul Kamzelas. Director: Sam Cadman at Rogue

Two spots from production company Eyeball NYC focus on Delta Airlines' "simplifares" deal for Cincinnati residents and travellers alike. Both spots feature cleverly animated line drawings and were produced from start to finish in just under three weeks. Creative director: Limore Shur; executive producer: Mike Eastwood; producer: Beth Vogt; designer: Johan Wiberg; CG: Stuart Simms; agency: BrightHouse Live, Atlanta, GA; producer: Halle Griffe; art director: Tia Lustig; copywriter: Scott Biear

Don't just copy everyone else, buy a distinctive Skoda Octavia instead. Creative Team: Dave Masterman and Ed Edwards. Ad agency: Fallon. Director: Frederic Planchon. Production company: Academy

Rutger Hauer growls about the kaleidoscope's influence on the Smart forfour's 30 colour combinations. Agency: Farm. Creatives: Christian Bunyan, Gary Robinson, Owen Lee. Director: Simon Green, Large

1. Two buggies go head-to-head at Singapore airport, from a project by Julian Wolkenstein. See more at www.julianwolkenstein.com.au

2. Thurrock never looked lovelier: Jason Orton was commissioned to produce a photographic portrait of the area to go alongside essays by Ken Worpole and Chris Baines in Thurrock: A Visionary Brief in the Thames Gateway. The document, designed by Kerr Noble, formed part of a project looking at culturally led regeneration in an area that will be transformed by London's shift eastwards, curated by General Public Agency. It was distributed to architects, artists, environmentalists and community workers invited to the area to consider its future.

3. Drive By Shooting is the latest book from photographer Max Forsythe. It features photographs taken by Forsythe from moving vehicles, such as as this serendipitous shot taken on a London bus. As BBH's John Hegarty says in his introduction, Forsythe's photography "reminds us that life doesn't happen in black and white. It happens in colour and sadly, for so many, it passes them by." To be published in November by Booth-Clibborn Editions, £25

Ralf Obergfell, Maxine Beuret and Jet, from the London-based collective Photodebut, all share a passion for the classic London Routemaster bus. Routemasters on the historic 73 route were recently replaced by the new "bendy buses" and now the same fate awaits routes 19 and 38 (the last Routemaster was scheduled to run the 38 route in July 2005). "It's a London icon, a design classic with all its wonderful round curves," says Obergfell who spent six months photographing bus exteriors (indicator, shown, 4) and passengers. Jet documented the working lives of bus drivers and conductors (her portrait of conductor Chris Tesaga shown, 5). "The ultimate aim is to publish our project in the form of a book and launch this with an exhibition," says Obergfell, "probably around the time when the last Routemaster will disappear." Beuret has also been working on a project that documents the demise of another classic mode of British transportation; the slam-door train, currently being phased out across the UK (image shown, 6). In consultation with several train companies, the project, says Beuret, "is creating a visual record of an important, yet overlooked, part of our cultural identity."

7&8. From a personal project tentatively titled Cover Up by Carter Wong Tomlin creative director, Phil Carter. 15 was taken in Stockholm while 16 is in Chiswick. Carter hopes to publish a book of his shrouded cars next year

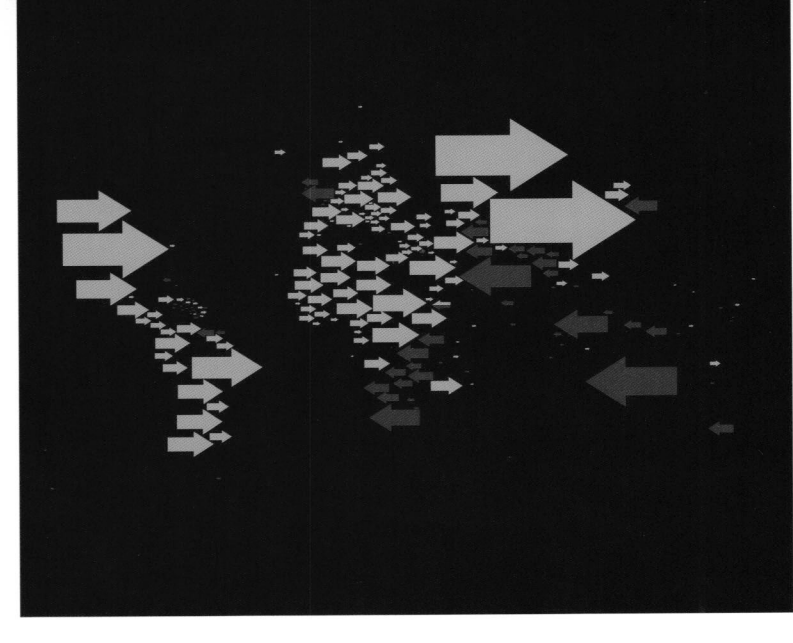

Drive yourself italic
cruise the linguistic
highway
open the throttle
FOR AN UNEXPLORED
typographic
PALETTE OF 3 ITALICS
IN 4 WEIGHTS [INCL. ROMAN, SMALL CAP AND SMALL CAP ITALIC FONTS AS WELL]
A FLAT TIRE
IS OUT OF THE QUESTION

1. Auto is a triple italic sans serif font from Dutch foundry, Underware. Having three different styles of italic to use together helps "solve more complex typographic tasks" such as designating a quotation within a quotation or identifying different speakers in a play.

2. Yorgo Tloupas created this map for Intersection magazine, indicating which countries drive on the right and which on the left.

3. Identity for the regional transport authority of Asturias, in northern Spain. The logo can be rearranged when the need arises: vertically or at a slant for example. The three circles refer to the three main towns at the heart of the region (Oviedo, Tijon and Aviles). Akzidenz

Grotesque medium was selected as the logo font since it had to be both standard and functional. The regular version of the font is used for the core corporate typeface. The project had particular appeal for designer Fernando Gutiérrez at Pentagram as his family hails from the region.

4&5. Johnson Banks' Michael Johnson and Julia Woollams used transport-related imagery in the Design Partners Annual Review, the relevance being that the body helps generate overseas business.

6. The Kelvin 40 concept jet from Marc Newson, commissioned by the Fondation Cartier, Paris. See it for yourself at the Design Museum, London, from 23 October

©–C–T–A Consorcio Transportes Asturias

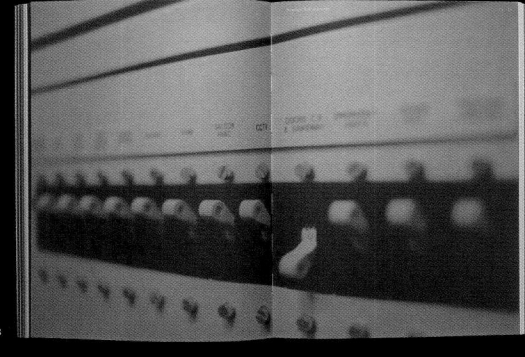

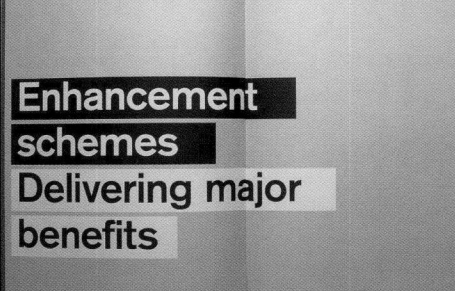

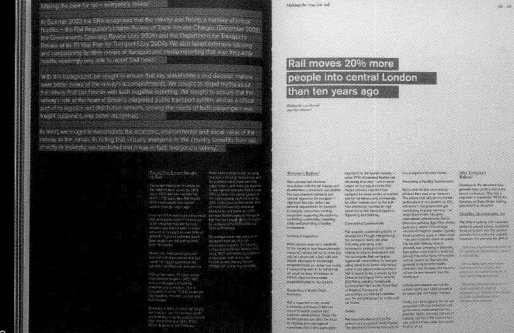

The Strategic Rail Authority's Annual Report 2003-2004 was developed by design consultancy Spin. The aim was to convey the serious, factual nature of the information within. Decoration of a superfluous nature, we're told, was absolutely not permitted. "Highlighting key points of information and the linear nature of rail architecture," informed the look of the brochure, explains Spin's

Ian Macfarlane, who worked on the report. "A system of blocks was developed which remains consistent across the title and introduction pages. A bold typographic style was developed for the title pages with a serif typeface used as a counterpoint," he adds. Abiding by the no-nonsense style of the report, a colour palette of greys was used throughout, softened with a pastel

lilac. Shots of railway environments from photographer Lee Mawdsley (8&9) are generously spread across double pages. The report was printed on two uncoated paper stocks: white for the financial section and grey for the report. "The grey paper was specified to achieve a grittier feel for the front end and extend the limited colour palette," comments Macfarlane

1

1-3. Pentagram New York partner Michael Gericke developed this system of wayfinding and identification signage for Terminal 1 at Toronto International Airport. The new terminal building, by architects SOM, features a curved, swooping roof. The signage had to complement the architecture and yet be simple and easy to use. Due to the restrictions of the Canadian Language Act, it also had to accommodate both English and French. Gericke created two elements: tall aluminium pylons to carry gate numbers and other information which are intended to recall air-control towers and overhead signage which is curved to echo the swoop of the terminal roof and is split into two to carry both languages. Designers: Michael Gericke and Lior Vaturi. Consulting designer: Wayne McCutcheon/ Entro Communications. Photographs: Peter Mauss/Esto.

4&5. Michael Gericke was also in charge of wayfinding and environmental graphics for the new PATH Station at the former site of the World Trade Center in New York. PATH is the commuter railway into Manhattan. This temporary station will serve until a new transportation centre is finished in five years' time and includes a surviving pylon from the original station. To acknowledge the city's resiliency after the traumatic events of 9/11, memorable quotes about the city run on the station's perimeter walls. Interior walls have been covered with maps and overhead views of lower Manhattan

1

2

1. Sweden's Forsman & Bodenfors AB have designed the latest site in Volvo's online portfolio: it features guides to the S60, V70 and XC70. Flash production and sound by Kokokaka Entertainment. See www.volvocars.se/74nyheter.

2. London's 20:20 created a cleverly customised campaign for Audi's A3 Sportback. A viral campaign (stills shown) was sent to 50,000 people, each one tailored to name the recipient in a DNA matching sequence at the end. A mailing house is then prompted to send out a direct mail pack which includes personalised print items.

3&4. Connexxion is the Dutch equivalent of London's Oyster card public transport payment system.

Design Bridge created and implemented the full Connexxion identity system and were then asked to work on the introduction of the OV chip card system. Three different cards were designed: a personalised card (for frequent travellers), an anonymous card, or a disposable card for tourists. Different Dutch quotes were placed on the cards to inspire the traveller. Illustrations feature the Dutch scenery.

5&6. Lumsden Design Partnership created these fetching posters for Transport for London. Filling vacant poster sites around London Underground, they highlight London sights made accessible via the transport network. The posters can be purchased through London's Transport Museum Shop

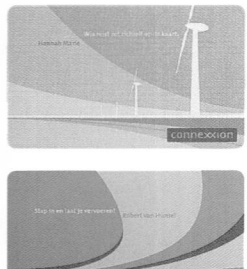

3

4

5

6

Type

1. Michael C Place of Build is currently completing Thread – a typeface that he conceived when exhibiting at a show of the same name in Australia. "I thought it would be a challenge to do a piece of type that is one continuous line," explains Place. "Plus,

I'm a glutton for punishment." He plans to make Thread available soon through Build Type. 2&3. James Goggin of design studio Practise created this catalogue for the Barbican's Colour After Klein exhibition. The typeface used is a redraw of

German typographer Rudolf Koch's 1931 multiline face, Prisma. Goggin took this all-caps typeface and used it as the basis for a modular system. For the Barbican project, he used an outer-edge outline version plus a solid weight, in all-caps. Goggin is collaborating with

Tokyo-based designer Alex Rich on extending this into a family of 12 weights and variations entitled Prismaset, plus a full lowercase character set. They plan to release this through foundry Lineto, later on in the year.
4. Poster by Pentagram's

Fernando Gutiérrez with Susan Jamieson for a student competition to design a Hermes window.
5. Philippe Apeloig designed this poster promoting Typo/Type, an exhibition held in April at the Museum of Russian Art in Kiev. 6-8. Identity for

film/video editors Trim. Designers Multistorey recreated the visual impact of staring at a screen for long periods of time (as editors are wont to do) with these maze-like typographic blocks, created from concentric lines, that visually vibrate like the

frequency of a monitor. "The shapes of the letterforms were drawn to fit into each other's negative space, creating a seamless modular unit, an expression of editing pieces together to make a whole," the designers explain

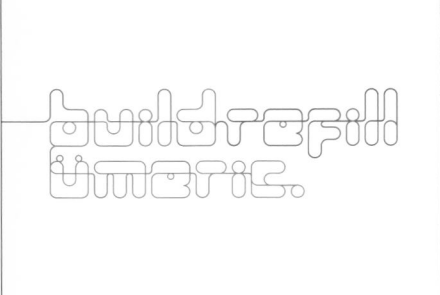

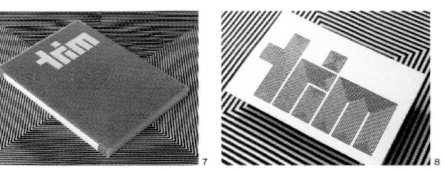

9. Delicate, overlapping outline type forms the artwork for the sleeve of Adapt or Die, a collection of remixes of Everything But The Girl tracks. By Stoke Newington-based design duo I Want. 10. Briefed to create an identity for 3D design and manufacturing company Standard 8, Browns created no less than 8 logos – each made up from multiple number eights taken from one of eight different typefaces. Says Brown's Nick Jones: "There will be eight different backs to business cards and promotional postcards will be printed with each logo foil-blocked in fluorescent orange to create a set. One logo has been chosen for use on the letterhead, again foil-blocked in fluorescent orange." 11&12. Spreads from a charming little typographic tour of Clerkenwell, London. This pocket-sized booklet was developed by Fontsmith to mark the launch of font, FS Clerkenwell. Designer: Ian Whalley. 13. NB:Studio created the marketing material and exhibition graphics for Joshua Reynolds: The Creation of Celebrity at Tate Britain. In collaboration with architects Muff, they were tasked with filling a long corridor that leads into the exhibition. The curator was keen to have a timeline of Reynolds' life and career, which became a 20-meter-long typographic diagram, linking to political events of the time. This left a blank wall opposite: NB:Studio decided to focus on the idea of the creation of celebrity and introduce quotes about fame from the era on the wall. They commissioned hand-lettering artist Alison Carmichael to add some flourish to the quotes which were then applied by sign-writer Kevin Glashier

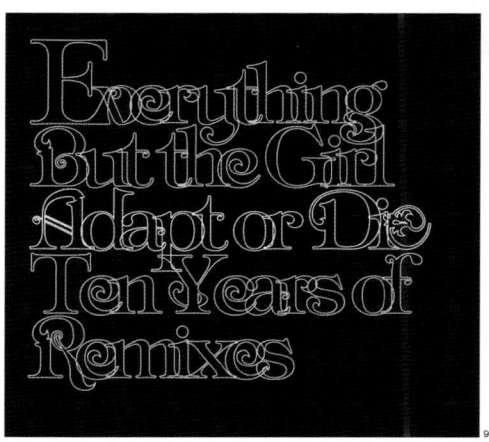

9

10

11

12

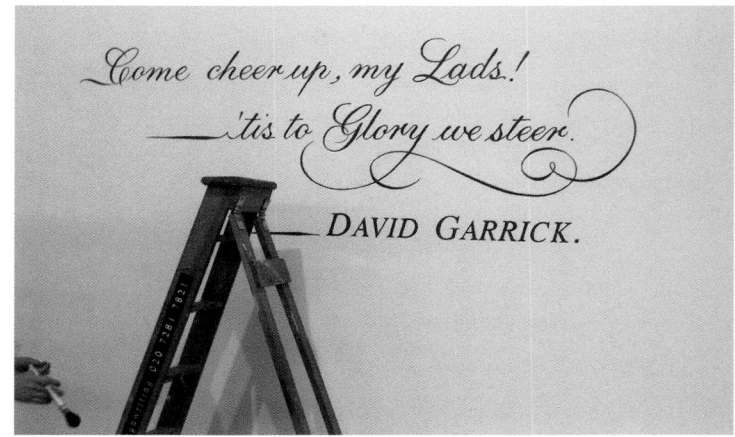

13

1-5. Many an ex-graphics student from Camberwell College of Arts will be wishing they'd thought of doing this: Graduating student Martin Zähringer created a typeface based on the grid of the architectural facade of the main Peckham Road college site. This typeface has been used in all the signage to direct visitors round the college during the show (18-24 June) and on the invites (designed by dddesign). The envelopes which invites were sent out in also show a representation of the architectural grid (5). Fellow students James Finch and Marc Cowan created 215 plastic shells: the perfect shape to fill the not-quite rectangular holes of the grid, thus spelling out Summer Show 05 (shown, 1) on the front of the building. Darren Wall created the sleeve artwork for Spy 51's album, Play For Your Life, released on Double R Records (cover shown, 6). "After realising that the singer and myself shared a love of colourful Japanese model kits," says Wall, "I constructed a typeface from abstracted photographs of the kits and of various toys."

7&8. Hat-Trick designed this kilometere-long hoarding celebrating Samuel Johnson's two hundred and fiftieth birthday. It surrounds a large new office and retail development by Land Securities, near to Johnson's house in London. The design, set in typefaces Baskerville and Caslon, features original definitions from Johnson's famous dictionary. All the words are to do with building or walls and run as a series of ABCs. The X has been omitted as it wasn't in Johnson's original dictionary. In a competition organised by Neville Brody's experimental type event/ publication, FUSE, designers were asked to create a typeface and poster around the theme of Security. The four winners are

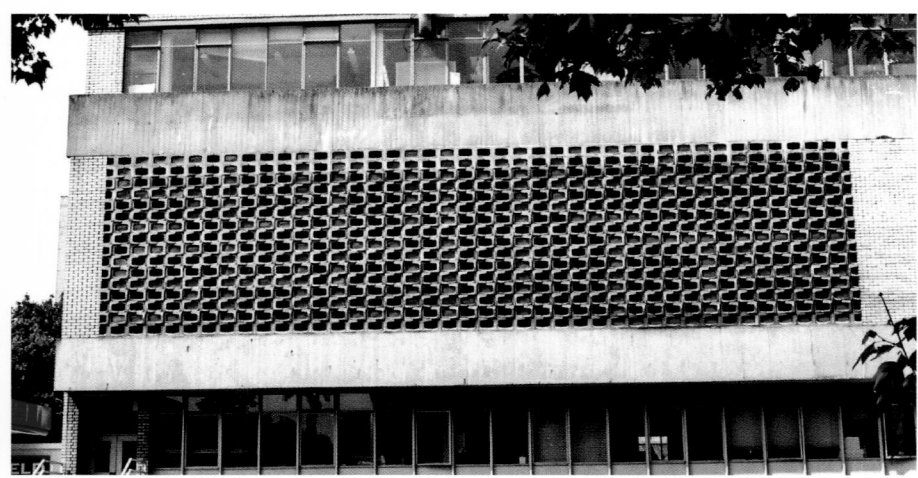

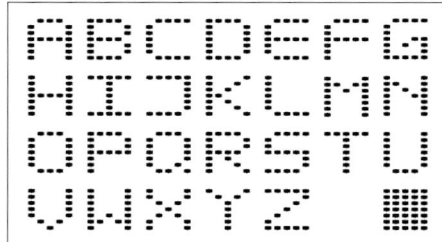

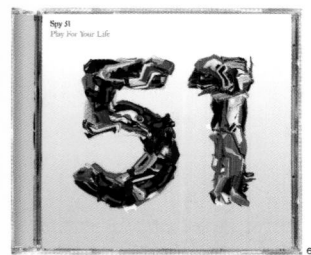

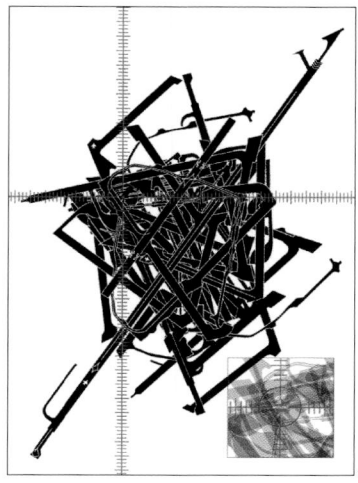

9

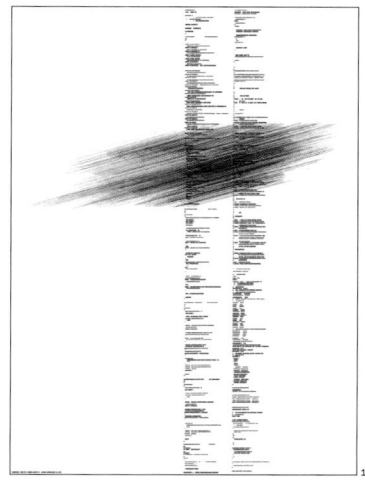

10

FUSE

11

12

Adam Gravely (9), Coil Graphics (10), François Moissette (11) and Lee Hasler (12). Visit researchstudios.com/home /fusecomp/fusecomp.php for more information. 13. Multistorey packaged and re-branded this range of products from trichology clinic Philip Kingsley. "The logo consists of a newly drawn font, incorporating a letter K made from lines that resemble hair," they explain. "Type is positioned vertically on both boxes and bottles inside so that it wraps round like fringing, again to suggest hair." A colour coding system defines product groupings. 14-16. Hyperkit created this signage for Quayside Studios, near Chelsea Harbour. The hand-drawn dot matrix face was applied directly onto the walls

13

14

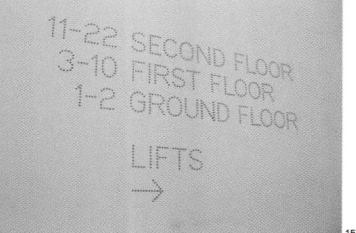

15

16

Tokion magazine's art director, Deanne Cheuk, designed these spreads for issue 47, which included features on several internationally renowned artists. Mariko Mori was photographed by Alex Freund (1) and Maurizio Cattelan by Jason Nocito (2).

3. The Beautiful Script is the title of an exhibition to be hosted by PlayStation Portable (PSP) at London's The Dray Walk Gallery just off Brick Lane in August. Several artists, including calligraphers, graphic artists, designers and a photographer, have been commissioned to interpret the words Beauty, Desire and Freedom visually using Arabic calligraphy as their primary inspiration. This piece is by Raadiyah Bint-Safar. Find out more at pspthebeautifulscript.com
4. From a personal scrapbook project from Why Not Associates' Andy Altmann (entitled The Big Book of Shite) this page was created from the kind of cards most commonly found in telephone boxes.
5-8. This book, Summer of Love – Art of the Psychedelic Era, accompanies an exhibition of the same name at the Tate Gallery in Liverpool. Developed by A2/SW/HK (Scott Williams and Henrik Kubel) the cover is composed of 12 letters, laser-cut from sheets of coloured Perspex. "The composition was carefully arranged and photographed on a light box in order to achieve a fluid effect," comment Williams and Kubel. A set of bespoke typefaces were also developed by A2/SW/HK for use throughout the publication.
9. Poster by Belgian design studio, Coast, for a free jazz festival at deSingel in Antwerp. It is based on ITC Avant Garde

1

2

3

4

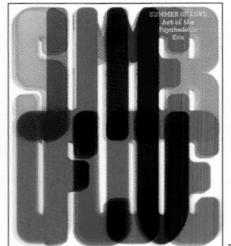

5

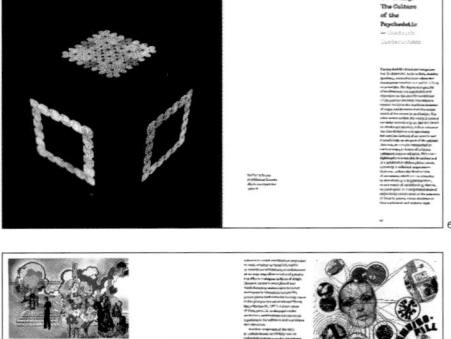

6

7

8

9

10-13. New website for font foundry, FontSmith, designed by Craig Thomas and team at Carter Wong Tomlin. Fontsmith.com uses mock personal ads to convey the tongue-in-cheek attitude of the studio. 14-15. Creative Type provides an illustrated account of the impact of the digital era on modern typography (spreads shown). Showcasing 34 classic typefaces created between 1985 and 2004, it also includes comments from the designer of each one. In addition, there is also an historic look at some typographic classics ranging from Garamond (designed in 1530) up to Akzidenz Grotesk (1969). Published by Thames & Hudson, Creative Type is priced at £29.95. Also just out is 1000 Type Treatments (cover shown, 16) published by Rockport at £27.50. The wealth of contemporary typefaces, all photographed in-situ here, is impressive and the book reads like a catalogue of great type usage (spreads shown, 17&18). The particular fonts used in each execution are credited clearly, while the design of the book, by Paul Burgess of WilsonHarvey/Loewy, makes for easy navigation. Design/research: Paul Burgess and Ben Wood. Artwork: Peter Usher. 19&20. These posters from Paula Scher at Pentagram New York, will eventually form a complete series running from 1 to 9. Each number is being printed in a limited edition run of 125 silkscreen posters, measuring 30 inches x 46 inches. A single poster can be purchased for $400, or a whole set of ten (numerals 0 to 9) for $3000, from screenprinters, Grafx. For information on purchasing the posters, contact Bob Jones on bob@grafxsp.com or check out www.grafxsp.com

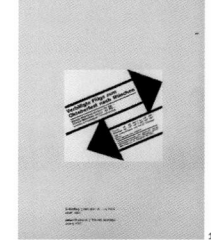

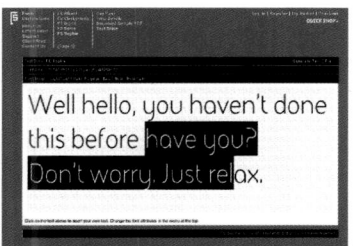

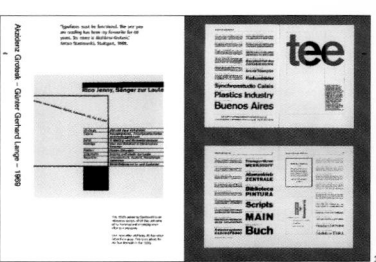

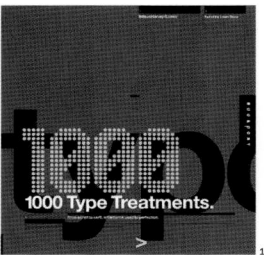

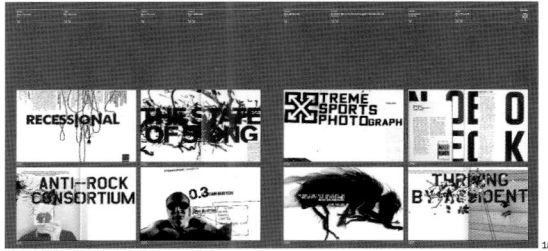

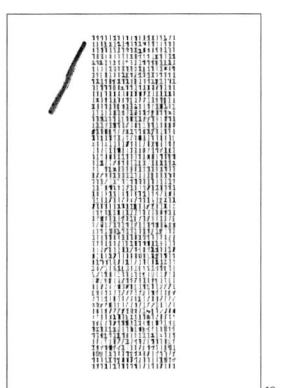

Spread design, including text, by Supermundane

1. Pea is designer Corey Holms' latest typeface which is available at www.veer.com. Explains Holms: "When you see it small, it's pretty clunky, but the bigger it gets, the more elegant it becomes."
2. A recent graduate from the London College of Communication, Paul McNeil has been a graphic designer and typographer for nearly 30 years. Now a lecturer at the LCC, he has established his own type foundry, from the which the commercial output is his Bone family. "The design celebrates notions of progressive 'modernity' explicit in late eighteenth and early nineteenth century typefaces such as Bodoni and Didot," he says, "whose letterforms were structured on technological frameworks rather than calligraphic, historical and visual orthodoxies."

3. Baksheesh was designed by Stuart Brown of the Identikal Foundry and comes in three weights with accompanying italics. A part of the Identikal Summer collection, it references a system built for typewriters during the 70s. Baksheesh is exclusively availble from www.identikalshop.com.
4. Kenn Munk is somewhat of a specialist in non-text typefaces. Karmaflage is a dingbat system with which ornamental camouflage patterns can be built by layering characters in Illustrator. Numerals produce one type of camo, upper case another and lower case yet another. Download it for free from www.kennmunk.com
5. Cézanne has long been one of the most popular handwriting fonts from the P22 foundry. However, P22 were concerned that it was

① PEA

Hold this for a second It was warm and unfamiliar. I was going to ask what it was but she took it back before the words came out.

② BONE

"I've never done this kind of thing before" — BONE
He proclaimed honestly, but of course she — BONE STENCIL
couldn't reply, not with the tape over her mouth. — BONE LIGHT

③ BAKSHEESH

The trees before him in the wood spoke in a language — BAKSHEESH BOLD
of the wind he didn't understand. Kicking his chainsaw — BAKSHEESH ITALIC
into life, he thanked God for this blessing. — BAKSHEESH LIGHT

④ KARMAFLAGE

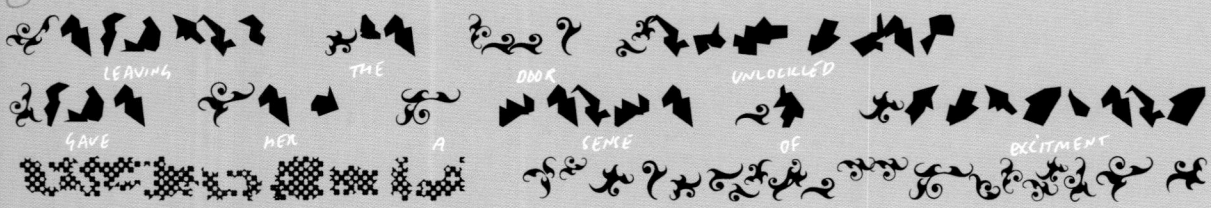

LEAVING THE DOOR UNLOCKED
GAVE HER A SENSE OF EXCITMENT

⑤ P22 CEZANNE PRO

The phone rang & it was not through coincidence that he answered it.

I DON'T UNDERSTAND

becoming too recognisable and regular. James Grieshaber has tried to resolve this by producing a version in the OpenType format. Cézanne Pro offers an expansive suite of options that allows for up to six different versions for each character. There are hundreds of automatic substitutions programmed into the font but designers can also hand-select individual letters for just the right look. Available at www.p22.com. 6. Lines is a new font by Supermundane. "It's an experimental font with seven variations that can be combined to create about 40 different font varieties," he explains. See more of his type and design at www.supermundane.com 7. Munich-based designer Gert Wiescher has just released Bodoni Classic Stencil through his Wiescher Design foundry. The stencil weights are the latest addition to the extensive Bodoni Classic Family which includes text, display, ad, condensed, deco, chancery, swash and even Cyrillic variants. Available from Fontworks (www.type.co.uk). 8. Freight by Brooklyn-based Joshua Darden has just been released through garagefonts.com and philsfonts.com. It comprises three families, Freight Sans, Freight Micro and Freight text, each with five weights, which support a wide range of usage from signage to extended text articles in journals. 9. With a nod to the schoolroom, Just van Rossum's FF Schulschrift is a handwriting font that comes complete with ruled lines. Although it's been available for some time, a newly expanded package with 12 styles can now be had at www.fontshop.com.

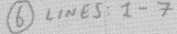

6 LINES: 1-7

WE RAN THROUGH THE HOUSE TO THE BACKYARD JUST TO FIND THE NIGHT WAS EVERYWHERE

7 BODONI CLASSIC STENCIL

The idea of baldness terrified him, — BODONI CLASSIC STENCIL FAT
"I don't even like eggs" he told the barber. — BODONI CLASSIC STENCIL

8 FREIGHT

Being able to see his breath in his freezing bedsit — FREIGHT MICRO BOLD
was something of a comfort to him. "At least I know — FREIGHT TEXT BOOK
I'm still alive" he said out loud watching the clouds — FREIGHT SANS MEDIUM ITALIC
of mist rise and disappear. — FREIGHT SANS BOLD

9 SCHULSCHRIFT

"She would never understand" he said to his reflection. His eyes — SCHULSCHRIFT OT LINIEN ZWEI
SCHULSCHRIFT OT NORMAL
drifted to the floor; all he could see were his bare
SCHULSCHRIFT OT ERSTES VIER — SCHULSCHRIFT OTA NORMAL
feet squeezed into her shoes. — SCHULSCHRIFT OTA ERSTES ZWEI

I THINK I LEFT THE OVEN ON!

I'M INVISIBLE

Spread designed by Marcus McCallion

1. Akkurat Mono is the latest weight to be added to the Akkurat font family, available exclusively from www.lineto.com. Its designer, Laurenz Brunner, is currently finishing his diploma at the Rietveld Academy in Amsterdam. 2. A set of bespoke typefaces, A2-SOL, by A2/SW/HK for use in the publication Summer of Love – Art of the Psychedelic Era. "The typeface is rooted in the typewriter tradition but departs typographically by not being mono-spaced," explain A2's Scott Williams and Henrik Kubel. "The individual characters have been opened up, serifs omitted and a single-storey 'a', 'g' and lowercase 'l' with a curved ending added. There is a true italic plus small caps and non-aligning figures, totalling six typefaces," they add.

3. According to its designer, Marcus McCallion of üNDT, Puritan is "a brutally geometric sans design" which comes in two weights. It will be available from www.myfonts.com and www.undt-type.com shortly. McCallion also designed this spread. 4. Book& (Bookend) is now available from hollandfonts.com and was designed by Max Kisman for the identity and stationery for a small antique bookstore in The Netherlands. 5. Laurentian is the most recent release from Agfa Monotype. The face was designed originally by Rod McDonald for Canadian magazine title, Maclean's. 6. House Industries' Paperback has been specifically designed to perform well across a wide variety of point sizes and paper stocks. With digital technology, it is possible to use any

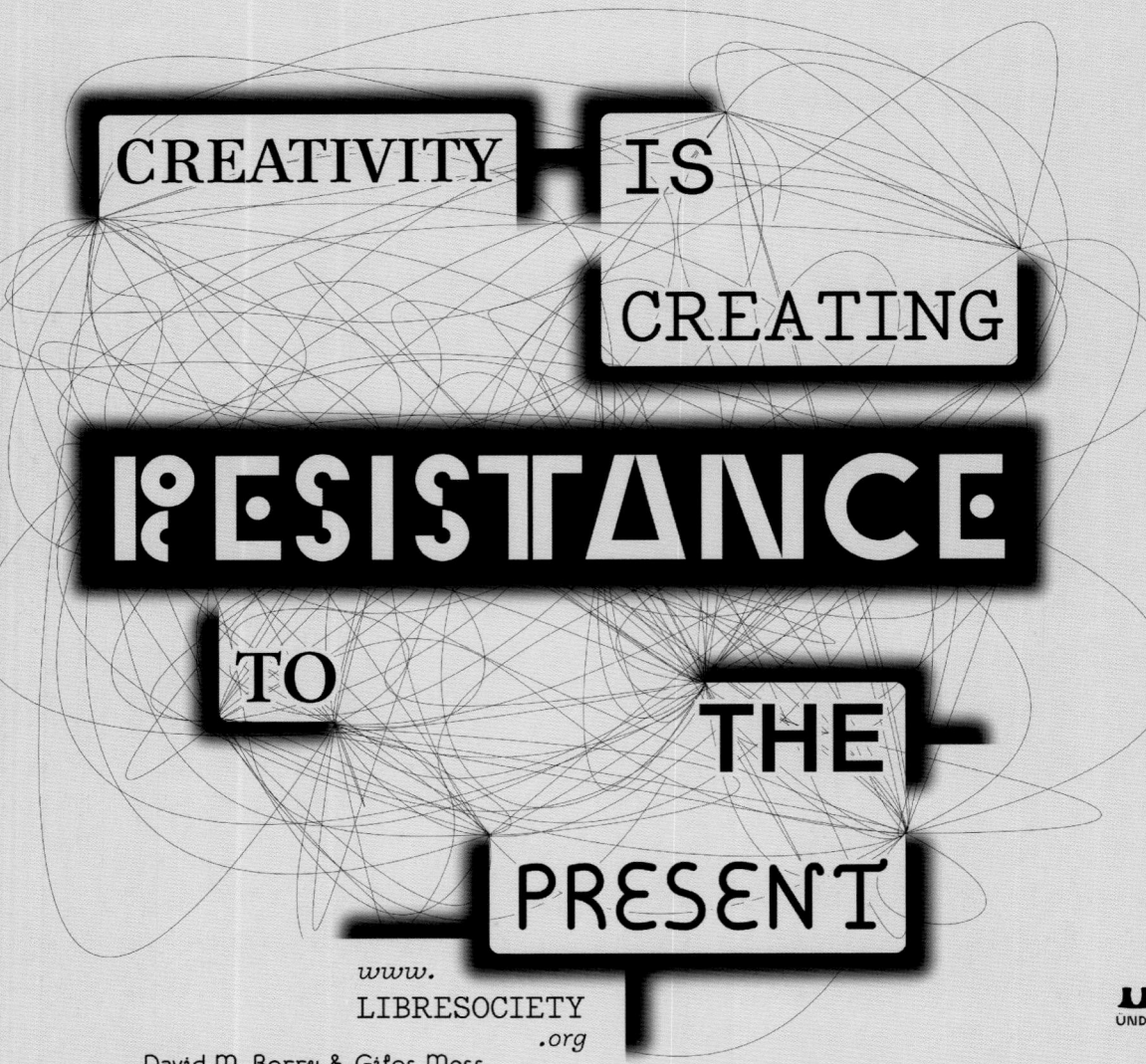

CREATIVITY IS CREATING RESISTANCE TO THE PRESENT

www.
LIBRESOCIETY
.org

David M. Berry & Giles Moss

ÜNDT

typeface at any size, a habit which does not always yield optimal typographic results. On Paperback, designer John Downer went back to the days of metal type by drawing different versions of the face optimised for different point sizes. Paperback also includes 25

decorative embellishments designed for use as repeat patterns, enclosures, rules and flourishes. www.houseindustries.com 7. Julian Morey has almost completed new face Sigma. It is, he tells us, a revival of Grotesque, an early twentieth century sans-serif

originally manufactured by Stephenson Blake for letterpress. "I've admired the font for some time and have always wanted to revive it," explains Morey, "because, although there are several derivations of Grotesque available, none for me retained the quirky

personality found in the original hot metal cut." Sigma will be released later in the year through Morey's own foundry, Club-21: www.typeclub.co.uk

"To forget one's purpose is the commonest form of stupidity.", Friedrich Nietzsche

"Language is made not to be believed but to be obeyed, and to compel obedience.", DELEUZE & GUATTARI

"Every tool is a weapon if you hold it right", ANI DEFRANCO

"Should 1 bite the hand that starves me so that it will throttle me?".

"Murphy" by SAMUEL BECKETT

"The first man who, having fenced off a plot of land, thought of saying, 'This is mine' and found people simple enough to believe him was the real founder of civil society. How many crimes, wars, murders, how many miseries and horrors might the human race had been spared by the one who, upon pulling up the stakes or filling in the ditch, had shouted to his fellow men: 'Beware of listening to this imposter; you are lost if you forget the fruits of the earth belong to all and that the earth belongs to no one.' ",

JEAN-JACQUES ROUSSEAU

"He who receives an idea from me, receives instruction himself without lessening mine; as he who lights his taper at mine, receives light without darkening me.",

Thomas Jefferson

REMEMBER
Sagittarius,